FEVERLAND

FEVER

LAND

A Memoir in Shards

ALEX LEMON

MILKWEED EDITIONS

Published 2017 by Milkweed Editions
Printed in the United States of America
Cover design by Anders Nilsen and Mary Austin Speaker
Cover illustration by Anders Nilsen
Author photo by Ariane Balizet

First Edition
17 18 19 20 21 5 4 3 2 1

Milkweed Editions, an independent nonprofit publisher, gratefully acknowledges sustaining support from the Jerome Foundation; the Lindquist & Vennum Foundation; the McKnight Foundation; the National Endowment for the Arts; the Target Foundation; and other generous contributions from foundations, corporations, and individuals. Also, this activity is made possible by the voters of Minnesota through a Minnesota State Arts Board Operating Support grant, thanks to a legislative appropriation from the arts and cultural heritage fund, and a grant from the Wells Fargo Foundation. For a full listing of Milkweed Editions supporters, please visit milkweed.org.

Library of Congress Cataloging-in-Publication Data

Names: Lemon, Alex, author.
Title: Feverland : a memoir in shards / Alex Lemon.
Description: First edition. | Minneapolis, Minnesota : Milkweed Editions, 2017. | Includes bibliographical references.
Identifiers: LCCN 2017011038 (print) | LCCN 2017029387 (ebook) | ISBN 9781571318428 (ebook) | ISBN 9781571313362 (pbk. : alk. paper)
Subjects: LCSH: Lemon, Alex. | Poets, American—21st century—Biography.
Classification: LCC PS3612.E468 (ebook) | LCC PS3612.E468 Z46 2017 (print) | DDC 811/.6 [B]—dc23
LC record available at https://lccn.loc.gov/2017011038

Milkweed Editions is committed to ecological stewardship. We strive to align our book production practices with this principle, and to reduce the impact of our operations in the environment. We are a member of the Green Press Initiative, a nonprofit coalition of publishers, manufacturers, and authors working to protect the world's endangered forests and conserve natural resources. *Feverland* was printed on acid-free 100% postconsumer-waste paper by Thomson-Shore.

For Ariane, Felix, and Alma—my everythings

Contents

How is it that you live, and what is it you do?
—WILLIAM WORDSWORTH

Thus strangely are our souls constructed, and by such slight ligaments are we bound to prosperity or ruin.
—MARY SHELLEY, *FRANKENSTEIN*

My ambitions are very old and simple and almost always unvoiced. I want to be whole. I do not know what this condition would feel like and there is no advice on the matter that convinces me. I am not exactly sure what whole means, and to be honest, it sounds too much like being finished.
—CHARLES BOWDEN, *SOME OF THE DEAD ARE STILL BREATHING: LIVING IN THE FUTURE*

If at home, sir,
He's all my exercise, my mirth, my matter,
Now my sworn friend and then mine enemy,
My parasite, my soldier, statesman, all:
He makes a July's day short as December,
And with his varying childness cures in me
Thoughts that would thick my blood.
—WILLIAM SHAKESPEARE, *THE WINTER'S TALE*

EKG

I heart the rock-and-roll stardust, steroids that let you live, all the spilled love and still being alive. I heart Twizzlers, tangerines, until the stomach can't take any more. I heart knots, the perfect peel. I heart the heaving. I heart banging my head when I fall in the shower, banging my head on the curb. I heart making out in the ghosting cold. I heart the lips warm. I heart shame on me. Novocain, hydrocodone is what I heart. Ativan, Percocet, I heart you, too. Heart a handful of heart-shaped candies. I heart the moist perfume of Whoppers on the fingers I kiss. I heart the past—drinking through the blackouts and onward, crashing ass over piehole down the apartment stairs. Pills, I heart pills. I heart waking with my head's dried blood glued to the pillow. I heart asparagus-and-beet salad dusted with manchego. Not remembering speaking to you, that is what I heart. What did I say? I heart. I heart it all wrong, I heart it until it shatters into a thousand sharp hummingbirds. I heart my mother pushing my wheelchair through leaves along the barge-clanging Mississippi. I heart muggings, the quick cut, the knockdown. I heart shame on you. I heart it right. I heart keeping my fingers crossed. I heart going for long, cane-dragging walks, smoking cigarette after cigarette in Minnesota's winter air—puffing myself light-headed, until I fall into the snow. Too deep, I heart, too long. I heart having nothing while pretending to have it all. I heart every last joint that I've smoked, every pop, every line. I heart the pretty. I heart instead, maybe, might. I can't see, I heart you. I heart walking blindly into traffic. I heart still believing in something better. Still believing, I heart. I believe, I heart. I heart dead animals beneath my bed, in the walls. I heart visitors. I heart I am not home. I heart songs that go on too long. I heart a tight chest. I can't breathe, I heart. Numb face, too, I heart. I heart amphetamines, amphetamines, amphetamines. The shock of the coldest water, I heart. The ugly, the ugliest, I heart you, too. The belly-up flies on the windowsill, I heart, the orange peels drying in the sun. I heart making love premorning. I heart that assemblage, the way it all falls down. I heart never getting tired. I heart not being able to get out of bed. Codeine my heart, I heart. I heart the bed spins that come each night, the vertigo that makes me claw the air. I heart the butcher beneath my ribs. I heart it all wrong. I heart no speed limit and flicking my headlights off. I heart swerving beneath the moonlight. I heart the kitchen with the oven baking bread. I heart the midnight inside me, nail-holed with starlight. I heart the slowdown, the traffic jam. I heart gutting walleye along the shore, the turtles sunning on rocks. The guts, I heart. I heart your body. Your body, I heart. I heart the darkness my boy tells me he knows. His thundering run through our home, I heart—the way he starfishes in his sleep. I heart the bruise of watching him grow up too fast. The good burn and blister of my daughter's fat-cheeked grin, I heart. I heart knowing I can do nothing about the pain the world will deliver upon them. I heart trying to soak up as much hurt as I can. I heart there is no time to give up, there is so little time. The art of the impossible, I heart. The heart, I heart, I heart. Each ache inside me, I heart. Open windows in winter and blue skies, I heart. That hard work of the heart, I heart. The heart overripe, I heart, the heart always raw. The heart churning, I heart, the heart aflame. The good heart gone bad, I heart, the good heart always coming back. The chandelier heart, I heart, its wicked sparkle, its champion gleam. I heart this heart, this last, this only, this heart glowing swollen because always, we are all about to die.

FEVER

LAND

I WAS ALREADY READY WHEN I WAS DEAD

> I have seen such things as they occur
> in some remote and improbable time.
> —C. D. WRIGHT

I'm trying to read poems, to find solace in language, but really I'm just sitting in my living room with the TV on. "BURN IN THE USA" is stamped across the ticker of the ten o' clock news. A slideshow of images—charcoal drawings from the day's Zacarias Moussaoui trial—run alongside it. I flick the TV volume up. Listen as the blindingly white teeth of the anchor snap and click over courtroom drawings, as audio of 911 calls crackles over the video everyone has seen a hundred times more than they'd like to: the jet vanishing into the thousand-eyed building, smoke billowing into the New York morning as leapers drop to the earth, dust-faced gawkers pointing at the shuddering tower as it begins to fold downward.

Cut back to the news desk. The newscasters stare wordlessly, motionlessly, into the camera for a second, then another—so long the moment seems frozen—until something signals the two to churn back to life. The woman turns to her coanchor. The camera zooms in on his mannequin face. Another death statistic drops woodenly from his mouth. I hit mute.

Above the TV, one of my stepfather's paintings hangs half-cocked, a beautiful landscape of bruised woods shrouded by night. The trees are Giacometti-like, black-and-blue apparitions. Slatherings of moonlight crawl between the trunks and branches. Often I imagine clambering into it. The moonlight hot, rushing the blood. Boughs snapping above and around me, as if the cage of my life had been welded together from millions of breaking ribs.

Though my brain surgery—in which a vascular malformation was removed from my brain stem—was seven years ago, still my entire body hurts. My health is detonating. Each day my disabilities seem to worsen.

The cat head-butts my blistered hand, prodding and ramming until I cup her tiny skull. She purrs and pivots in my palm, and kneads her claws against my belly. It is hours past her feeding time. On the coffee table in front of us, atop a pile of tattered magazines, my cell phone jumps. My entire body jolts in surprise. Catface leaps off me and sprints out of the room. I listen to her scamper down the basement steps, scrabble up a mound of unpacked boxes, and then claw and slink into the paneled ceiling, and I am reminded of my aloneness. Lonely in the silent house and a stranger to myself.

I've been waiting for months to be told if I have a tumor-growing syndrome that I'd likely pass on to any future children. Waiting to be told whether I will ever have a family.

The glass screech of the bird feeder swinging against the window scissors apart the quiet. The phone's screen blinks as I rise from the couch.

Nights are the worst. Sleep will be impossible and the

phone is blinking again and suddenly my chest is tight. It feels as if the world is collapsing down on me, strange and hot breathing in my face.

The phone jukes sideways. In the basement ceiling below me, Catface is skulking. *Scree-scree-scree.*

The calamity parade is unstoppable this year: All the torture, the poor handling of Katrina. Miners trapped miles beneath the earth who die, already buried, and are forgotten within a week. Mudslides, earthquakes, stampedes. Another shooting spree, another family murdered. Each day a roadside bomb, a sunk ferry. Mass graves. And the vice president shot his friend in the face.

I need to talk, want someone to assure me that this place isn't as fucking horrible as I think it is.

> The unbreachable gap between the pathos of the art-work—an aesthetic quality—and the experience that produced it and that it produces—a moral quality—means that there is no straight path from the artwork to life-action. The two—aesthetic impression and moral sympathy—cannot coincide in themselves, though they may find temporary coincidence in the mind of one responding to the artwork.
> —HELEN VENDLER, *INVISIBLE LISTENERS:*
> *LYRIC INTIMACY IN HERBERT, WHITMAN, AND*
> *ASHBERY*

It's not even spring yet in Minnesota, but already the kitchen air is cottony and humid. In the distance—somewhere across the bridge, on the other side of the

Mississippi—sirens winnow. The melting ice fills the air with groans and drips and clatterings. Out front, earlier today, the muffled conversation of walkers taking advantage of the warmth.

It is so beautiful. The lazy weeping of winter as the world inches itself back into the dirt. Pearls falling from the eaves, growing larger and larger holes in the snowbanks.

But I can hardly see it. I can hardly see anything. Another day chewed apart by medical appointments. Another week on medical leave. My face sweat-greased, burning beneath the eye patch in the razor-sharp strap. No urge to do anything, no heartbeat in my chest.

I am alone, lonely—waiting, always waiting, and getting sicker. I want to lose myself in poems tonight. Have them swallow me whole.

Next door the British lady's porch light winks off. She's just home from the hospital. This morning I saw the top half of her face in her window, peeking out at the street. Her cigarette smoke seemed to rise from a pyre of hair.

Tomorrow it will be more of the same. Joggers in the slush. Melt gurgling in the slicked streets. Rivers along the curbs. Breaking tree limbs falling from the sky.

And all over again, surely, more bad news.

Good Friday. Good God. Goddamn.

When I tear open a package, wet cat food spoots into Catface's dish. The last tuna-flavored squeeze dribbles over my fingertips. I streak the chunky paste down the thighs of my jeans—the same ones I've worn all week—and pick up my phone. The text is from my fiancée, who right now is sitting in a hotel room in Philadelphia reading Shakespeare. I have to squint, close one eye to read it. Six digital words, all buzz-sawed twenty-first-century language.

Tomorrow I will again use this phone to call the doctor, again ask the receptionist if the results of the genetic test are in. Again she will say not yet—that they will call me when it's time.

> Your gesture which is neither embrace nor warning
> But which holds something of both
> —JOHN ASHBERY, "SELF-PORTRAIT IN A
> CONVEX MIRROR"

After refilling the Groveland Tap pint glass that Catface laps water from, I watch her hunch over the food dish. Shoulder bones press from her cobalt fur. She takes a bit of the mush in her incisors, looks up at me, then whiplashes her skull backward. I open my mouth and thrash my head, mimicking her—to know the pleasure she gets from that kind of car-wreck eating—but it only makes me dizzy and nauseous. I steady myself against the countertop, sigh as she throttles more food into her mouth.

I take the trash out back and stand in the snow-glowing yard, listening to the rumble and blink of my neighborhood, Prospect Park. Jets landing and taking off a few miles south, the constant hum of the campus down the hill, cars passing through the slush on University Avenue.

Drifting slowly through the porch shadows, I think about the photos my fiancée e-mailed me this afternoon. In one she's grinning, crouched over the hole Benjamin

Franklin buried his shit in. In another she's giving the camera a thumbs-up. I start laughing and round fist-size snowballs in my hands until they are concrete hard and slam them off the garage door. My fingers and hands go numb and disappear in the blackness. From the dryer vent in the neighbor's basement, steam chugs into the cooling air.

Back in the living room, the flashing screen wrenches me forward. I turn the volume back on and slump on the couch. The news footage is of a high-speed chase filmed from a cop's dashboard camera. Blue-shadowed jumps, and cars yanked to the shoulder of the road before the Lexus misses its turn. Its headlights pierce the air as it vanishes into a ditch and then twists around a tree on the other side. Smoke and flames wisp into the tree's limbs.

The news isn't worth watching—I know this—and it's probably making me worse, but I can't turn it off. The apartment feels almost comfortable, like a home, like a place I can be OK in, when I turn up the TV loud enough to be clearly heard from down the block.

To make the days feel as if they have substance, I want—need—everything to be worth it. I want to twist everything out of this life, slurp from it every last drop.

I pick up my collection of Ashbery's poems. I let the lines twist and tumble me through them. I have so little, barely even words, but art is a bomb shelter packed with dynamite, the bottom of an ocean where somehow I can breathe. When writing, I can make my own livable world, a safe house, a hideout.

∴

When I next look up at the TV a man in a Minnesota Twins hat is weeping into his hands, sputtering out half words because the Ford assembly and production plant on the Mississippi River in Saint Paul is going to shut down soon. Downsizing. Going international.

"I had the same job my father did," he gasps, red cheeked. "I can't do anything else." Video of an assembly line of Ford Explorers follows, then an interview with a union rep, a curved scar over his lip and cheek.

"After the shock, we'll all be OK," he says. "It will all be OK." The way he speaks, the undertow of his voice, reminds me of a Saturday morning in college when I woke up in the woods near that same Ford plant. "Somehow," he says slowly, "it will all be OK."

My T-shirt was nowhere. My shorts were down, torn. Scratches crosshatched my forearms.

I do not want to remember that man, the person I was, that sometimes I can't seem to stop myself from being. I want him to stay in the past tense. But always I think of him. There is too much failure inside me still, too much slippage and hook. I try to love him, forgive, but it's impossible.

I stare at the TV, look down at the cat, ask her how one reshapes the world around oneself so one can get better. "How?" I ask her. "Huh?" This world makes it so easy to be a bad person. It excels at making you feel worthless. To see brutality and become brutal. Perched on the coffee table, Catface licks her paw before looking back at me and turning her head to the side, quizzical, asking what the fuck I am talking about now. I swat at her with my book. Throw a pen at the TV.

The best way to survive the sleepless dark is to never get

into bed. All night I will read Celan, Vallejo, Dickinson. Squeeze from them all their blood and dirt. Gulp it down.

My uncovered eye burns. The one beneath the patch stings. I dab at the sweat that pools beneath the patch, gag at its wet rot stink. I rub the long scar on the back of my head. I go to the bathroom and scrub my eyes with a washcloth, pressing the coldness into them.

In the mirror above the sink, there I am.

Hello, stranger. Hello, dead friend.

Sports begins with a wrinkle-heavy man monotoning to a room of sixth graders about the day he played a doubleheader with Babe Ruth. His blue suit sits spiky on his wasted bones. His neck tendons stretch, but the rest of him is motionless as he gazes blank eyed above the kids. He quiets and looks for a moment as if he doesn't know where he is. The cross-legged children fidget, look away, mouth words to each other, or make faces at the camera. One girl looks down at the baseball in her hands. A boy in the front row is picking his nose. And then the old man yanks himself back from whatever dark place he'd been drifting toward and his near shout rattles—"Babe would stay forever, you know, if you promised there'd be beer."

This genre is distinguished from the lyric of solitary
meditation (which also can have a Utopian motiva-
tion) by the intensity brought to it in its surge toward

an invisible other who becomes the site where urgent
questions of guilt, love, home, and trust can be
explored and even resolved.

—HELEN VENDLER, *INVISIBLE LISTENERS:*
LYRIC INTIMACY IN HERBERT, WHITMAN,
AND ASHBERY

My phone chirps again and again, so finally I pick it up
and squint at the tiny numbers and display. I fuck up
my text the first time. I am nearly blind after reading for
hours, and my fingers feel like bananas. I mash the buttons and slam the phone against the table.

I just wish I could speak—say *hello* and *I miss you*
and *I am weak and need help*—ask, *Would you help me,*
please? But even if she were right beside me, lips pressed
to my neck, it wouldn't matter. My mouth cannot find the
shapes for the words.

My fat fingers tub over the numbers—erasing, trying again—until finally: L-U-V U M-O-R E-V-E-R-Y
D-A-Y.

And then one green-button push and the letters spiral
off into the ether. Far away to a woman who, somehow,
makes me want to figure out how to be alive and good in
this terrible world.

But tonight, all night, I am alone. A whole week—and
it will be impossible to leave the house, it will be the cat
and I, calling every day for the results, becoming each
second frailer. All my listening, all my trying not to hear,
at the same time. Everything so loud it drops like a black
sheet over me.

How to be here, now? I want to know. *How to be here,*
good?

I am alone, all day, all night. I am here and nowhere at all.

Hello, stranger. Hello, dead friend.

The TV flickers from a Levitra commercial to *Nightline*. There are more court drawings—a pastel Moussaoui leaning back in his chair, his too-large hand cradling the long beard he's grown in jail; the judge hunched, glasses clutched in her fingertips—and as I turn the volume up the program's host is coughing over video of the plane-wrecked field, where suits stand around, pointing the wobbly end of a tape measure down the charred stretch of debris, pens drooping from their lips, before the screen flashes back to Moussaoui's orange-suited mug shot with the voice-over explaining how, today, Moussaoui said he's running over with a new faith from what he saw in a dream—that he knows in his heart that he will be pardoned and sent to London, where he will go on living into eternity—and wishes that it could all happen again and again and again, every day.

MIGRANTS IN A FEVERLAND

"Please?" the kid begs. He squeezes the safety bar so hard his eight-year-old fingers look bloodless. The Ferris wheel is stopped; two stories beneath them a teenage couple is being loaded onto the ride. The gondola is rocking back and forth because the teenagers on either side of the kid—his new brothers—want to scare him.

Below, the carnival is daylight bright. The kid is too scared to look down, but he hears the bustling: shouts and laughter, popping cap guns, and carnies yelling at every passerby.

His brothers swing their weight forward, shaking the gondola up and out like they are trying to make it fly into the night air. But each time, just as it feels like it might break off, it suddenly stops, hangs a sick feeling in the kid's gut, and drops backward into the dark. The kid's stomach flops. He's seasick, airsick, about to throw up. He wishes he hadn't chomped down fist after fist of cotton candy earlier, because now it's coming back up, scalding his throat.

"Wheeeeee," the oldest brother squeals, loud and long into the high dark. "Let's go! Wheeeeee!"

The kid stares at the boat lights on the far side of the lake. Red and white orbs floating miles away. He knows that if he looks down at the boats bobbing right off the beach at the edge of the carnival, he'll puke. He focuses on the farthest of the dots and imagines fireflies, glowing hummingbirds.

"Hello, Clear Lake!" the other brother shouts. He slaps the kid's thigh. The kid looks down in the dark, sure the pain must be making it throb with light. "Are we having fun or what?"

"Don't. Don't. Don't," the kid pleads. "Come on, please?"

His new brothers howl. They swing and sloop in the bug-thick fringe of light.

The kid starts sniffling, says, "Please don't," and then is crying softly as the Ferris wheel jerks into movement and stops again to let another group on. "Please?"

He tries to swallow his sobs.

"You scared, Hemmy?" the oldest brother asks, nudging the kid with an elbow. It's their nickname for him, short for Hemorrhoid. The kid knows they are poking fun at him when they use it, but usually doesn't care because it makes him feel special. "Wow, we're pretty high. You can see everything up here. I reeeeeaaaaaallly hope we don't fall!"

The kid closes his eyes. He wants to be back on solid ground, to leave Iowa, to go back to his mother's house in Minnesota. The younger brother huffs, but stops swinging his legs. Finally the Ferris wheel rattles to life and rotates smoothly.

"Hey, hey, hey. We were just messing with you." The older brother leans down and speaks softly. He puts an arm over his shoulder. "Didn't mean anything by it. Come on, we're sorry. You're our brand-new little brother!"

The kid wants so badly for his new brothers to like him. He's done everything they've tricked him into this weekend, shadowed them every second of the day, asked them thousands of questions, even sat on the toilet in silence while they took baths. But right now he wants his new brothers to die, for their dying to hurt so bad, to last longer than anything.

The Ferris wheel loops, machinery clacking with groans.

The kid refuses to speak or open his eyes. He is far away, alone in a field of glowing light. They ride the giant hoop in silence. Down into and then above the jubilance of Clear Lake's Fourth of July Carnival.

The kid is still overwhelmed by everything that has happened these last two months. One morning, a week after he asked about his father, his dad showed up for the first time since the kid was a baby. They went to Hardee's for burgers and milk shakes and followed it up with an afternoon of toy shopping. He had never had a day like that—was entranced by this new way of living—and asked if he could go home with his father for the weekend. This is the third such weekend since.

Yesterday, while his father and stepmother were at work, his brothers stripped him naked. One held down his writhing body while the other squirted two full bottles of mustard all over him. They shoved him out the front door, locked it, and waved from the picture window as the naked and soiled kid cried in the driveway.

Afterward he scrubbed and scrubbed his skin but it just turned sickly, a deeply flushed yellow. The smell of the mustard is inside him still, overpowering the sugary smells of the carnival, all the junk food his father happily gave him money for—a twenty—the most money he's ever held in his hand. He bought and ate everything: bags of saltwater taffy; an elephant ear as wide as his chest, caked with powdered sugar; a sock-long sleeve of caramel corn.

His hands are sticky with sugar but all he smells is mustard.

The Ferris wheel orbits over and over, their gondola rising high above the other rides, and the kid imagines he is the Incredible Hulk, smashing each of his brothers' heads in a fist with the same ease with which he can flatten a roly-poly. He will launch them off the gondola, far out into the lake, where they'll sink to the muddy bottom and become food for catfish.

In the quiet he hazards a look down. Seats are filling in front of the band shell. On the other side of the street, the grassy shoreline is quilted with the blankets of people who, before the sun set, hunkered down in the best spots for viewing that night's fireworks.

It will be a concussive barrage of an hour—and he will be scared and confused and some kind of happy he can't understand. The fireworks will be shot off a barge anchored a few hundred yards from shore. The fireworks will streak cherry red and willow white across the sky. Laceworks of crackle and burst will reflect off the lake.

The kid will imagine the world is shattering, that all of it is on fire.

When their gondola stops at the bottom, a rail-thin carny with forearms like scabbed straws lifts the safety bar from their laps. As soon as he can squeeze out, the kid makes a break for it. He leaps down the ride's steps and is sprinting before his shoes touch the ground. He runs away from his new brothers, away from the corner of the fair where the rides whirl and clank, where everyone smells like an electrical fire, like a car garage.

The kid hears his brothers yell and start after him, but the street he runs down is lined with midway games and food stands. It's jam-packed with everyone who lives in northern Iowa. The kid squirrels and eels through the masses without slowing down. His new brothers have to stop running, say excuse me, pardon, pardon, to pass through the crowds, because tonight—the biggest night of the summer at the lake—all the assholes are out.

Too many people have crazy thoughts fizzing through their heads. Too many want to start a fight, trying to impress the boys or a girl, especially after failing to win the human-size panda bear, especially after slamming the gigantic hammer down on the scale and watching the game show mercury rise up to "Mini Man!," the surrounding crowd slapping their knees with laughter.

The kid goes and goes. He flies past everything. Ring toss. Water gun horse races. Throw a dart, pop a balloon! A few seconds later—beside a stand hung with ziplock bags of goldfish—he passes the same game, but with BB guns.

He hooks around the side of a stand selling fresh

lemonade and peeks out from its edge. Can't see his brothers anywhere in the crowd. He catches his breath, and as he watches, everything slows down. The kid doesn't know any of the thousands of people at the fair— including, he thinks, his brothers.

He feels like a spy, someone on the run, an outlaw. Bliss lightnings down his spine. From his pocket he pulls a twist of saltwater taffy and stuffs it in his mouth. He walks into the shadows and drops the wrapper. Never in his life has he eaten so many sweets. Later he will wake in the middle of the night and rush to the bathroom. He'll turn himself inside out throwing up. But right now he untwists another piece of taffy. He feels electric. He might not sleep all weekend.

He disappears between two stands and comes out the other side. Suddenly he's on an empty street, lined with the plastic back walls of the midway games. It's dark except for a flickering streetlight. He's amazed at how quiet it is—all the people and games and rides are just a street over, but they sound a thousand miles away.

Up and down the pavement, thick electric cables twist from the stands to the mobile home–size generators lined up in the lot one block over. The kid imagines they are snakes, enormous anacondas and pythons slipping through the slim darknesses of the midway.

Buzzed on sugar, the kid runs the dark streets that surround the fair until he's back at his original point of exit. He stops to catch his breath and notices, far down one street, RVs pressed together like boxcars on a train.

He tiptoes down the pavement. Each smashed street-light dangles glass teeth. Closer, he hears people, and, stepping back, hides behind a tree. The RVs are ram-shackle, with duct-taped mirrors and windows covered with cardboard. Standing on the steps of one of them, backlit by its insides, a man pisses into the street.

"Look, Ma," he shouts. Hands on his hips, pants crumpled to his knees. "No hands!" The loud splattering goes on forever before, finally, slowing to a dribble. The man grabs his penis and shakes it. From the shadows comes a woman's voice, ghostlike, saying to put that thing away. The kid can hardly breathe.

The man on the steps waggles his penis for his invisible audience until a full can of beer rockets off his chest.

"Fuckers!" he shouts, leaning down to reach his pants. A lake of foam grows around the can in the street. There's laughter, hoots that turn into phlegm-webbed coughs, and someone spits against the side of the RV. The kid thinks he somehow crawled into another world. Like Narnia.

"I'm empty." The man on the steps zips up and opens the door of the RV. "Who needs one?"

After he's gone, a cigarette is lit, and the kid sees clearly that there are two other people standing in the street—a woman and a man. "That fool's gonna get him-self cut," the man says. His face is tight but puffy, like the bags of goldfish on the midway, and his voice sounds like wrenching metal. "Better watch it."

"Don't be like that," the woman says as she steps toward him. "Don't." In the half light of their smoking, the woman unbuttons her shirt, opens it wide, and presses her breast to the angry man. The kid feels as if he should look away but he can't.

"Let's go," she says. The two hurry down the street, toward the lake, into the farther dark.

The kid feels all weird and tingly, outside himself. He's played around with his friends secretly, touched the privates of all the girls and boys and let himself be touched in return. But he's never seen a grown-up's penis like that. Nor has he seen the real live breasts of a stranger. He also didn't think someone could pee so much for so long.

He isn't really sure what he saw, but he knows he wants to see it all again.

Just as he's about to crawl out of his hiding spot, the RV door opens. The man steps onto the landing, hands filled with beer cans. He stops and looks slowly around the street.

"Shit," the man says to the empty darkness. "Where the fuck did y'all go?" he shouts.

After reaching into the RV for an electric lantern, the man sits heavily on the bottom step. He sets the light in front of him and hunkers on the edge of its halo. He lines up four beers on the pavement, and from his hip pulls a knife as long as the kid's forearm.

The kid is antsy and ready to go—he needs to use the bathroom, too—but now he's scared. He is sure that the man will see him if he crawls out from behind the tree. He wishes he hadn't been so stupid. Suddenly he doesn't care if his brothers bully him some, if only they'd find him.

The man stabs the knife tip into the top of a beer can, then brings it to his mouth and tilts back his head. A second later he flattens the can in one fist, lets out a long burp, and throws it beyond the circle of light. There's no clatter. The kid never hears the can land.

The man does the exact same thing two more times.

Just as he reaches for the last can, he looks up like he's heard something out in the dark. He shouts—and then a mountain of a man, slumped deep in a wheelchair, appears in the too-bright lantern light. The man on the steps stands, hands the beer to the wheelchaired man, and then bends over and offers a hug. They speak quietly. The kid can't make out any of it. And now he's more confused than ever.

The man in the wheelchair looks exactly like Governor, a man the kid sees back home in Red Wing. Each day the kid and his friends ride bikes for miles, all over town, and they see Governor, in his wheelchair, everywhere. They think he must have some superpower that allows him to wheel around town at ever-higher speeds. The kids all know that something is wrong with the man—he's a little slow, sometimes he says stuff that doesn't make sense—but they also think it's just his disguise. They love him. If they see his wheelchair rolling in the distance they'll pedal as hard as they can to catch up. The kid has no clue why the man's called Governor. And he doesn't understand why Governor calls everyone—boy or girl, man or woman—Pretty. But he loves it. "Hey, Pretty, how's it going?" "Be careful crossing the street, Pretty."

He is lost in this coincidence, all of this strangeness. So he steps out of his hiding spot, without thinking, and shouts hello to the men. But they don't smile as he expected them to. They are staring at him, hard. The one with the big knife steps toward him.

"Hi, Governor," the kid hollers, waving, bewildered by the awesome power Governor must have to travel the hundreds of miles from Red Wing. But after taking a step closer, he sees a scarred and red-bumped face. The man is not Governor.

The bottom drops out of the kid's guts. Fear freezes him in place before his body takes over, decides that it is time to run, and then he's going as fast as he can. The men yell as he dashes down the block, sprinting until he finds a sliver of dark to slip through. He scrambles into the crevice, teary eyed, about to wet himself. A second later he's back in the carnival's cacophony. He stands upright, blinking at the brightness. Stunned.

Almost immediately he feels a hand grip his shoulder, and he's about to scream—because the man has got him and the man has a knife and the man is going to pop the kid's head open like a beer can.

But the hand relaxes and an arm drops over him and gently turns him around, pulling him into a hug. He feels like a spinning top. He's delirious. So confused and scared. But his ambusher is his oldest brother. The kid knows he's in deep trouble. His new brothers will probably never like him now. He looks at his feet and waits for them to call him names or swear at him.

"Where'd you go?" the oldest brother asks. "We've been looking all over for you. You OK?"

The kid looks up. The oldest brother is smiling. Around the three brothers games bling and carnies bark and people shout. Music blares from speakers on the rides. There are people crowding around them, everywhere eating and spitting and laughing.

"I'm fine." After a pause he says he's sorry he took off. He just hated the Ferris wheel so bad.

"We're sorry," the oldest brother says, looking at the

other brother, who agrees—they were only trying to have some fun with their new little brother.

The kid grins at this. He did kind of have a little bit of fun. And then he says he needs a bathroom, but after he goes, could they try the Ferris wheel one more time?

"OK, Hemmy," the oldest brother says. They all laugh together. Around them the carnival pinwheels with light, clamors with life. "Sure thing. One more time, then one more treat. Then we gotta go."

KISSING GOD

> You forget what you want to remember and you
> remember what you want to forget.
> —CORMAC MCCARTHY, *THE ROAD*

I

My son is born into a Caravaggio painting. At 3:34 in the morning, my wife labors in the doom light of a hospital room in Fort Worth, Texas. There are pools of blood and hushed murmurings. Sideways voices curl through the darkness. It is the middle of January 2011. In less than two weeks I will turn thirty-three, and most days I am amazed to be alive. My boy—who does not yet have a name, who will not be anything but *baby boy* for the next seven hours, who is simply my son, my grime-slicked boy, my wailing and blood-roped son, my boy, blinking, teary, how much pain you look like you're in, my son, my son, my crumple-fleshed son—the head of my son appears in the muggy space between his mother's knees. I swear to you: there was nothing there, and then, suddenly, there was. Blinding shine of the silver bowl and I move to stand at Ariane's head, her black hair frizzed with humidity. My knucklebones grind as she crushes my hand in hers. Slick skin and the darkening light of ecstasy and oil paints. My field of vision narrows into a tight circle around my wife's pelvis. The nurse and doctor and doula hunched at Ariane's feet, urging her on, all vanish into the shadows. Everything slows, and the room gets even darker, darker, darker, slowed way down, so slow that the weak feeling in my knees is already gone, has turned into *Maybe. I'm. Not. Feeling. Anything. At. All? Maybe. I'm. Feeling. Too. Much.* And then everything ratchets back up, it gets louder and louder. It's palpable, all the life in this room; it teems with noise. Grimacing, smiling, hurting, my wife stares as a wrinkly boy appears, some trick of birthing-room light, smoke and mirrors, a movie's special effect—I swear to you: there was nothing there, and then, howlingly, there was. A *person*, much too large to fit inside another person, to have lived and grown inside my wife for months. A *whole human being*—can you hear me over the crying? over my screaming son?—like pulling a bonfire out of your mouth, a white tiger out of your hip pocket, a magic trick, in the keening air, a *baby boy* materializes in a red-soaked towel.

And then, less than a year later, it is spring and beautiful and I'm blowing through stop signs to get to the same hospital. I'm staring big eyed around the ER's waiting room. I lean against the receptionist's desk and the wall of Plexiglas she's sitting behind. My chest feels as if it's being jigsawed apart. I have a wife and a baby boy at home. I am going to die. I put my ear to the circle in the Plexiglas to hear her next question. I press the flat of my hand to my heart to show her where the pain is, run a hand down my left arm, fluttering the fingers when I describe the way it hurts. I fold the readout of the EKG performed at Emergency Care two hours before and pass it to the receptionist. It shows that I'm having an irregular heartbeat—peaks and valleys and lines—something about one of the ventricles, something that's not beating correctly, the nurse said, before adding that I needed to go to the ER immediately for more thorough medical procedures, to be sure, to make myself right. I drove straight home from Emergency Care, slowly, with both hands on the wheel. In the driveway I tried to figure out what I was going to say to Ariane, but then, trying not to cry, flatly told her that my heart was fucked up. I kissed her shocked face as Felix clambered up into my lap and grappled my neck.

"What's going on? What is it?" Ariane had asked. "You need to bring your MRI." I wouldn't have thought of it myself, so I tried to smile at her. I sat down, said, "Sure thing, thanks," and stared at our reflection in the kitchen window. Felix laughed, and then leaned toward my cheek with his mouth open and kissed me wetly.

Before I left, crying, I kissed them both again.

In the ER waiting room I don't look directly at the receptionist because my nystagmus—the uncontrollable bouncing of my eyes—has gotten more severe. I have diplopia, or double vision, too. I can't focus on anything; it looks like I have eight fingers, a blur of digits, on each hand. I raise my arms and say that earlier in the day there was a limb of pain branching down the entire left side of my body. Right to my fingertips. Both of my hands are numb, my face, too.

"Or," I tell her, trying too hard to suggest it's no big deal, "it might also be my brain."

She looks up, nonplussed, from the chart she's filling out.

"My brain." I notice—starting to blush—how loud I am. I'm making big arm motions at her. I drop the hand I'd been pointing at my ear. "My brain stem," I say. "I had a bunch of brain bleeds, brain surgery over ten years ago."

I run my finger down the scar on the back of my head, then lift the MRI films I've carried in with me.

"When I was twenty-one. I have my MRI films here. I just got one a week ago. Haven't even gotten the results yet."

II

"I think gold would be good," the dentist says. He's just a voice emanating from the blinding light above me. His rubbered fingers push in my mouth and over and against my teeth and lips. It feels as if a cuttlefish, a squid, is trying to get inside me.

I am twenty-seven and life is good, only getting better. After my dental appointment I'm going to walk out into the California sunshine and breathe deep the flowery air and get fish tacos at the restaurant that's a few storefronts down in this strip mall.

"Gold, gold, gold," the dentist mutters to himself, as if I'm not there at all. The room is thick with his honeyrot cologne. My head snaps each time he jabs my teeth with the tiny metal hook. The dazzle off his diamond-and-gold bracelets, his heavy gold chain, makes me squint. He stops scraping my gum line and stares out the window at the shine of the Lexus-packed parking lot. "Good value, gold. Good keeping."

Like someone trying to catch a snowflake on their tongue, I nod, open mouthed, ask, "Really?" but it comes out "Aaaaaaaaaaaeeeeeeee?!?"

As a little boy I dreamed of tigers. I'd be sitting right behind the animal's colossal, mawing furnace of a head, controlling its loping by tugging its ears, urging it forward, faster—or to slow down, or stop—with the fragile bones of my ankles. Two bluffs cradled the part of Red Wing I lived in. The Mississippi River snaked by on the other side of Barn Bluff. Wisconsin was just a bridge away. It was all very Huck Finn and I was already one hundred years old. I rode my bike to the craggy mouths of caves charred black by old fires, which were littered with the starlight of Bud Light cans; empty soup cans and shattered liquor bottles littered the deer paths I hiked. I scrabbled up the slopes of loose rock to the brittle grass on top of the bluffs.

For whole days I hung my legs over edges, hundreds of feet straight down. I lay stomach-down on hot flat stones, my head lolling over sandstone lips.

From Barn Bluff, like some tiny impotent god, I watched all of Red Wing buzz and weave below. I felt burnished with the sensation that I almost, just almost, could control what I saw down there. The cars and people just toys for me to move—four steps forward, four steps back—around the board game that was my days.

I can't figure California out—the beautiful tedium that bleaches the day of sorrow while beneath the illusion a gnarled pit of sadness grows inside you—but I think some part of me loves it, this gorgeous shitshow. A perfect day—the cloudless, bluest sky above Thousand Oaks, seventy-two degrees and a breeze shuffling the pomegranate trees—will be followed by weeks of calamity. Midnight earthquakes. Rain, rain, rain, rain, and then mudslides. Then the world will go inferno. For a month ash will darken the air, a gloomy gift from one of the dozens of uncontrolled wildfires spreading through southern California. Hundreds of thousands of dead fish will wash ashore and the beaches will shut down. Two days later the same sand will be foaming with raw sewage that leaked from a water treatment plant in one of the cities along the coast.

Each day from high above Red Wing I counted the houses on my block. The neighbor lady in the wheelchair that I visited each day—that I ran errands for. The bullies' big house on the corner. Colvill, my elementary school, and the blacktop field where we played kickball. The lot that froze into a skating rink each winter after the fire department hosed it down. I let my arms marionette in the wind, watching hawks that lazily hooped through the air. Brown-gold swoops in the blue sky above the Mississippi, above the small Minnesota town.

Yesterday was one of SoCal's flawless days: sun soaked, dozens of radiant oranges in the light-gemmed tree. And today started even better, but an hour after breakfast it started to shred apart. The kombucha smells off, a puckering, vinegary sweetness, and these new pills my doctor prescribed are giving me what Ariane calls "the yawn." The kefir I'm making in the kitchen has started expanding exponentially. The first forty-ounce batch was perfect with a splash of mango juice, but the quantity of finished kefir doubled the next time, and that doubled the next— again and again—until now two levels of the fridge are packed with forty-ounce jars of curdling milk. My wife doesn't like kefir, and Sam, the only friend I have here, lives an hour away in Ventura. I'm not sure he trusts my batches of homemade fermentation anyway. In a couple of days the kefir will be a rot-chunked soup. I will not let it go to waste, I will drink it all if I have to.

My dream tigers effortlessly churned up the bluffs' hillsides. I bravely rode them into the caves I hardly had the courage to creep into by day. As the tiger looked over the graffitied walls, the rocky contours lit up, as if its eyes were headlights. When the animal closed its eyes the world went dark and I clung to the heaving, furred body that hummed warm beneath me like a foundry. Some nights my dream tiger would sprint right off the edge of the bluff and we could fly.

But now, each sun-drenched afternoon, I'm falling deeply and suddenly asleep. This kind of gone-forever sleep has never happened before. It's a being-swallowed-into-the-belly-of-a-whale nothingness.

It always starts the same: beneath the orange tree, I meditate on my recovery, on my body healed of all brokenness.

There's an ocean breeze, the peppery smell of my tomato plants.

An hour of mindfulness, sometimes two, and then blackness. From out of nowhere. I am nothing. I don't exist. And time is an endless train of bruised boxcars.

What feels like months pass before I'm waking, bewildered, gasping—the sapphire bowl of sky above the orange tree, the aloe plant blossoming in this place, this wherever the fuck I am, this backyard—and then fiercely I am jammed back into my body.

The grass needs to be mowed. Hornworms are making Wiffle balls of the tomatoes. I listen to the neighbor's radio—the Dodgers are up by two—and at the same time a sort of shamefulness starts crawling up my chest. I'm struck with the sense of satisfaction a policeman must feel snapping the cuffs on a burglar, as if I'd caught someone doing something wrong.

The dream tigers appeared throughout my childhood—and I loved them. Bengals, Sumatrans, Siberians, Malayans. Almost always, each new dream brought me a different tiger—a thicker, more golden coat one night; an ear that kept flopping down the next time; a huge-headed, five-hundred-pound Siberian after that—but somehow they were also all the same. In the first dreams, when I pressed my forehead against the tiger's enormous head, the plush orange fur seemed to cave and curl around my bones like a mask or scarf or stocking cap, and in the heat I could hear my own thoughts.

I heard, in the tiger, whatever I was thinking. I was eavesdropping on myself. *Climb the bluff. Hunker through the tall weeds along the stretch of swamp before the power plant. Wonder if David is home.*

Early this morning, on my jog through Thousand Oaks, hours before my dentist's appointment, a motorcycle cop pulled me over for jaywalking. After getting my lecture, I ran up into the hills on the distant edge of town.

At night coyotes sprint through this scrub. Falling asleep, we listen to their maniacal ululations as they stand in a pack over whatever frozen-eyed animal they are rending apart.

The howls are the purest bloodlust, a gnashing bacchanal.

I followed the horse trails to look down on Simi Valley. Plops of horseshit speckle the dirt. It's lined by prickly pear and gnarled, bone-dry brush. Occasionally wildflowers, vibrant fists of color, peek up.

I don't usually pause for whatever's left of what the coyotes killed during the night, but today, starting to lasso back and forth down the other hillside, just a few miles from the Ronald Reagan Presidential Library, I stopped short—and the raptor looked up at me like *What the fuck are you doing here?* before knifing its black triangle of a head back into the blood puddle at its talons.

It hopped, hopped, hopped through the muck like it was dancing.

When awake—my dream tigers crouching in the sleep that I would fall into that night—I loved pop-up books, Superman and the Lone Ranger. The Man of Steel emerging, chest thrust forward, from the Metropolis phone booth Clark Kent had just entered, after I tugged the paper tag of the booth's doors. The Lone Ranger *Hi-yo, Silver! Away!*-ing atop the white stallion that I whinnied across the page via a wheel that fit my index finger perfectly.

With no TV in our home, books turned to confetti in my hands. I read in the bathtub. I slept with whatever books my mother brought home from the library.

But sometimes, after falling asleep, I pressed my face into the tiger's fur and couldn't tell what it was thinking. A blank chalkboard. The surface of a lake on a breezeless day. Into the black gap I yearned, but I couldn't hear what was going on inside me.

Then, as I got older—sometime around first grade— the dream tigers started ignoring me. Little things at first. I'd think *Go right around that fallen log* and the animal might go left. Instead of slowing when I asked it to, the rippling beast would keep sprinting ahead. To stay balanced atop it, I'd clutch and scrabble while it zigged or bucked.

Once, ignoring my pleas, it leaped straight off the edge of Barn Bluff and instead of flying us high over the Mississippi, the huge warmth beneath me vanished. The tiger was gone. And I plummeted. Choking, my stomach in my throat, as the murky water raced up at me.

With a jerk of its head, the bird hops at me before flaring into the air. Up it flies, a barking arrow, curling in the updraft. It circles and swoops above. The mess left behind makes it look as if a *real* animal—something three or four times bigger than a rabbit—exploded all over the dirt. On the side of the trail, the breakable weeds are red freckled.

Flies buzz over the splay of meat and blood.

Because I'm a little boy, what I'm completely bewildered by—what, as a thirty-three-year-old, I still can't make sense of, what, maybe, I'll always be writing about, what I'll always be trying to understand—is why my teenage cousin would want to repeatedly sexually abuse his sister and me. I'm three, maybe four years old. His sister is four, too, and she is my best friend.

These memories are mercury poured into my cupped hands. My attempts to fathom the flesh and cruelty are eating fire, choking a bonfire down.

The sexual abuse happens while I'm living with my cousin's family in Oregon.

There is a knife in the room each time he unzips his jeans.

The blade shines.

My cousin's zipper shines.

Rain fingers down the bedroom window. Beyond the glass, the gray sky.

My cousin points the knife tip at me, threatens to murder my mother, the most important person in my world, the one who's raising me by herself, the one I'd do anything for, before he'll come after me. Before he'll kill every person I love.

So of course I'm not going to tell.

At the time I'm not even sure what exactly is going on. Don't know if what is happening to me, what I am being forced to do, is really bad.

Maybe I deserve it, like he says. Maybe a part of me likes it.

"If you tell," he says, "I'll kill everyone." My cousin smiles, taking his belt off. "Then you."

I showed up to the dentist's early. I walked around the strip mall to feel the sunshine on my face and then checked in at the front desk. On one side of the waiting room, a man sat hunched toward a blaring, wall-mounted plasma TV. A game show was on. As if I weren't even there—a ghost, an invisible presence in his living room—he hardly looked up when I entered. I said hello and then sat on the other side of the room.

I flipped through my book's pages, unable to focus through his laughter, the gunshots of his knee slaps. Each time the show's audience laughed the man clapped once, percussively, which was followed by the sound of his hands rasping away from each other, like a tennis shoe tearing away from melting-hot blacktop.

For fifteen minutes I tried not to sigh as he thundered and roared.

And then, at eleven fifteen exactly, the man stood, flattened his track pants with a few swipes of his hand, and tucked in his bright-yellow T-shirt. From the back of a chair he swooped up a doctor's overcoat, then stepped toward me. He grinned and reached out to shake my hand, introduced himself as my dentist, and said he was happy I was there.

III

At some point in my life I realize that I do not see the world exactly as it is—that I do not see what the people around me see. That my vision is skewed and I stare at what's not there, or what no one else is looking at.

Often I feel like I'm living inside a cage, watched in truth by no one, but paranoid that others are out there, staring in at me.

Always it seems that I'm waiting for the results of a procedure that will tell me how close I am to death, if I am dying again.

Around me the world is terribly alive.

Around me the world is not equally loved.

KING OF THE RATS

> When the Rio Grande is flowing, the starry skies are
>   bright,
> She walks along the river in the quiet summer night:
> She thinks if I remember, when we parted long ago,
> I promised to come back again, and not to leave her so.
> —FROM "THE YELLOW ROSE OF TEXAS"

paranoid—New Latin, from Greek, madness, from
paranous "demented," from *para-* + *nous*, "mind."

R ats are taking over the garage. There's nothing to
be done.
      Boot-size rodents sprint straight up the walls
and then tiptoe along the roof beams. In the wall or the
attic, they sound like the Sunday newspaper being crumpled and lit aflame, but out in the open they are silent, a
crawling mannequin's hand. When I go into the pass-out
heat of the garage—the loaded-down laundry basket held
in front of me, banging through the kitchen door—I *feel*
them up in the rafters, lording over me, disease eyed. My
flesh shivers.

The neighbors up and down the street all seem to
have dogs, and all those dogs are barking.

Inside the garage I look up and see the one that always

seems to be there. Big, slumped lazily as if on a throne, fearless, smiling down at me. In January I will be thirty-three. Soon I will be a father, to a biracial son due also in January. I was born in Iowa, he will be born in Texas. My wife says something must be done about the rats and *I know*, but nothing I do succeeds. I look up and see shapes moving in the dimness and know that I am the master of nothing, the king of weakness.

A *rat king* is a group of rats whose tails have knotted together. In January 2005 an Estonian farmer named Rein Kiiv found one. After Rein's son killed the sixteen rats, the two men realized they'd been fused together by frozen sand. Imagine a Ferris wheel constructed from rats. Imagine the carny at its controls. And imagine, beneath the wheeling assemblage and the grandstand, smaller rats, nubs of stale popcorn and chunks of taffy in their sharp-toothed mouths. Inside these rats there is even farther down: garbage and blood and guts. My attic churns with the noise the rats make. I imagine rat kings in our walls, in the crawl space beneath the floorboards.

In January 1971, Black Sabbath's second album, *Paranoid*, was released in the United States. Two of the band's biggest hits are on the record: "War Pigs" and "Iron Man." An anti-Vietnam song, "War Pigs" was the band's choice for album title, but Vertigo Records thought it too provocative. *Rolling Stone* has often called Black Sabbath "the heavy-metal kings of the 1970s." I have bought T-shirts, seen posters that said as much: "Kings of Heavy Metal." In high school we'd go "gravel-jamming" on Iowa's back roads—we'd get lit up and drive around listening to Black Sabbath or *Blizzard of Ozz*, lost, playing the Lizard King for hour after hour. *The future's uncertain and the end is always near / Let it roll, baby, roll.*

Yes, I will turn thirty-three this winter. I cannot stop thinking about the rats, the horde of them, unyielding. Their crackling keeps me and my wife sleepless. In 2010 I am at war with the rats, while on the other side of the world the United States is also at war, sanctioning torture. I dream of being handcuffed nude to a chair, a barking dog set upon me. Soon, I will be a father. So soon, I will be. So soon, I will be a father.

Elvis Presley, the King, or the King of Rock and Roll, died thirty-three years ago. He was also born in January. As were Hall of Fame pitcher Nolan Ryan and advocate of torture Dick Cheney. When I think of Elvis, I think of the movie *Viva Las Vegas* and pills and sweaty muttonchops. Nolan Ryan was almost bald when he put Robin Ventura in a headlock and punched his head, over and over again, after Ventura charged the mound in a game between the Texas Rangers and the Chicago White Sox. Dick Cheney was thirty-seven when he had his first heart attack.

Four years away: from heart attacks, from saying *You bet* to torture, from saying *Go for it, do what needs to be done, do whatever it takes for them to tell us what we want to hear.*

Counting each bone in my coccyx, I have thirty-three vertebrae in my spine—a spine that was slightly curved in my youth. A spine that ladders up to a brain that has been observed, kicked, kissed, cut into, swollen, photographed, punched, fallen upon, head-butted, dashboard smashed, beaned by a curveball, split apart, x-rayed, beaned by a fastball, held, injected with dye, concussed, massaged, and prayed over.

Thirty-three is also the atomic number for arsenic. In a study published in *Epidemiology* in 2003, a group of seven scientists found that pregnant women who are exposed to arsenic through drinking water will have children with lower birth weights. Arsenic's effect on pregnant women is similar to that of tobacco smoke and benzene. Lewisite is an organoarsenic compound named after the American chemist Winford L. Lewis. "A dark, oily liquid producing an irritant gas," lewisite was developed by the US Army as a chemical warfare agent in the early twentieth century. It causes blisters similar to those of mustard gas, but is more effective because it seeps into the skin. It is sometimes odorless and can appear amber if it's impure. In "Why Not Gas Warfare?" a 1939 op-ed piece in support of the use of chemical weapons, Lewis argued that "the advantage in this mode of warfare goes to that country which is more highly developed in chemical industries."

The crows swoop and dip, dark commas tornadic in the drafts between bluffs. It is 2004 and I am visiting friends in the Navajo Nation in New Mexico. I'm years away from being able to care about anything or anyone more than myself. I've been lying down on this rock for only ten minutes and already the thirty-three vertebrae in my spine, all of my back, are numb. A pickup chugs off in the distance, out along the horizon, maybe in Arizona. A dog barks. A door slams. Earlier I'd gone to the abandoned uranium mines, to see deep into the ground where, for a long time, many Navajo worked without much protection. On the reservation there's generation after generation of sickness and death and very little help. But the rez dogs wouldn't let me get a close look. They chased me up to this rock formation and frenzied while I clambered up.

Each dog is mangy, covered with open sores. After chasing me they jawed and snapped at each other, and then, as if they heard some crash in the distance, stopped. They drifted off into the culvert, a spread of trash-strewn snow: torn garbage bags; an old Clorox jug, like an enormous busted tooth; two pieces of a sink; some PVC piping. Now a dog with a pulpy bloom of fresh blood where one of its ears used to be noses into a bag and a black flash streaks out. While the three dogs chase the rat, I watch two other rats inch out of the white plastic. And then they're muzzle and jaw down in the weeds and gone, invisible in the ditch's dried grass. I hold my stocking cap to keep the wind from stealing it. The same wind that had hundreds of US flags straightened out above the cemetery yesterday, as if they'd been pinned to the air. One of my gloves is already gone, sinking into the icy slush in the ditch far below. The dogs are back. One has the rat hanging limply from its mouth.

∴

If you walk into a garage in which rats have chewed open your lewisite reserves, and the gas is drifting down on you like a comforter, this is what you should expect: "large, painful, fluid-filled blisters, especially on the extremities, back, and scrotum . . . swelling, inflammation, and destruction of the lining of the airways . . . pulmonary swelling, diarrhea, restlessness, weakness, below-normal temperature, and low blood pressure." In the 1940s the United States was making lewisite in Pine Bluff, Huntsville, and the Rocky Mountains. At decade's end production was halted and the United States dumped over twenty thousand tons of lewisite into the oceans: "One of the 1948 dumping operations was referred to as Operation Geranium because lewisite has a geranium-like odor." In 1991 an Iraqi prisoner of war reported that Saddam Hussein had stockpiled lewisite munitions.

On May 13, 2004, Steve King, an Iowa congressman, compared the torture at Abu Ghraib to fraternity hazing. In the same press release he references prostitute Heidi Fleiss, serial killer Jeffrey Dahmer, and Iowa senator Tom Harkin, and says, "charred," "dangling," and "ballpark." King attends St. Martin's Church in Odebolt, Iowa. This is just over an hour from where I was born.

On the gorgeous, sun-dappled day I decide all the rats must be killed—no matter what trap or poison it requires—a bird flies into my open garage. It swoops down again and again to peck me on the back and neck. I run from the garage but the bird stays, flies up into the dark, and roosts in the eaves. I leave the garage light off and a door open when I go, hoping the bird will know to fly out into the pink Texas twilight. At dusk, when the bird sees me looking through the garage window, it yells, "Cracker Jacks." My wife says it is a mockingbird. I say I know; the fucker is making fun of me. Tomorrow the garage will be oven hot. If it doesn't fly off tonight, it will die. Or the rats might get it.

All night I walk around the house. I flip the garage light on and peer up into shadowed beams. The bird is gone. In January I will be thirty-three. I see the rats scurrying through the dark. In January I will be a father. I am as naked as the day I was born, a bag over my head, handcuffed to a chair, and there is a dog snarling atop me. In the morning I will have to sweep up whatever the rats have left of the mutilated bird.

The summer after my freshman year of college—the summer of 1997—I had an internship at a television station in northern Iowa. Each morning I'd blearily drive to work. Check in. Get an assignment. Check out a video camera. All day I'd drive a TV station car, most often a falling-apart white station wagon, to sporting events across the state. I'd shoot video until I had a few highlights—home runs, a triple in the gap, double play, backward K's—and then it was off to the next town. The next game. At night, bone-sore from driving all day, I could hardly stand.

That summer I read only Nabokov and often, instead of going straight on, I'd hang a right after leaving town and drive aimlessly down a gravel road. I'd pick a spot where the corn was taller than the roof of my station wagon and then lie back on the hood, smoking cigarettes and reading.

All summer it was Cedar Rapids, Garner, Hampton, Odebolt, Webster City, and Aplington. It was also the summer that I began brushing my teeth on long, solitary drives. The radio up—probably Black Sabbath or Ozzy Osbourne again—and the windows open to the humid choke of the corn and soybean fields. I'd brush them again and again. The toothbrush's white whiskers going pink with blood.

Martin de Porres was the first black saint in the Americas. The Saint of the Broom was famous for his work with the poor. Levitation and the ability to appear in two separate places at the same time were among his miracles. November 11 is the feast day of Martin of Tours, who, before being baptized as an adult and becoming a monk, was a Roman soldier. In Estonia the day marks the beginning of winter and the end of the Soul's Visiting Time. *Collectio orientalium canonum, seu Capitula Martini* was Saint Martin of Braga's collection of eighty-four canons.

"The Fox and the Cat," one of the Grimms' fairy tales, begins with the cat admiring Mr. Fox for how well regarded he is in the world. "Good-day, my dear Mr. Fox," she says. "How is it going? How are you?" The fox looks the cat up and down. He takes a long time to decide whether or not to even speak to her before calling her a "wretched beard-cleaner" and a "speckled fool." The fox thinks the cat is stupid for understanding only one way to escape. The fox brags about knowing hundreds, about his "sackful of cunning." "I feel sorry for you," Mr. Fox says to the cat. "Come with me and I will teach you how one escapes from the dogs." But when the hounds come, the cat uses that trick and leaps into a tree's safety. She yells at the fox, telling him to open his sack. But the fox is already being torn apart.

Outside in the Texas dark, the dogs are barking. All the beasts are coming. All the beasts—the cat, the fox, the dogs, and the people—are torturing one another. In the garage there are hundreds of rats. I see them in double, two by two, a parade of them. I look at the cat, ask why she doesn't do shit, and she looks away from me, disgusted. I will be a father soon. I will be thirty-three. Somehow I am still alive. The rats blur straight up the walls.

Rat kings are sometimes bound together not by frozen sand, but by a glue of blood. *A glue of blood.* When I close my eyes and am lucky enough to sleep, I see the first of the rats that were snapped almost in half by the traps set in the garage. Roiling with maggots, their flesh churns, seeming still alive, and the garage is so hot the stench—the unbearable death scent—seems lacquered on. The rats that aren't cracked instantly dead wriggle, pry themselves from the traps, and then drag their bodies across the concrete, leaving a wake of dark syrup. *A glue of blood.* Maggots, "no one gets to heaven / Without going through you first."

❖

So here I am, barely able to go on in Texas, a state where fifty years ago I couldn't be married to my wife because of miscegenation laws. Soon I will be thirty-three—I will be father to my son, something so recently illegal. The state flower is the bluebonnet and for the few short weeks it blooms during the spring, Texas is dazzling. Then there is drought. Halliburton. Lockheed Martin. The mockingbird, which comes to my home to die, is the state bird. The Gulf of Mexico is our lowest elevation; it's where they dump what they want to hide or ignore, without a worry for what it kills. This is where everything spills. We are the buckle of the Bible Belt and everything is bigger here. Magnolias. Church steeples. BBQ ribs. There's been so much drilling for natural gas that there's benzene in the air, and Texas has the largest uninsured population in the nation. All the fracking might be causing the dozens of earthquakes occurring in the region each week. The Texas Troubles—a panic about the potential insurrection of slaves—presaged the Civil War. Someday my child will have to confront that backwardness because it's still swaggering around. The racism that grins through every hello and sharpens every minute with hints of violence. Echoes of the voices that put a "WANTED" photo of JFK on flyers distributed in Dallas the day before he was killed.

There are the rats, always arriving, no matter how many are snapped to mush. The dogs are howling. Torture, torture, torture. I am sleepless and the king of failings.

But I am also right here, half-awake in this Texas of Blind Lemon Jefferson. The Texas of Janis Joplin and Buddy Holly and the first black heavyweight champion, Jack Johnson. The live oaks are bursting and emerald and throw shade over the backyard and each afternoon a child bikes down my street and each afternoon that child waves and I'm going to become an ordained minister on the Internet and someday soon I'll become a father and all of this is so much I often feel like I'm diving into the swallowing sun—for it is again and always and somehow, through all our revolting failures, our endless cruelties, still amazingly beautiful—listening to "War Pigs" on my headphones, my back unfeeling as I work in the oven-like garage, out here killing, ending the endless rat after rat.

MIGRANTS IN A FEVERLAND

They stumble loose limbed up the grassy median, Summit Avenue dappled with spring sunshine. The sick boy wears a baseball cap pulled down like a trucker's. It masks the bruises beneath his eyes and his insomnia-carved cheekbones. When he lifts the cap his shaved head is blinding except for a weepy red scar. He kicks at the tulips that bloom on the boulevard. The heads of the flowers rooster-tail high into the air, shattering into a thousand shards of light, and he runs beneath them, petals raining on his shoulders and hat. His friend—taller, tan, goateed, also in his last year of college—strums an invisible guitar. Hums and croons to no one.

It's late April, the first beautiful day after a winter that would not end, and Minnesota is drunk on sunlight and good weather.

Everyone in Saint Paul is outside. Students from Macalester, St. Thomas, and St. Kate's throng the side-walks. Outside Coffee News the tables are packed, and thick crowds are gathered like rubberneckers outside Dunn Brothers. Cars whip by the median. Blurry faces and shouted greetings. Every other car honks. At all times someone, somewhere, is screaming with joy.

The day whirs, jade green and full throated, around

the two boys—but they are oblivious. They barely acknowledge each other. Yesterday they spent the entire afternoon with a men's group they formed with a baseball teammate. They spent hours talking, unspooling their guts, and crying. They held each other's quaking bodies. Afterward the sick boy was exhausted but couldn't sleep. His eyes stung. The sun rose as he watched from the couch and still he was bewildered by the traumas they'd all shared. Overnight he'd become sure that everyone carries catastrophe around inside, and imagined himself the only one able to see each person's hurt, a pulsing organ within.

On the drive home, the boys had decided to dedicate today to getting fucked up, throttling themselves toward blackness. Letting the world swallow them for a few hours.

A pair of runners divide around the singer and then merge seamlessly, like magnets. Their long strides twinned. The singer waves at their backs, then grimaces and rocks out a solo.

Looking out from the darkness of his cap brim, the sick boy sees a hugely blossoming lilac bush on the next block and sprints through the red light into the street. A northbound driver lays on the horn and swerves to miss him. The car skids to a stop and the one behind it runs onto the curb, but the sick boy doesn't look back. He swims into the lilacs, does not hear the man yelling from the open car door, asking what kind of stupid fuck he is. Instead he shrouds himself in the thin limbs and sickly sweet smell.

The singer waits for the light to turn green before crossing the street but he, too, ignores the complaining drivers. When he stops suddenly and stares into a gigantic red oak, a pack of joggers have to sidestep and collide into one another to avoid him. For minutes he doesn't look away from whatever he sees high in the limbs.

"Let's burn another one down and cut across," he says to the lilacs, where the sick boy is digging finger runnels in the dirt. He shades his eyes and, like the captain of a doomed frigate, stares south toward Grand Avenue. "Onward. We go that way!"

"Sure," the sick boy says quietly. "Let's do it." He can't tell how loud he's speaking or if what he's saying is making any sense. "I'm down for whatever."

He watches how his friend stands upright, in plain sight, pouching rolling papers with weed. No worries, not a care in the world. When the joint is sealed, the sick boy stumbles from the lilacs, right in front of another group of runners. The women, all clad in St. Thomas gear, scream and scatter. He screams, too, louder than all of them as he flinches back and away. He didn't see them coming and the surprise strangled his heart. Creating a wall of his arms, waiting for the first kick or punch, he topples onto his butt.

In seconds the sprinting girls are a half block away, but turn back to shout. "Fucker!" "Creep!" "Psycho!" They give him the finger and yell that they're gonna call the cops, and then cross Selby Avenue and are gone.

On the curb of the frontage road, the two boys smoke the joint down to a roach that the singer pops into his mouth. They have to force themselves to get up from the plushness, to not give in to the urge to nap. They swipe

grass and dirt from each other's shirts and pants and
continue plodding toward campus. On a normal day
they would have been there an hour ago.

The sick boy suggests they turn right off Grand at Ace
Hardware—a block before campus—to avoid the college
kids cramming the sidewalk. They can access campus
through the side doors of the art department. He's a
super-senior, thanks to his brain surgery, and most of
his best friends have already graduated. His girlfriend
lives on the other side of the world. He feels left behind,
ashamed for still being around. Each day on campus
someone is sure to ask him how he's doing, tell him
that he's looking great, that it's so nice to see him—and
instead of letting their kindness in, he feels pitiful.

The two spent all morning in the basement of the singer's
apartment, where he lives with the teammate from the
men's group and another one from Montana. The sick
boy crashes on their couch when it is impossible for him
to get back to his apartment on the other side of campus,
or when he doesn't want to walk home in the dark. If
the couch isn't available, he'll sleep on the floor or in the
yard. During the day he might go to class, but usually
he's at their apartment. Someone might play piano or
guitar and sing, or they might meditate for a few hours
before talking long into the guzzling and bleary-eyed
night.

Earlier today the two painted the cinder block and
chipped-wood basement with the kaleidoscopic vision
the singer has been working on for weeks. The sick boy

is awed by his friend's intensity and wishes that he could
care about anything half as much. The frenzied dedi-
cation he sees in the singer reminds him of the Watts
Towers, the passion they were built with. For weeks he's
been thinking about them, remembering the little boy he
was, overjoyed by their mad beauty each time he visited
his aunt in Santa Monica.

With only a crack in the cellar window for ventila-
tion, ten minutes in they were woozy and cotton ball–
skulled. They smoked up every hour or so and didn't
speak between bowls. The sick boy thought about boogie
boarding, how it feels to sacrifice oneself to the waves
and tumble beneath cascading foam. To gasp to the surface. When he felt the urge, he rested the paintbrush on a
step and went upstairs to lie in the yard and watch monkeys and pit bulls and tractors in the clouds. Each time he
boarded in the ocean, grit and beach sand would line his
scalp—and as he lay on his back that feeling returned,
and he fingertipped his shaved head.

The sick boy prays they don't run into anyone they know.
His brain is burned toast and there's no feeling from his
waist down and that's just the way he wants it right now.
He knows he needs to stop trying to escape from the
world. But there are days it feels unbearably hard—as
if he is making his body a home for rattlesnakes—and
yesterday was overwhelming. Reliving his past, taking
on the colossal pain of his friends, drowned him in sadness—made being alive feel impossible.

Before the doors to the gallery where the curators are

in the process of hanging the senior art showcase, the singer looks back. The sick boy can read his mind: *Are you coming? Come if you want, man, if not, it's cool. I'll see you.*

"I'm coming," he mumbles. The singer bows and holds the door open wide. "Here I am!"

The art department is abandoned on such a beautiful day. Even the student worker who is paid to greet visitors is gone. The boys wander through the empty labyrinth, staring long at each figure drawing and still life pinned to the wall. They stand on the platform for nude models in the center of the studio; surrounded by easels and silence they pose absurdly.

Through the floor-to-ceiling windows they watch campus buzz. Frisbees fly across the softball field. Students lounge on blankets in the outfield grass, sundresses pulled knee high, reading books or sleeping behind sunglasses. Some boys are shirtless. On the small hill above the infield fence, a gamer—still wearing his black trench coat, black jeans, and dark sunglasses—sits smoking. A trio of soccer players are gathered on the grass right outside the studio window. They dribble the ball from foot to knee to foot, then pass it to the next person, and it is hypnotizing how the ball goes up and down and around without ever stopping. A football zips through the air. Another Frisbee whizzes into the group relaxing on the grass. Some guys from the baseball team are playing long toss, too, throwing from one end of the field to the other. Someone on a unicycle, juggling bowling pins, rides by.

"So many fuckos on parade," the sick boy says. "I don't know where I'm going. But I'm so ready to be gone. I hope that kid crashes into that light pole."

"If he doesn't," the singer says, "someone somewhere in the world will." He takes a wad of gum from his mouth and, left-handed, whips it at the window, where it clings for a second before tumbling down the glass.

Decapitated heads stare from each workbench in the sculpture studio. The sick boy inches close enough to kiss every clay bust and misshapen, steel-welded skull. Some mouthless, others grinning with hollow eye sockets. A headband of bottle caps. Glass shards for lips. The singer leans close and mimics their contorted mouths: silent screams and yawns, big hollering O's.

"Any second they're gonna start whispering crazy shit," the sick boy laughs, trying to ease the horror show fear crumpling his chest. He feels their blank eyes following him past tables and tools. They're terrible and uncanny, these half-finished faces of people he can't name but feels he knows intimately, old friends that appear in recurring dreams. "Tell us to start canning dead birds, or worshipping Prince."

"Oh no, let's go crazy!" the singer yells as they wander into the empty print studio.

They turn knobs on the presses, spill ink and roller it out on the tabletops, and scratch random letters into engraving plates before wrapping themselves in handmade fibers. Almost every print pinned up is inscribed with a political manifesto: "Meat Is Murder," "Free Tibet," "The Personal Is Political." They laugh at the strident righteousness of so many of their classmates.

The sick boy thinks about the piece he liked, the back of a stolen stop sign graffitied with "Try More. Suck Less. Shut Up," as they return to the front hallway for the free coffee that's always sitting on the rickety nightstand there. The coffee is cold and sour—yesterday's brew—but he pounds one cup down, fills another, and chews the Styrofoam between bitter sips.

What would it feel like to be zealous about something, anything, like the printmakers with their sloganeering lithographs? He makes confetti of the cup, then gulps another empty. His mouth tastes of vinyl, burned couch. More shreds of Styrofoam blizzard the floor around him. The singer raises his eyebrows and asks if he wants another one.

In the empty ceramic studio, the singer tosses a ball of clay to the sick boy, who rolls it in his hands and throws it down on a worktable. He kneads it until all the air bubbles are gone, then pat-pat-pats it into a perfect sphere. "Man, I used to spend all day in here," he says to himself. The singer knows it all already—how the sick boy would skip class and throw bowls and mugs and teapots all day; how he would help the ceramics professor with every firing, and built a raku kiln. But something happened during his surgery and he can't throw pots anymore. Bending over the potter's wheel gives him the bed spins.

"Just feel this," he says, tossing the grapefruit of clay back to the singer. "So nice." His words come out sad sack and they both hear how much he misses it.

Before leaving the art department, the singer wants to go back to the sculpture studio. They are standing in front of a bust that's been mosaicked with glass slivers and safety pins when a faculty member—the mustached one with a bonfire of hair, who doesn't teach any classes and always looks surprised—walks into the cavernous room. He stands behind them without speaking. The three of them stare for so long at the sculpture that the sick boy's mind goes blank. He jumps when the faculty member asks if they've heard.

"Heard what?" the singer asks, leaning closer to the bust's thumb-smudged cheeks. The sick boy feels how cold the air-conditioning is, how not high he suddenly feels.

One of their classmates was home for the weekend, they're told, back east somewhere. She was riding her bike when a city bus hit her, flinging her into the air. She lost her leg, and her insides won't be good for a long time. Who knows when she'll return to school—if she will at all. It's too early to know much of anything.

The sick boy is about to cry. He's always about to cry.

But then the singer stands up rigidly, like a robot, and says, "Man, that's a bummer," and turns from the sculpture to the sick boy, a huge, unhinged smile on his face. "A bummer," he repeats, an eye twitching above the crazy grin. "For sure."

At this the sick boy begins to giggle. He flutters his fingers good-bye and bolts, crashing through the art department's doors like the Kool-Aid Man. A second later the singer is outside, too, and they are both laughing, horribly, uncontrollably.

"What the hell was that?" the singer asks, incredulously. "Did I just say that?"

On the steps above the parking lot, they call themselves assholes and heartless pricks. But they can't stop laughing. They laugh so hard they are both crying.

"That's a bummer," they shout at strangers who walk past. Again and again. The dreadfulness of it does not stop being funny until somehow the afternoon is dimming around them. They are bone tired.

"Think I'm gonna go home," the sick boy says. He gives his friend a high five. "I'll be by later."

"Right on." The singer plays a solo on his air guitar and then jumps into the splits.

The sick boy sprints through the parking lot. Before turning into the tennis courts, he yells, "A bummer!" one last time. A second later, in the failing light, he hears back, "A bummer!" It echoes off the science buildings around him.

He scales a locked fence to cut through the track and soccer field. He jogs halfway across. At the high-jump pit the sunset reflecting off the bleachers freezes him. He's filled with a memory: when he was a kid he used to see perimeters of color around people. Gold and orange and blue and green, every color in the rainbow. They sometimes went fuzzy or changed hues. He falls backward onto the high-jump cushion and it folds around him. He says a word out loud. "Auras." Again, "Auras," feeling his mouth hum.

For the first time in years, he thinks about Reiki, how he could once heal with his hands. A few miles from where he's sitting right now, he'd go with his mother to energy sessions. Their group would sit in chairs around a massage table, and each would lay their hands on the person lying there. Focused softness. He remembers the way his entire body heated, furnace-like with joy, and how that strange jubilance made it hard to sit still. But he was the only kid in the candlelit room and he learned to control and lovingly whorl that energy through his hands.

He takes off his baseball cap. The wind caresses his stubbled scalp. He cradles his hands together and stares hard at his woven fingers. When did he last see those colors? Those auras? Why did he stop seeking out the hues that saturated the air around strangers? He doesn't know. He can't remember. He looks at his arm, hoping to see it gloved with color. But there's nothing.

The pillar lights that dot the campus walkways start easing into their all-night brightness, and a spray of fireworks scatters the sky to the north, up where the Saint Paul Saints play. Bugs flurry at the lights, and he decides he will not go home tonight. He will stay right here. He presses his hands hard into his eyes and is fading toward sleep, but half wakes himself giggling. *What a bummer*, he thinks. Fuck it. This life right here. The life that was supposed to be, that never could have been because his body fell apart, keeps breaking this life happening now. What a motherfucking bummer.

Tomorrow there will be auras. He wants to see colors, to heal and be healed. He will palm the face of a friend, spend an entire day cradling the bones of another, because it is all horrible and hilarious and no one knows anything about life or death. He curls into himself on the high-jump mattress—unafraid for a few seconds at least—as he falls and falls and falls into a dreamless black.

MY MISOGYNY

> There is a deeper, Strangelovian logic to such happy holocausts.
>
> —MIKE DAVIS, *ECOLOGY OF FEAR: LOS ANGELES AND THE IMAGINATION OF DISASTER*

Oh, Bride of Frankenstein, I say. I chuckle, then groan about the hideousness of what's on the Oscars. A grandmother's sack-skinned head medically scaffolded atop the lithe and taut body of a swimsuit model. Oh, Sophia Loren, what have you done? Raising my hand, I cover the top fifth of the TV, Wite-Outing her face. Blood pushes into my groin.

I have made love to Sophia Loren thousands of times in my dreams. My wife and Courtney glance up from the couch. Ariane grimaces like she's got a bad taste in her mouth. They look at each other wordlessly, for a half second too long—it is official: I am King Asshole—before turning back to the TV. I sidestep out of the room, a magazine hiding my erection.

The day's plates are stacked in the sink. On the other side of the wall, Sophia presents the Oscar. My wife and our friend begin talking about plastic surgery and the gendered unfairness of beauty ideals. Both women are dedicated feminists. Courtney is the author of a brilliant book called *Perfect Girls, Starving Daughters: How the Quest for Perfection Is Harming Young Women.* I stare out the window. Across the street the parking lot lights look like swans frozen in the air. I turn the lights off, close my eyes, and scrub the dishes by feel.

The film that's winning all the awards is filled with played-out tropes: love and redemption and comeuppance. But it's *other.* It's vibrant. And it's set in a different country, so it makes people feel doubly good. *Who wants to be a millaneeer?!*

Oatmeal and banana and polenta are caked on the bowls. My fingernails can't grind the crust away. Listening to the women talk about the Oscars, I feel a familiar shame pulling at my insides. I laughed, but would I really care? So my Sophia is half-mummified. *Put a paper bag over her head, and I'd fuck her.* I stand back from the sink and fling the steel pad against the window.

Sophia Scicolone was born in Rome in September 1934. She was forty-three when I was born in 1978 in Iowa. I first saw *The Pride and the Passion* (1957) as a teenager. In the film, Sophia's hair always seems to be tousled. The top of her tight shirt is open. Her lips pout. Her eyes are angry and sad and passionate. *Fuck you, Frank Sinatra. Eat a dick, Cary Grant.* That look meant that *she* wanted *me.* From that moment on, even through and past her femme fatale role in *Grumpier Old Men*, she was my sexual Mr. Potato Head: she looked any way I wanted her to. She didn't have to touch me. It was better that way.

It was perfect.

But my breath had caught in my throat when she walked onto the Oscars stage. With each step she metamorphosed—left right swish, left right jiggle—changing from the fantasy of a broken thirteen-year-old to an exhibit in a museum of grotesqueries. And I felt like a monster was the most I deserved.

In the dark kitchen, I fondle each thing left on the counter. A pyramid of bowls. The detritus of chips and salsa. Sesame crackers and hummus. Half-finished glasses of Italian soda. I touch whatever's left in them and bring my fingers to my lips.

Pile the years I've been a miscreant, the years I've mistreated women, on one side of a seesaw and the time I've known how to love fully on the other, and the sumo wrestler of my malice would have one end of the seesaw buried in the ground. At the opposite end the small boy of my love would be crying in the air.

I didn't have sex without being inebriated until I was nineteen. I celebrated my twenty-first birthday at the University of Northern Iowa—hundreds of miles from my girlfriend—and somewhere in that night's snippets of memory is a faceless woman in the bathroom of a bar. Sometime later that evening a bedroom door closes, vanishing all my partying friends, and a sixteen-year-old girl and I rip the clothes off each other. And still later, sometime after the fight in the street, after Jonny jumps off the balcony, that same girl and I wrestle into the bedroom again.

I'm positive I've done things in blackouts that in

another life would have me waking in handcuffs. In a hotel bar, my first year of graduate school, I kissed a man, but refused another's plea to give me a blow job. I've been tossed onto sidewalks in front of bars and looked up just as bouncers thwacked my own cane against my skull. I've been jumped in an alley because I groped someone's girlfriend on the dance floor. As I woke in a pile of trash, a mask of blood on my face, my first thought was about what lie I was going to tell my girlfriend. To get sympathy. To get some love.

Before turning twenty-six, I cheated on every woman I was with.

And all those years, I hated myself the morning after. I spent my sober hours manic, afraid and teeming with rage.

In the dim room where I was repeatedly molested, there was a knife on the bed.

As I write this today, my hands tremble. My chest feels filled with wasps.

In 2006 almost seventy-eight thousand children were reported traumatized. According to Darkness to Light, an organization dedicated to "confronting child sexual abuse with courage," one in six boys is sexually abused before turning eighteen. These boys are more prone to sickness, posttraumatic stress disorder, and depression; are 70 to 80 percent more likely to be addicts and/or boozers; and often have suicidal thoughts and/or attempt suicide. These boys are more likely to violently victimize others. When the sexually abused boy reaches adulthood, he is more likely to become a perpetrator of felony assault, domestic violence, and a litany of other crimes.

When I was a boy, my urge to hurt myself seemed inexplicable. Lightning spiderwebbing down from a blue sky. Caresses were not pleasurable. They were painful, unnerving. But in my all-American world, you had to be tough. You had to soldier on grimly even if the land you walked was flecked with your own blood.

So what was the mal-American boy who yearned to be the all-American boy to do?

I was violent. And though fucking further barbwired my insides, I tried to get as much ass as I could. For years the only way to go on was by erasing myself. To drag myself forward I filled my bleary nights with as much flesh as possible.

In his book *Waking the Tiger: Healing Trauma*, Peter A. Levine writes that "learning to work with the felt sense may be challenging. Part of the dynamic of trauma is that it cuts us off from our internal experience as a way of protecting our organisms from sensations and emotions that could be overwhelming."

In my struggles to recalibrate my "felt sense"—what, without thinking, I know through what my body feels— I've cut and punched myself. I've lifted weights, starved myself. Imagined my own death and, for years, wanted violence to orbit around me.

I had to get fucked up to feel something.

Anything at all.

When the pendulum swung to the other side of my new "felt sense," TV commercials made me weep. Feverish, I'd lie in bed. All day. Sleepless, all night. Bus rides gave me panic attacks. I'd stare at the cobwebbed ceiling of my apartment, paralyzed, depressed, because it was all too much. I could feel every single word I heard. Every heartbeat around me. Branches snapping and singing birds. Blades of grass whispering.

Flushed, I half listen to what's happening in the living room. I think about how much I love my beautiful wife. But I'm shivering. My reaction to Sophia is rooted in a part of me that most days I pretend is gone. The part of me that is torn and shaken, rattled and scarred. It is the thing locked in the attic. It is one of my multitudes. The worry that one day I'll punch someone I love or find myself on *To Catch a Predator*.

For a decade, when I squinted, I'd see them both. The sumo wrestler. The little boy. Frozen in the blur of my eyelashes.

No matter what antidepressants I'm on, no matter how many times a week I get my head shrunk, I'm not sure that the fear and darkness will ever recede. Not fully.

But a few years ago that still life behind my eyes, *boy trapped in the air by pain and anger,* slowly began to change. The little boy slid down the seesaw and began walking toward the giant man. He wrapped his frail arms around the enormous belly.

It is unquenchable, this love.

Done with the dishes, the Oscars blaring on, I flick through songs on my iPod. What has been done to me, what I've done, will never not have happened—it will never go away. It is an extra rib, a heart valve always about to fail. Here, where I *love* the dark joy that bubbles in me when I listen to 50 Cent's "Heat." "It's a fact, homie—you go against me you're fucked."

"Going outside," I singsong to the women in the living room. "Filling the feeders. Love you."

I jump down the back steps, spilling birdseed over the walkway. The night sky throbs. Filled with beacons and warning lights and high-power tension lines. Day or night, it's always there. The stars are razor edged tonight. Sharpened by the torque inside me. Done pouring sunflower seeds into the plastic tubes, I crumple the bag and toss it on the porch. Through the picture window I watch the women on the couch, laughing and talking about Beyoncé's song, Penélope's kiss.

The gas station lights blink off down the street. A teenager sprints through the parking lot, pushing and pushing and pushing a shopping cart until he's going so fast his hair pulls back from his head like a black flame. He shouts, then hops on the clattering cart as it sails into the flickering shadows.

HEARTDUSTING

For all the history of grief
An empty doorway and a maple leaf.
—ARCHIBALD MACLEISH, "ARS POETICA"

I

A feeling of fullness, discomfort in the digestive area,
weight loss, and vomiting: these are signs you might have
stomach cancer. John Wayne died nine or ten times in
the movies before dying, one last time, on June 11, 1979,
from complications of stomach cancer. Usually the stomach is J-shaped and lies between the esophagus and the
duodenum. Wayne was born in Winterset, Iowa, halfway between Lorimor and De Soto on Highway 169.
His given name was Marion. Iowa was named after the
indigenous Iowa Tribe. In Sioux it means "sleepy ones." I
was born five hours from Winterset the year before John
Wayne died. Like Alex, Marion is also a woman's name.
Marionberries.

At the last minute my parents decided to name me
Alex instead of Sam. I do not know why. In sixth grade
I was an uncomfortable boy who wore the same yellow

sweatpants half the week. I was in love with a girl named Samantha. Each morning I'd eat a bowl of oatmeal and think of myself as someone else. Sam in love with Samantha.

Quaker Oats, one of the largest cereal companies in the world, has a processing mill in Cedar Rapids, Iowa. The Cedar Rapids of my mind is gelled and lumpy and congealed—I've awakened moth eyed in Cedar Rapids hotels dozens of times. Ninety-nine percent of these mornings, sitting on the edge of the bed, I stared blank and hungover at Wilford Brimley in TV commercials for Quaker Oats. He always seemed to chew on his crusty mustache, muffling his words, as if to emphasize the importance of mastication. I'd imagine he was my grandfather.

Wilford Brimley was actively opposed to the banning of cockfighting in Arizona and New Mexico. Laws against cockfighting are most lax in Alabama, Hawaii, Kentucky, Idaho, and Mississippi. Cockfighting is one of the oldest sports in the world. It is a felony to own a fighting bird in Iowa. Chickens are the descendants of the Southeast Asian red jungle fowl (*Gallus gallus*), a tropical pheasant that was first domesticated around 8000 BCE. When you eat chicken, the stomach-wall muscles keep the gnashed-apart flesh moving round and round to break it down into a thin paste. At the same time, more digestive juices are added. *Cement mixer. Washing machine. Centrifuge.*

In the ten years that have passed since my brain surgery, swallowing has become painful. My doctors do not know why. They say, "Inexplicable," and list the endless maladies that can occur when the brain stem is cut open.

When I gulp, it feels like a chunk of glass is caught in my throat.

In *The Path of Emancipation: Talks from a 21-Day Mindfulness Retreat*, the Buddhist monk Thích Nhất Hạnh says, "Each morsel of food is an ambassador from the cosmos." Last year I tried to chew each bite of my meals fifty times before swallowing. It felt like a countdown, like facing the firing squad. Often my wife finished eating a full half hour before me.

II

In *The Cowboys* (1972), John Wayne dies after being shot a number of times, at least once in the stomach, by Bruce Dern's character. The poet Archibald MacLeish was Dern's great-uncle. MacLeish was appointed assistant secretary of state for cultural affairs in 1944. According to Urban Dictionary, "chicken chow Wayne" is a "reference to a Chinese person with [a] lower back/leg injury, hence they walk like John Wayne." The ninth song on Terry Scott Taylor's 1998 album *John Wayne* is "Chicken Crosses the Road."

In 1995, on a road somewhere between Iowa Falls and Winterset, I sat in the backseat of a car, chewing cherry Skoal, eating a Snickers bar, and drinking a Coke. Jonny and Brown laughed in the front seat. In the middle of a sentence, I vomited sweet-and-sour chicken into a winter boot. As Jonny's Oldsmobile whizzed down Interstate 35, I threw the soggy boot liner out the window.

Bruce Dern's 1981 movie *Tattoo* (tagline: "Every great

love leaves its mark") was panned by critics. Dern plays a tattooist who kidnaps and repeatedly tattoos a model he's infatuated with. In the film's closing minutes, Dern and the model (played by Maud Adams) make love, and then she kills him. Promoting the film, Dern said that they actually had sex in the scene. Adams vehemently denied this. In 1960 Dern's godfather, Adlai Stevenson, was defeated in his bid for the Democratic presidential nomination by John F. Kennedy. George Dern, Bruce's grandfather, was a two-term governor of Utah and Franklin Delano Roosevelt's secretary of war. Eleanor Roosevelt was Theodore Roosevelt's niece. Theodore had a tattoo of the Roosevelt family crest on his chest.

I got my first tattoo around my eighteenth birthday. Now, at thirty-one, half my body is inked and there is a black box inside me filled with Polaroids. Ghostly shapes and fogged windows. Electrical tape, blank rectangles over the eyes. Faces without names. Headless bodies with names. I am handicapped, and will never fight in a war. No one would have me.

US chicken consumption increased during World War II due to a shortage of cows and pigs. In Britain, consumption of chicken rose and consumption of beef and veal declined in 1996 due, in part, to consumer awareness of mad cow disease. Bovine spongiform encephalopathy is the result of cattle being fed other cattle. In humans it is known as variant Creutzfeldt–Jakob disease. The onset of vCJD is marked by psychiatric symptoms, including agitation, anxiety, delusions, and hallucinations. Physical problems then manifest: jerky movements (myoclonus), balance and coordination dysfunction (ataxia). So does dementia.

At one time or another I have suffered from each of these symptoms. For months after reading a book about cannibalism, I dreamed about eating human flesh. But I do not have mad cow disease or vCJD. My sicknesses are more gossamer and ethereal, veiled behind previous conditions and a matrix of medical causes and effects. The opening of the body. The opening of a box. With the box open, so much can come out.

III

The day after John Wayne's death, Chuck Berry pleaded guilty to income tax evasion. He was later sentenced to four months in prison. When asked about his song "Maybellene," Berry responded, "The only Maybelline [sic] I knew was the name of a cow." Think: duckwalk, Berryland, "Johnny B. Goode." AC/DC guitarist Angus Young cites Berry as a major influence and is known for duckwalking across the stage while he plays. Mouth agape, eyes closed.

One of the last things I did before my brain surgery was listen to AC/DC's "Highway to Hell." Mouth agape, eyes closed.

Angus cattle are hornless. There are two types of Angus beef: red and black.

In American slang, *beef* can refer to fighting someone or being aggressive toward a person or thing. *I have beef with that muthafucker.* It can also refer to the penis. *Stop grabbing your beef.* But also flatulence, assorted drugs, falling down hard, and *beef curtains*, a derogatory term used to describe the female genitalia. *Camel toe. Moose knuckles.* In the early part of the twentieth century, a womanizer might be called a *chicken butcher.*

For a number of years I often found chicken breasts in my jeans the morning after blacking out. Dozens of times. Whole flocks of chicken. As if hoarding for the end of days, I'd wake with sweat-damp food, money, or drugs—all of it stolen—and not remember how it got there. Like Walter Benjamin fondling his books, I'd spend hours fingering, tasting, staring at the curios my pockets disgorged. *Andrew Jackson, Rx bottle, thawed chicken breast.*

Chickens sold in US stores are first subject to inspection, carried out by the US Department of Agriculture or by state groups with similar requirements. Each chicken is checked for disease. The USDA's Agricultural Marketing Service is responsible for establishing chicken-grading regulations and standards. Grade A chickens have "plump, meaty bodies and clean skin." These best of the best poultry are "free of bruises, broken bones, feathers, cuts and discoloration." According to the USDA, "inspection is mandatory but grading is voluntary."

Long before my days of poultry gathering, I was a name collector. From the beginning I was Ali, Ali Baba, Little Babaloo; then Al or Lex, Lem, Lemmy Lem, Lemwah, Tiny, Tinacious; and then, in college, Alphonse, Leroy, Motlow, Chet, Chester, Blackjack, and Happy. It's what everyone seemed to call me, even people I didn't know: Happy. But on the inside I called myself *pussy, chicken.*

In a Northwestern University study, *Helicobacter pylori*, the bacterium that causes ulcers, was found in almost 40 percent of a sample of chickens from a Chicago supermarket. *H. pylori* infects the stomach lining and causes an inflammatory response that increases the risk of not just gastric ulcers but also gastritis and stomach cancer.

Now I'm a hoarder of sicknesses, and through each, my attachment to pain has grown. Tattoos have manifold functions: punitive, decorative, religious, magical. Think X's tattooed between a thief's eyes or Mike Tyson's face tat. From gangbangers to sea captains, inked skin has been a symbol of identity, community, class, occupation, and ownership. *Ownership*, "The fact or state of being an owner; proprietorship, dominion; legal right of possession. Also: the condition of being owned (by a particular person, institution, etc.)." *Ownership*, from the noun *owner* and the suffix *-ship*. *Owner*, from the verb *to own* and the suffix *-er*. And then the oceanic depths of *own*: "To have or hold as one's own"—this body is mine, no matter how distant it feels, it is me—"To make (a thing) one's own; to gain possession or control of; to appropriate, seize, win; to adopt as one's own"—I have learned to love these broken days—"To acknowledge as having supremacy, authority, or power over oneself"—between night and day I choose night—"To recognize or profess obedience to (a greater power, a superior, etc.)"—I am a toothy gear in an enormous machine made of all of us—"To acknowledge (a person or thing) as affecting oneself; (more generally) to acknowledge (a thing) to be as claimed, or to be a fact; to confess to be valid, true, or actual; to admit"—doing unspeakable things and filled with love I have died and lived and lived and died. It is true—"To acknowledge as approved or accepted; to declare or indicate acceptance or approval of; to countenance, vindicate"—this me, this sometimes here, this sometimes gone, this whatever it is, is good.

IV

When the gastrointestinal doctor showed me my endoscopy results, I was thinking about what it meant to be a week from my thirtieth birthday, to still be alive, wiped out from going to near-weekly medical appointments. In the pictures my ulcer looked like a face. Wraithlike, red rimmed, and faintly smiling. The visage seemed frozen, trying to recede into the pink mucus of my stomach. The doctor grinned, then asked if I could come in next week for a colonoscopy.

After Dr. Simoni sauntered away, I lay back in the hospital bed. The nurses said that if I looked OK a half hour after the procedure and if there was someone in the waiting room ready to drive, I could leave. Brilliant white, the recovery area was so bright it hurt to keep my eyes open. The edges of my vision blurred. While the nurse removed my IV, an old man shuffling by the foot of my bed looked into the small recovery bay I was about to leave, stopped, and hacked into the air. The spittle on his lips was dark red, burgundy. Like he was wearing lipstick or had been drinking blood. The nurse didn't look up, only asked about my tattoos and said something about my thin-walled veins, while I stared.

The day before I'd been reading about people who drink menstrual blood. The Vaishnava Bauls, of Bengal, ceremoniously give up many of the strictures of daily life for even harder ones. They've removed themselves from the Hindu caste system. They sing—about Krishna, other facets of their spirituality, and the power of the "seed," which is found in all bodily fluids, especially, and most potently, menstrual blood—while begging for enough food to live on. It is a sacred arrangement, a powerful transfer. Vaishnava Bauls endow strangers and passersby (sometimes in train stations, on trains, or in other communal settings) with strength and intimacy and love and light through their music.

In the foggy drug slippage, my brain kept telling me that the patient wheezing his way out of Thousand Oaks Endoscopy was a Bengali holy man. That somewhere in the hospital he'd soaked blood-stained cloth in cow's milk (another holy fluid), coconut milk, camphor, and palm juice, then added a spoonful of white sugar before chugging it down.

I was imagining the pink-milk sweetness when the nurse asked what kind of juice I wanted. Hidden behind the sheet that separated our hospital bays, a man next to me asked a doctor what all the polyps meant.

That afternoon, still buoyant from the "twilight tonic" they'd pumped into me, I lay in the plush backyard of my California home. Sufjan Stevens's album *Illinois* washed through the open windows. Oranges cluttered the fruit trees like a thousand trapped suns. I felt stoned, unhinged from my body, and warm. I could barely feel the knife in my hand as I peeled mangoes. Gorging myself, I felt like I was in slow motion—at the same time both out of my body and deeper within my own flesh than I'd ever been. As if each of the mangoes' fibers were my own. As if I were eating my own heart. I didn't know the sticky juice was streaking my chin until the droplets began plopping into my lap. One of the Vaishnava Bauls spoke about the emptiness that comes from singing. "A melody contains a thing [*jinish*], endowed with a life [*ekta jiban*] or life force [*pran*]," she said. The song blossoms from, and is a part of, the life force, and, in the singer's breath, it passes to the listener. I wiped the syrup from my face, then wiped my hands on the lawn. Grass stuck to me like sickles of light exploding from a supernova.

Weeks later my wife would ask what was wrong with me—had I even looked at the album?—before pointing out that my favorite song, the most wrenchingly beautiful and melodic piece of music that I swore I had ever heard, was about John Wayne Gacy.

V

So here I am, the person in each black-box photograph, the singer, the patient, the passerby, the click in John Wayne's limp. The backyard grass is manicured a Disney green. A soft breeze spills down from the Malibu hills. The orange tree's limbs swish, the fruit vibrates and then stills. On the brick wall a lizard moves in time with the sun's glacial crawl across the sky. I have an ulcer, a burning hole inside me. Blood in my cough and stool. But this is California. This is America. Everything is fine. The clouds scrawl across the sky. Power lines dissect the air. My head is cottony and luminous. I'm not sure what to think about all the blood that wants to come out of me. The doc says that ulcers are not directly related to stress, but I should relax more—eat gentle foods. I tell him that it tastes good only if it burns some. He laughs kindly, says, "That explains a lot."

The clouds stretch threadbare above me.

VI

A Fela Kuti CD starts inside my home and I wake up. The stereo seems louder and the Afropop is relentless and pummeling. The clouds have vanished. The California sky is blindingly blue. The lizard on the wall has not moved.

I have been reading about Lazzaro Spallanzani, but I can't find a portrait of him. An eighteenth-century Italian biologist and physiologist, he was best known for experimental studies on live animals and his own bodily functions. Also a priest, he earned extra money by conducting Mass in nearby churches. In his attic he hung bats from strings. Spallanzani "blinded the animals, sometimes by burning the eyes with a red hot wire," or just plucked the eyeballs out. He'd pour wax into their skulls. In his studies Spallanzani describes swallowing "bone, cartilage, and tendon, concealed in perforated wooden tubes," meant to stimulate digestive juices that he could later vomit up for his experiments.

Maybe Spallanzani is the ghost face in my ulcer. Maybe I need more painkillers, a handful of pills. Maybe I will peel an orange and feel like the only person still alive in the world. Rind falling weightless, like confetti.

I settle into myself on the bread-stone warmth of the concrete patio. Bees bounce in and out of the orange blossoms. In my mind, inside the black box, there is a deck of cards—like the *lotería*—and each is painted with one of my illnesses. *El Cerdo. Los Enfermos. La Botella. El Corte.*

A velvety memory starts to open inside me, blooming

from the bees' stop-and-start hum. The power lines. A branch whispering against the fence. The bright orchestra of bees, the Afropop drifting from my home, the pungent waft of whatever animal is dying in the nearby aloe plant.

I'm nineteen again, back in Iowa, waking on a wet deck beside a pool.

Twenty miles from any town. Black sky. The snuffle and grunt of hogs in the confinement buildings around Lurch's farmhouse. Muffled music, partying voices from inside. Red cups and beer bottles are strewn about, glowing like Halloween skulls on the slick wooden deck. Bathing in the pool was balmy and slow, like dipping into heated paint or honey. My skin is molten. A naked woman is glistening in the moonlight beside me.

Her fingertips dance electric over my stomach. She asks if we should take another swim. The moon is the moon is the moon and I'm not sure I'm ever going to die. Thudding bass fills the rank hog-lot air, and fifty yards away a house door bursts open. The music quickly drowns out the pig sounds. One of my friends yells my name, then, "Here you go, buddy," and heaves something into the air. The door slams. There is the silence of the hogs. The pool mouths wetly. Wind hushes through the cornfields. Somewhere out in the dark, a car rumbles over the country road. She asks again, "A dip?" and then, from the dark above, a bottle explodes like a gunshot into the water.

I CAN HOLD MY BREATH FOREVER

How long it takes to do all the things that can't be undone, sharpen the antlers and polish the cracked hooves, taxidermy yourself monstrous; how long to staple and stitch pieces of the body together, to electrocute it back to life; how long to learn you are not behind the steering wheel but still you are driving the ambulance, this riot of burned rubber and spun cherries; how long to fall asleep with starlight glittering your face, to wake from the suck of the bottomless black; how long to let sweetened air whole the broken, to climb into the flames and breathe; how long to wellspring, how long for those jangled legs to spring well; how long to swan dive into your wreckage and weeping, your kingdom of heaped garbage, of nails and creeping dirt, how long your wreck, your wrecking, your wrecked; how long to scour blood from your fingernails, to scour your fingernails bloody; how long to still not finish this story, to confess, to say *No no no it wasn't me*; how long to say you've done every last thing; how long to see it all for the first time again; how long the pain zigging the spine, hot-wiring the nerves; how long to lean into the hurt; how long the fall is, for pulling it close; how long to feel lucky, for the sky to go mirror ball, for it to go black; how long to bulletproof the face; how long the staggering, the glowlight all around you; how long, how long; how long to sing to the endless end—for the darkest nights to go hot and pleasurable, visible with song.

THINGS THAT ARE: ON PLEASURE

1. Once upon a time, a guy limps into the Outer Edge's glit-ter-spinning darkness behind a pack of backslapping fools in a bachelor party, looking too young to be there, like a kid really. He staggers with a cane, wearing an eye patch. He has the swollen look of sick people.

Shit, he's some kind of fucked up, the bouncer thinks. *Poor ugly fuck.*

One of the strippers sees the sick guy enter, too, and frowns in the dimness. She might almost feel bad taking his money, she thinks. If his fingers shake as he nuzzles bills into her panties, she might throw up. But watching the rest of the group, their foolish swagger, she gets over herself. She will take his money, she decides, and she will do it in a way that he will never forget. She will hold his hand and lead him into the back and make him wish he could give her more, give her everything.

Barely inside the dizzying and cavernous room, the sick guy drops his cane and starts to go down. Another bouncer snatches the back of his shirt and steadies him. Has he been drinking a bit too much already? The guy shakes his head no, emphatic.

His cane strobes in the stage lights as he shuffles to catch up with the group. The men have camped out at the two tables closest to the elevated stage, pulling wads of bills from their pockets, counting the singles into stacks on the damp Formica. Over the Whitesnake song they shout out drink orders to every topless girl who saunters by. The guy's pulled-down stocking cap makes it look like he's trying to hide his pallid face.

After AC/DC's "You Shook Me All Night Long" ends, the carouseling lights dim and slow to a stop, making Monopoly money of the explosion of bills that a dancer, now on her hands and knees, panties dangling from her teeth, snowplows into a pile with her arms. The DJ screeches that everyone is so lucky to be here tonight, surrounded by so many lovely ladies.

"Pour Some Sugar on Me" blasts. The mirror ball starts whirling. Everyone in the group is staring at the sparkling legs that cord and vine around the pole, at the lotioned skin of the girl licking her lips as she hangs upside down.

The guy's face is a sheen of illness. No one sees him fall, unable to rise from the sodden floor. Under the bass and the sounds of the dancer slapping her own flesh, no one hears him cry for help.

2. Now, take my glasses away, snap them in half, and demand that I look, and *pleasure*—the word—blurs fuzzily. I see the names of the extinct: plesiosaur, an ocean reptile that had a long, ropelike neck and a tiny head, and lived during the Jurassic period; or pleurocoelus, which was once the official state dinosaur of Texas. Or, because I'm only getting worse—between the diplopia, nystagmus, and deterioration of my vision over the last five years—when you tell me to look again, the second half of the word jams and smears and gives the appearance of

repetition and I see Peterville, a town on Prince Edward Island, an inn in the United Kingdom, a hotel in Saint Petersburg. Blink: Peterbilt. Blink again: *Pleasantville*, of which director Gary Ross said, "This movie is about the fact that personal repression gives rise to larger political oppression."

3. "*Pleasure*—1: desire, inclination; 2: a state of gratification; 3a: sensual gratification, 3b: frivolous amusement; 4: a source of delight or joy." Comes from the Old French *plaisir*, which means "to please," changed in Middle English to *plesure*. Think: content, delectation, delight, enjoyment, gladness, gratification, happiness, satisfaction. Depending on your pleasure, it rhymes with *glazier*, *leisure*, *measure*, and *treasure*.

4. As a little kid, I lived in a Wonderland where pleasure did not exist. Tipped forward over my tricycle's handlebars, chipped a front tooth. Tripped and fell face-first on a cooling iron's point, the metal piercing the skin just inches from my eye. Pleasure was unknowable to me, yes, but I also refused to believe it was enjoyed by anyone else—in my child's eyes pleasure just *wasn't*. The lights in the room are either on or off. Because I could not stand being touched, I assumed everyone around me must feel the same way.

That freckle-necked boy being hugged tightly by his father hates it—ignore the smile stretching his face! It is fake, hollow, a grimace if you really look—because being enveloped like that makes his insides coil and slither. Tearing long shreds of paper from each gift, the pink-crowned birthday girl wears a mask of happiness. What she feels, I know, is *nothing*, is *whatever*, is *I am so tired of this, of all these people*. Everyone eats the layered chocolate cake with a scoop of vanilla ice cream and always it is so sour with raw eggs, so sweet sweet sweet, that I, like everyone around me in our stupid tasseled hats, cannot stomach another bite but always stuff another forkful in, smiling, about to blow chunks.

5. "Pleasure is our first and kindred good," Epicurus, the ancient Greek philosopher, says in "Letter to Menoeceus." "It is the starting point of every choice and of every aversion, and to it we come back, inasmuch as we make feeling the rule by which to judge of every good thing." He details two anxiety-inducing beliefs that people live by, beliefs that can either soak life with joy or flood it with pain. The first: the gods will punish us for our bad behavior. The second: death is something to fear. But Epicurus thinks these beliefs are senseless, that the dark feelings they produce are self-generated, apparitions, fictions, rooted in nothing of the world. "Death is meaningless to the living because they are living," he says, "and meaningless to the dead because they are dead."

6. So what happens to pleasure when you are already dead, dead but still walking in the world of the living? What if you've been punished without understanding what it is you are being punished for? What if, for months on end, you are forced to get naked in a locked room, to touch and be touched? What if this braids and knots with your not knowing, and all the pleasure the world contains is whipped, whipped, whipped, and then hog-tied and carved into pain? What are you, Epicurus,

if there is no place in the world for you? If you—just
a child—have been ground down, finely powdered into
nothing?

7. Pleasure is a fundamental part of mental life. Honey
squeezed out of a plastic bear, Blow Pops, a perfectly rip-
ened clementine—their sweetness gives pleasure, but the
pleasure doesn't come from the sensation of taste alone.
Eight pieces of carrot cake or a tub of neon-pink Betty
Crocker frosting can be sickening. The depth of pleasure
comes from *glossing* the sensation, understanding the
feeling through a lens. Limbic circuits—systems comprised of different regions of the brain—contextualize
the sweetness so the single piece of cake is understood,
both neurologically and psychologically, as pleasurable,
while more is too much, maybe even terrible.

8. Still there were books, a tarnished enjoyment I took in
the work of reading. From *Where the Wild Things Are* to
Old Yeller and then *The Electric Kool-Aid Acid Test*, I lost
myself in stories, and my fear and anxiety and sadness
receded while I was immersed in another's life. Reading
satisfied my need to be alone while paradoxically, without my knowing it, connecting me to others.

9. By middle school I began to see the truth in the faces
of the people around me. From the way my friends talked
about how hungry they were for each other—how it felt
to get it on, to touch and be touched—I started to realize that pleasure was indeed an amplitude of the world.
An unattainable one for me. Pleasure was a secret room
in the building of our lives, where my friends rollicked,

where zippers were undone under the cover of darkness and blankets, where there was hot breath, moans. I was not invited into this room. Outside, I was cold, felt less than numb.

10. Anhedonia is the inability to experience pleasure in what is usually found pleasurable. So that loving touch—that body pressing into your own—doesn't melt your insides. It burns. There is no after-workout glow, only a cinching decay. Friendships fill you with a stinging anxiety. Whatever is playing on the stereo—Bob Dylan, Ben Harper, Billie Holiday—is noxious. Your bones crave silence. Anhedonia is characteristic of many kinds of mental illness, including borderline personality disorder, schizophrenia, and mood disorders.

11. Almost everyone—at one point or another—loses their way in middle school, and only fiction can keep them glued together when high school begins. So you tell yourself stories about who you are, about what happened. You were molested by a girl, not a young man, not your cousin, but you liked it because she was gorgeous, and you weren't *really* molested because you wanted to do it, and anyway you liked it, liked it so so much. And to make sure no one around you sees what has been done, you decide to do what the world expects of you, promise that you will do it better than anyone else, that you will be a god. So there is more and more aggression and compulsion and violence. It doesn't matter that you are dead—you are expected to be a *man*—and so you decide to do everything you can to make yourself real in the world. You swear that if you do it hard enough you feel

something; it might not be pleasure, but it's *something*. You get fucked up and fight and fuck and play sports and scream *fuck* and never tell anyone how you really feel and why don't you ever tell anyone that you are sad or feel worthless? Because you are too busy kicking ass, or getting ass, or assuring someone that you are going to get fucked up this weekend, swearing, as you whip off your T-shirt and slap yourself in the face, that you'll fuck up any motherfucker who wants to come get some.

12. "Pleasure is never as pleasant as we expect it to be and pain is always more painful," Arthur Schopenhauer says. "The pain in the world always outweighs the pleasure. If you don't believe it, compare the respective feelings of two animals, one of which is eating the other." But what, Arthur, should we believe about the feelings of the animal trying to consume itself?

13. You know nothing of Schopenhauer anyway—at least not yet—so you go off to college, your body still defining pleasure by glut and a sort of psychotic hedonism. On the first day of orientation, you are standing in front of your new dorm with someone you just met when a cyclist streaks by, so close to you that you feel his breath. You turn but the bike is already a half block away. Rage is blistering your chest when you suddenly see the bike's front wheel get caught in the sidewalk and the bike crash—back tire arcing into the air and forward, sending the rider over the handlebars and face-first into a wooden bench. His face is a darkening red mask from where you watch, from where you start laughing as loudly as you can. He spits a glob of red yarn, and you point and turn

to the person next to you and cackle even louder. Every night you don't stay at your girlfriend's apartment you hook up with whoever wants to go home at the end of the night, then lie about the scratches that ladder your back, the bites and welts that surely must be happening at baseball practice. If anyone is using the showers when you're done bathing, you are sure to pluck something from their caddy—a razor, a shampoo bottle, or room keys—and stuff it into the bottom of the hallway trash bin before whistling your way to your room.

14. In *Le Plaisir du Texte*, Roland Barthes divides the effects a book can have on a reader into two groups: giving pleasure and causing bliss. He expands this thinking in *S/Z*, a deepening of his theories about readerly and writerly books. He argues that pleasure corresponds to readerly texts because they do not challenge the reader as a subject, and bliss corresponds to writerly books because they allow readers to break free from their position as subject.

15. Once upon a time, the front door opens and into the party slips a priest. Or some college kid dressed up like one—it *is* the Friday night before Halloween, and everyone *is* really fucked up. A woman at least ten years older than him watches from the stairs, where she's pretending to listen to the man leaning his too-close mouth into her ear. His cup sloshes as he talks and talks. The priest sneaks around the packed living room, orbiting the groups of two or three, ignoring anyone who speaks to him. It takes him fifteen minutes just to get through the boozy fog and all the people, to disappear into the

kitchen. The woman is still standing on the stairs when he reappears with a loaded-down paper plate in his hands. She knows he doesn't belong here. She has no doubt that he wasn't invited to this party of grown-ups; there's no way. Everyone here knows each other from work at Wells Fargo or is an invited friend of a friend. He's just a punk from one of the colleges nearby, up to no good. But she doesn't say anything. For some reason she doesn't feel like it, and as the priest tucks himself into a corner of the room, eating and watching all the party's goings-on, she catches the priest's eye, and before he ducks out of sight, subtly nods. Like *I see you.* Like *I know.* Suddenly she blinks—that timeless blink of a party's darkest hours—and the priest is brushing past her up the steps. She notices two things: the hugeness of his addled eyes and his smell. He stinks, a gumbo of sweat and pot and booze. A minute after the priest passes, she gives the man who won't stop explaining the world to her a fuck-me smile and asks if he'll hold her drink while she freshens up. There is no line for the bathroom when she gets to it, but the door is closed, a sliver of light beneath. She rattles the doorknob and hears a slight shuffling inside. She knocks. A voice replies that the bathroom is being used. She jams the door inward and the priest jumps back, dropping a handful of prescription bottles. She tells him that he isn't supposed to be there, and his shocked face doesn't change. "Are you?" she asks. He shakes his head. "Give me those," she says, lifting her chin at the Rx bottles. "Then don't move." The priest looks at her like she's the crazy one, eyeing the door that she's closed behind her. "Please," she says, softer this time. She points at the bottles on the mat.

"Give me those and the ones in your pocket and I'll put them back and I promise not to tell." She smiles at him as he hands them over. She puts them back in the cabinet, then tells him to start taking his clothes off, asking him, too, why he decided to walk into a house filled with drunk strangers and steal from them. He stands naked in front of her, trying to cover the erection his penis is bobbing into. "And not even lock the door?" she laughs. With a blank helplessness on his face, just before she locks the doorknob, turns the deadbolt, and flicks off the light, he whispers, "I don't know."

16. At night a whirlwind of voices racket through my head and sleep is impossible and I feel an unstitching begin in me, an unraveling of my stories, of myself. Nietzsche: One must pay dearly for immortality: one has to die several times while still alive. Shakespeare: To sue to live, I find I seek to die; and, seeking death, find life. Goethe: As long as you do not know how to die and come to life again, you are but a poor guest on this dark earth. Blake: We are in a world of generation and death, and this world we must cast off. Until one morning I try to rise out of my bed and instead tumble headfirst to the floor. Something in my brain is bleeding. This begins a long fall: more bleeds, more disability, brain surgery, and then a wheelchair and eyes that don't work and tingling flesh. It is a fall that strips me from my reliance on my body, leaving me suddenly alive and foreign in the world. It is a fall that some days I feel I've willed onto myself. It is a fall that some days I don't ever want to stop. It is a fall that some days makes me want to end everything. It is a fall in which a part of me is always in the ER, listening

blindly, as a young man in a hospital bay close to mine dies, slowly and loudly, from injuries he got in a wreck, and always I feel guilty because it is he who died, not me—and always, unsure as I am, I am glad it was him, that I've got another chance. At the same time, it is a fall that is terrifying and grim: they have sawed into my skull and cut pieces of my brain away and I can't walk or read and books are meaningless. Sometimes I can only see decay around me.

So quickly it happens.

I am twenty-one and I am beyond dead yet so alive in my new body, the new body that I will never, ever get used to, that I pulse with hurt. And always beside me—no matter how I try to get rid of it—is the shadow of my old body. Always calling out my old cravings, my old pains.

17. Once upon a time, hundreds of miles from Minnesota, he sits in a chair and a woman handcuffs his hands behind his back. They're clamped on so tight his fingertips tingle for just seconds before his hands go numb, as if they've been erased from his body. She takes off her T-shirt, drops it in a laundry hamper, and kneels beside her bed to say her nightly prayers. She stands and turns off the low-volumed stereo.

Outside they both hear sirens, a tree limb brushing the window—*scriiiitch, scriiiitch, scriiiitch*.

In front of him she wiggles her panties down her legs and flips them from her toes to her hands.

In the apartment below there is muffled music, a long low grind.

All the bedroom lights are on but there is nothing

to say. She smiles as she stuffs the panties deep into his mouth.

18. My old body, that dear old friend, my shadow, is a garment that I can't stop trying to fit into. Over and over until it becomes so threadbare, so tattered and shabby, that I can see right through it and I am forced to come to terms with myself. I must change my life or I will die soon, die one last time. And beneath the cruel monster I have been I see a sad child, and I peel back the frayed darkness even more, and there is a young man who really does want to be alive, cowering. Seeing him, I say hello. I welcome him to me.

19. Staring at death, I am no longer afraid. Of what happened to that boy, of what happened to me, of what I have done. I am not afraid of what will someday happen when it is my time and the good dirt sings. The world is a place that hurts, a place that I cannot control, that I will never truly know the right way to move through because there is no right way. I don't need to see that boy and that young man to feel good about them, to know that they are right here with me and my gorgeous wife, holding the red-cheeked new daughter who just this second has learned to grab her giant hooped earrings, and my son, leaning warmly into my side, whispering to me about ghosts and lizards and zombies and bugs. To feel good about what I am. Because there is no room to be afraid when I know the huge bliss of it all.

MIGRANTS IN A FEVERLAND

On the flight to California, the lost man thinks about how it will be his first time in Las Vegas since he lived there in fourth grade, when he was in love with the daughter of a showgirl. A girl with whom he spent every afternoon. All of her home was theirs. They could do anything they wanted to because her family was never there, not her father nor her brother nor the dancer mom he didn't meet once.

Years after moving away from Nevada, he realized how oblivious he'd been to his little girlfriend's sadness. Only in college did he finally wonder what kind of terrors tore through her because her family didn't seem to think she existed. He had suddenly worried about her—but her name didn't appear in any of the Internet searches he attempted.

It was as if she'd never existed at all.

In the fourth grade he had attended Lewis E. Rowe Elementary, was a Lewis E. Rowe Runner, but played Little League in the 120-degree inferno for the Red Wings, a team that shared a name with the town in Minnesota he'd just moved from. They'd won every game. At home he spent hours pretending to be Larry Johnson, his favorite University of Nevada, Las Vegas, Runnin' Rebel. He'd reverse-dunk on the Nerf basketball hoop attached to his bedroom door, then bellow and King Kong his chest while staring big eyed at his always-dying goldfish.

The lost man is flying from Minneapolis to Los Angeles with his roommate. After landing they are picked up by one of their best friends from high school, now a surfer who teaches second grade. When they get to the surfer's apartment, thumps and shouts are coming from a party inside. Sitting cross-legged in the surfer's "yard"—a slab of concrete no wider than a bathtub—a sunburned man takes swelling rips from an enormous bong. He nods at the three, falls to one side, and rolls out of their way. The surfer grins as they pass and tells them that the sunburned man's a lawyer. Inside the apartment their bags are taken away and huge drinks—White Russians in 7-Eleven Big Gulp cups—are handed to them.

The rest of the night happens in snapshots, fuzzy and blurred.

Stumbling after a girl, as if leashed, to a beach bar. Dancing. A pitcher and pints, glasses shattering on the sticky floor. Punches, a cyclone of them. A head butt. The world suddenly whipping out from under him. A table rising up, smashing—straight on—his face.

Later he wakes in the dark, still on Minnesota time, naked and knotted in a heap of sodden wet suits. A chugging hurt in his head. He touches his blood-caked nose, the grapefruit-size swelling over an eye. He lies back, but cannot sleep because of the pain. For three hours he watches the gradual reappearance of the party-wrecked apartment as the sun rises. Then the surfer walks out of his bedroom, scratching his shaggy head. He sees the lost man slumped in the wet suits, laughs, and asks where the roommate is.

The lost man grimaces and looks at the surfer like *Can you see me? What do I know of anything?* He tries to speak but his skin feels like crackling glass, so he groans at the surfer like Chewbacca.

The surfer says they need to pack up and leave for Vegas in an hour, no more than two. They are meeting another high school friend at a resort there. But the roommate is a ghost. He's not in the apartment complex, not sleeping in the bushes nor in the trash heaped on the curb. The two men stand on the boardwalk, their heads spinning.

"He just ran off into the dark last night," the surfer says, pointing toward the ocean. "He went that way. I heard him laughing." They walk up and down the beach, tracing the barely remembered steps of the previous evening. The surfer looks at the lost man thoughtfully and says in his teacher voice that he really, really looks like shit.

When they return to the apartment there's still no roommate. No phone message. No note pinned to the door. Nothing. Shit, the lost man mutters. He sees concern on the surfer's face and it stills his insides. The joke they'd both been anticipating changes to something bad—a body washed ashore, a man who is never seen again.

The surfer pulls two beer bottles from a cooler. They chug the beers in silence, then call the cops.

The roommate is sitting at a bus stop in front of the police station when they arrive in the surfer's pickup. The lost man somersaults into the back cab so the roommate can have shotgun. And then they are off, the lost man pulling more beers from the cooler and the roommate laughing as he fills in the details. Someone's bike. Police chasing him down the boardwalk. Tumbling face-first into the sand.

By the time the roommate's done with his story, they are an hour closer to Vegas and the lost man hasn't stopped drinking.

Las Vegas rises spirit-like and shimmery out of the desert. In the lobby of the Flamingo Hilton the lost man is already so fucked up he is speaking in tongues to strangers. The elevator ride to their rooms is one of the last things he remembers clearly.

His friends tear it up all day and all night. But he never leaves their floor. He locks himself inside the bathroom and wanders the hallway. He demands more alcohol and drugs each time the three friends return. He passes out in the bathtub and under the bed. He throws a chair out the window, crashes the dressers to the floor. In the hallway he stumbles into a group of party girls, who invite him into their room. They share all their booze and drugs. He thinks that one of the women is the childhood girlfriend he could not find. He talks her up, says he's missed her, that still he thinks about her all the time. "Where did you go?" he asks. "What happened? Did your mom ever come back?" Between kisses, he tells her that he has always loved her. He's been waiting.

Before the girls check out of the hotel, they return him to his bed and empty his wallet.

❖

The lost man doesn't want to wake up—wants to die—the morning they are supposed to leave Las Vegas. The roommate and the surfer have to lug him to the pickup.

Feverish on the drive back to California, he hallucinates and dreams. His Las Vegas childhood slashed together with images of the weekend. The hugeness of the Hoover Dam. Spinning slot machines. Sun blindness. Hostesses in bikinis. The day the ceiling in his school's lunchroom crashed down. Wading into the hotel lobby fountain. The explosion, a hundred miles away, of a factory where space shuttle fuel was produced. His face in the mirror morphing in fast forward, then sloughing off, slow as cold molasses, beastlier each time. Protesters chaining themselves to the fence of a desert military base where nuclear bombs were detonated underground. The way the pool at his childhood girlfriend's house swayed with each blast. The way—in the blackness—the lost man swayed and shook, too.

LIKE SO MANY NIGHTMARES

And that brief madness of bliss, which is experienced
only by those who suffer most deeply.
—FRIEDRICH NIETZSCHE, *THUS SPOKE*
ZARATHUSTRA

Today, before sunrise, I crept from the warmth
of my bed, leaving my wife and baby boy still
sleeping. In the living room I stared out the picture window at the sky, and the purple-black clouds were
boiling. My eyes are always worse in the morning, when
I'm acclimating to the vision of the living. It is the slowest part of my day. The ceiling juddering above me, but
never falling. A half hour of the pillows trembling on the
couch. And then, sipping yesterday's cold coffee, I read
Rilke: "I live my life in widening circles." The loamy smell
of the lentils we cooked last night still clung to the air, a
humid, dirty-dishwater morning in Texas. I started won-
dering about the shape of things—a pile of Sumo fruit,
tomorrow's hazy sky, the shadows inside me, the answer
to the question *What is there for us?* Again I looked at the
clouds, now turning orange. Again to Rilke: "I live my
life in widening circles."

⁂

Rilke was born on December 4, 1875. His given name was René. As if she'd given birth to a girl, Rilke's mother clothed him in dresses. Seventy-four years later, on December 4, 1949, the actor Jeff Bridges was born in Los Angeles. In *True Grit*, Bridges played the one-eyed Rooster Cogburn; in *The Men Who Stare at Goats*, Bill Django; and in *The Big Lebowski*, he is the Dude, Jeffrey Lebowski. Rilke changed his name to Rainer because a married woman named Lou thought it sounded more masculine. "Oh, the usual. I bowl. Drive around," the Dude answers when asked by Maude Lebowski what he does for recreation. "The occasional acid flashback."

Sometimes when someone says *recreation*, I hear *reincarnation*.

Rilke was secretary to Rodin, the sculptor whose *Thinker* is a kind of reincarnation, a monument to the traumatic birth of a thought. In December 2003 I visited the permanent collection of the Musée Rodin at the Hôtel Biron in Paris. My watch was still on Minneapolis time and I felt like a cow at the doors of the slaughterhouse. With a parade of other jacketed tourists, I trudged from room to room. The museum was too hot, syrupy with body heat. A wake of fragrance—tangerine and sun-hot tin—trailed the girl in front of me like a scarf. It was so strong I felt drunk and stumbled after her, away from my family, watching her beautiful mouth pop out incomprehensible Spanish, until, too strong, her perfume made me sour stomached.

Later in *The Big Lebowski*, the Dude breaks into the

Big Lebowski's mansion to confront him about a rug ruined by thugs looking for the other man. "Where do I fit in?" the Big Lebowski asks. "You mean," the Dude asks, "did you personally come and pee on my rug?"

Outside the Musée Rodin, Paris's first snow wisped down over long gardens. The air made expanding fists of my breath. I was alone in the cold.

I gaped at *The Gates of Hell*, all its torqueing muscles and scenes from Dante's *Inferno*, and at another reincarnation, the small version of the *Thinker* sitting fifteen feet up. The snow swarmed. I wanted to run a finger over the enormous bronze doors but was sure someone was watching from the museum. I kept my face tilted up and my hands tucked in my jean pockets, like someone lost, like someone waiting for a bus. Just me and *The Kiss* and *The Three Shades* and snow. Just *I Am Beautiful* and snow. Just me. Just *Ugolino and His Children*. Just snow, a falling halo all around.

Earlier in *The Big Lebowski*, the malice-faced thug Woo unzips his penis from his pants and says, "Ever thus to deadbeats, Lebowski," as he pisses. "Oh no, don't do that," the Dude pleads. "Not on the rug, man!"

The day of my brother's wedding, I woke outside, twenty years old, on the raft-size deck of his apartment. A bird's nest was crushed and scattered on my chest. I was bloody. My ribs felt like porcelain. My skull, drained of blood, another bird's nest, a vision of fire.

We'd spent the previous night drinking and going to strip clubs and drinking. Long after everyone had passed out, from his room, Jason heard a strange pattering. He flicked the bathroom room light on, and there I was. Pissing on his floor. "What the fuck are you doing?" he yelled. In Jason's version, I looked up like some beast caught drinking at a pool of blood, and then, deliberately, said, "It wasn't me." I pointed at the hollow-eyed boy in a mirror and cried, "It was him!"

Rilke spent part of the twentieth century's first decade in Ronda, an Andalusian town in the Málaga province of Spain. Within the next ten years, Rilke had an affair with another married Lou, the painter Lou Albert-Lasard. She is most famous for the *Montmartre* series: twelve chalked and colored lithographs full of wine or maybe absinthe, sharp noses, slashy eyes, and smokes. Sometimes her subjects are nude and often they're women, stark lined, triangle breasted, and cavorting. Albert-Lasard also painted portraits of Rilke, Cocteau, and Giacometti; she was a friend of many of the period's most important artists. Lou is addressed as Lulu in some of Rilke's poems: "Nothing but *being*. To the next stone asserting: / You are myself now, but this stone am I." Lou died in Paris in July 1969, the same month Neil Armstrong and Buzz Aldrin landed their craft on the moon during Apollo and then walked on the Sea of Tranquility.

I didn't sleep for much of my twenties. Alert way past midnight, I decorated my apartment with jars of neon colored water. I read and read and stared into the glossy pages of art books. I shaped coat hangers into figures or faces or just a knot—bending, crimping, twisting the wire until my hands were swollen and cut up. My little horde of starved, knife-thin characters, Giacometti-esque and stretched toward the ceiling by invisible cords.

The Gates of Hell was commissioned by France's Directorate of Fine Arts in 1880. Rodin was supposed to deliver the sculpture in 1885, but worked on it until he died in 1917. "It has been from the beginning," Rodin said, "and will be to the end, simply and solely a matter of personal pleasure." When the *Inferno* begins, Dante is suffering from a loss of faith. To rise into the Paradise of Heaven and meet God, he must journey first through the nine circles of Hell, come face to face with the Devil, and then climb the Mountain of Purgatory. "For a whole year I lived with Dante, with him alone, drawing the circles of his inferno," Rodin said. "At the end of this year, I realized that while my drawing rendered my vision of Dante, they had become too remote from reality. So I started all over again, working from nature, with my models."

The Men Who Stare at Goats, a book by the journalist Jon Ronson, is factual. It explores the intersection between psychological power and the military. The book is excellent. The movie is mostly terrible. Both show soldiers embracing new age mysticism, trying to run through walls, furiously staring at a barnyard animal while urging its heart to stop. But the book evolves into something sinister, as Ronson explores interrogation techniques used in the war on terror, how the theme song to *Barney & Friends* was used to torture Iraqi prisoners.

Often I've stared at an object, a bowl of rice or an apple, say, and tried to move it with my mind. I've made things happen. It's normal. Looking down from a second-story apartment I've urged a balloon to sail out of

a little girl's hands and then, a dozen yards down the
street, made a man jump off a fire hydrant to catch it.
I've said, in my head, *Do not start, car engine*, and for ten
minutes the starter wouldn't turn over, and I had a good
excuse to be late. And often I've stared at people—or
maybe it would be more apt to say *into* them—wishing
they would die. Myself in the mirror. The cousin who
molested me. The medical staff who hovered over me
before excising a piece of my brain.

Lou Albert-Lasard knew everyone. She was friends
with Bertolt Brecht and Paul Klee and Wassily Kandinsky.
She painted her portraits, and her brothel and circus
scenes. And she still found time to travel the world with
her daughter—Africa, India, Tibet. In 1940, after the
armistice signed by the Germans and the French, she and
her daughter were sent to Gurs, a Nazi internment camp.
Even there, however, she made art.

Early in the sketching work of *The Gates of Hell*, Rodin
envisioned something similar to Lorenzo Ghiberti's
Gates of Paradise: two columns of four panels each, all
etched with scenes of hell, the full column bordered by
smaller images. But as Rodin's vision grew, the borders
around the panels vanished and the entire piece, all the
grim suffering, grotesqueries, and embracing composi-
tions, began to look red hot, engulfed in flame.

For years I was sleepless in my ramshackle apartment.
I worked the wire sculptures until I had to get outside. I
was living with a great hole inside myself. Many nights I
packed a backpack with goodies and walked aimless circles
around Saint Paul, the diameter of my orbit growing with
each revolution. I'd curl up by the Mississippi and watch the
moon. Throw stones into the undulating black beneath the

Marshall Avenue Bridge. Like a wrecking ball I'd sprint into curbside trash bins, fountaining rubbish all over, and limp away as lights flipped on or dogs began barking.

You are made to wear a diaper and headphones. But you do not control the volume or what is played. Blacked-out goggles are placed over your eyes. The sound so loud when it comes on that your toes throb. Sometimes it's just voices, a woman screaming for a help, a baby crying endlessly, wailing, barely able to take a breath. You're handcuffed to the floor, so you have to squat, painfully. Something sharp cracks against your shins again and again for hours. You know that so much time has passed only because your diaper is overflowing.

On December 4, 1679, 196 years before Rilke was born and forced into skirts, the philosopher Thomas Hobbes died. "To understand therefore what is a miracle, we must first understand what works they are which men wonder at and call admirable," Hobbes says in the thirty-seventh chapter of *Leviathan*. "And there be but two things which make men wonder at any event":

> the one is if it be strange, that is to say, such as the like of it hath never or very rarely been produced; the other is if when it is produced, we cannot imagine it to have been done by natural means, but only by the immediate hand of God.

Each morning I shaved my head so all my scars looked raw and glistening. I was truculent, sorrow sharpened, and mean, but usually I aimed the rage at myself. I covered my body in tattoos. They felt almost good, what some might call pleasurable. Imagine: the skin just a small piece of some larger all-loving and powerful fabric. But most of the time I couldn't stand myself, and couldn't stand being alone, either. Friends would be gathered around me and I'd feel lonelier than ever, in agony.

Rodin populated *The Gates of Hell* with over two hundred figures, depicting not Dante's Hell for Christian sinners, but the nine circles where modern man's passions might bury him.

A cloth bag is stuffed over your head, jerked taut, and then taped around your neck like a collar. The clothes are torn off you. When water is poured over the fabric it feels like you're drowning. Again and again the tide rises in you, over you. When the bag comes off, a light scalds. A studded pink collar is constricted around your neck and you're punched and kicked and slapped. Your hands are tied to a pipe in the ceiling so far above your head you have to stand on your tiptoes. Hours pass into days into the end of time. You feel like you'd pass out if you didn't feel like you were burning alive, if you weren't always shitting yourself.

Rilke died at the age of fifty-one, on December 29, 1926. If I am still alive when I am fifty-one, I don't think I'll have any hair. Often, I expect, I'll wear a Minnesota Twins baseball cap. Maybe my hands will be covered in tattoos. Perhaps just the knuckles—"Love" and "Hate" or "Read" and "More."

One hundred and eighteen years before the day Rilke died, the seventeenth president of the United States, Andrew Johnson, was born. Eighty-one years before the day Rilke died, Texas became the twenty-eighth state in the Union. Andrew Johnson was the first president to be impeached. Thirty-six years before the day Rilke died, the US Army massacred hundreds of Sioux at Wounded Knee. As of 2004, Texas released more greenhouse gases into the atmosphere than any other state. Four years before the day Rilke died, William Gaddis was born in New York City. In 1942 the US Army Air Force forcefully took almost 350,000 acres of the Pine Ridge Indian Reservation—location of the Wounded Knee Massacre— and created the Badlands Bombing Range, a live-fire area that was used for thirty years. There are eighty-one "recognitions" in Gaddis's first novel, *The Recognitions.*

On my night walks I started wearing a gorilla mask. Blocks away from my apartment, I'd fade into the shadows between two storefronts, slide it out of my backpack, and then slip another face over mine. The gorilla mask was mostly a pliable black plastic, but it had red lips, sharp white incisors, nostrils punched through, and two nickel-size eyeholes. Up both jaws and across the forehead ran thick black fur. The mask was almost an exact replica of one I had as a little boy. Sometimes, with the plastic sticking to my sweaty skin, I was sure it was the same one.

Welcome, welcome, come inside! Within *The Gates of Hell*, folding in on itself: *The Kiss, Eternal Springtime, Adam and Eve, Ugolino and His Children, I Am Beautiful, Fleeting Love, Meditation, The Three Shades, Paolo and Francesca, The Thinker, The Old Courtesan*. Come inside, welcome, come. It is a screening of Cocteau's *La Belle et la Bête*. You are the beauty. Let me be the beast. It's Jay Z's birthday. Frank Zappa just died. Welcome, welcome, welcome. We're showing the slow-motion film that played on Buzz Aldrin's visor as, bouncing over the moon dirt, he saw Earth from afar for the first time. Matisse is painting scenes from Dante's *Purgatorio*. Gary Gilmore's wearing a bedazzled party hat, he's got a kazoo. Inside, come in, come in. Everyone is waiting for you.

You wake with nothing on—nothing but goose bumps, a swamp of bruises, the choking pink collar, and the zip tie handcuffs that have gloved your hands in blood. A woman shaves your entire body with a dull razor and your eyes are taped open so you have to watch her slowly drag the razor over your genitals and laugh, to feel the shame of seeing her see all of you. Cold water from a power hose punches you across the concrete floor. And finally you're stuffed into a box, a coop for rabbits, a toddler's coffin. Your ribs shatter as you're crumpled into it. You're like this for hours. You're luggage. A duffel bag of pain. Who knew bones could snap in so many ways? Who knew that they could sound like gunfire, applause? You are leaking so much blood and each time sleepiness is about to take over a hand slaps you awake.

Fourteen years after the day Rilke died, the Germans started dropping incendiary bombs on London. Forty-nine years after the day Rilke died, eleven people were killed when a bomb exploded at LaGuardia Airport in New York City. Over a million homes were damaged in the Nazi bombing campaign. Forty years after the day Rilke died, the Jimi Hendrix Experience played a show on the BBC's *Top of the Pops*. The bomb injured seventy-four people at LaGuardia; the crime has never been solved. Seventy-two years after the day Rilke died, Khmer Rouge leaders apologized for the 1970s genocide in Cambodia that killed over one million people. Jimi Hendrix was given a choice between going to prison or joining the army. Pol Pot, leader of the Khmer Rouge from 1963 until his death in 1997, studied in Paris for four years before returning to Cambodia in 1953.

Wearing the gorilla mask was sauna hot; it was like trying to breathe with a hand groping your nose and mouth. I loved that suffering, the panicky desire that knotted my chest. In the mask I'd ramble past bar and restaurant windows, turning, slowly, slowly, to look at whoever was on the other side. A lit joint or Parliament Light jutting from the plastic. On cold nights I could force my breath out the pinched nostril holes and see myself, ogling a couple inside O'Gara's, smoke funneling from the face of an enraged beast.

Rilke's first Lou, Lou Andreas-Salomé—she who wanted him more manly, more *Rainer*—was, like the second Lou, friends with a number of intellectual and artistic luminaries, Sigmund Freud and Friedrich Nietzsche among them. She was one of Freud's best pupils and one of the first female psychoanalysts. She wrote over a dozen novels and published a memoir about Rilke after his death. But in Freud's eyes, Salomé's finest work was a 1916 article on anal eroticism.

Rodin and Rilke were reincarnated as craters. They remain together now as they were in life. Both are enormous and located on the surface of Mercury. Rilke has a diameter of almost fifty-four miles. Rodin is almost three times as big, and inside the 142-mile-wide hole sit two craterlets. Black-and-white satellite images of Rodin and Rilke resemble paintings by Jasper Johns or Cy Twombly.

There is a hole 65 feet deep in the Kara-Kum Desert in Turkmenistan and it has been on fire for the last forty-six years, since a Soviet drilling rig punctured the roof of an enormous natural gas–filled cavern in 1971. The ground collapsed, swallowing the rig. Poisonous fumes began steaming from the spot. To avoid a catastrophe, to see what would happen, engineers ignited the gas; they imagined it would burn itself out in a few days. Locals started calling it the Door to Hell. Others nicknamed it the Gates of Hell.

Late in the nineteenth century, Freud shaped his psychological theories into the practice of psychoanalysis. He focused on hysterical symptoms and irrational behavior and believed problems were rooted in the unconscious, the result of sexual excitement during infancy. In the analyst, Freud thought that "the patient sees . . . the return, the reincarnation, of some important figure out of his childhood or past, and consequently transfers on to him feelings and reactions which undoubtedly applied to this prototype." Freud called this—the analysand's issue made manifest in the analyst—transference. In this charged transaction, Freud theorized that the analyst becomes one of the patient's parents. Freud thought that belief in reincarnation was a result of the denial of death. He was also addicted to cocaine.

When the Iraq War started in 2003, antiwar protesters gathered on both the Minneapolis and Saint Paul sides of the Marshall Avenue Bridge. I'd walk across the bridge toward Minneapolis, slipping the gorilla mask on as I crossed the empty center. On the other side bells jangled. Protestors chanted and waved homemade signs. The reactions among the rush hour commuters were split. Some cars honked their support. Others slowed, the window rolling down to reveal someone giving the finger. All the noise whirled and racketed and I ignored the few people who spoke to me. Silent, I leaned against the rail that separated the sidewalk and the road, staring into each passing car.

In *Civilization and Its Discontents*, Freud writes that "Men are not gentle creatures who want to be loved, and who at the most can defend themselves if they are attacked; they are, on the contrary, creatures among whose instinctual endowments is to be reckoned a powerful share of aggressiveness." Freud wrote extensively about a patient he called the Rat Man. The Rat Man was beaten by his father for masturbating, which, Freud theorized, led directly to the Rat Man's neuroses. The Rat Man worried that he spoke aloud without knowing it, that his words would implicate people close to him, and that these people would be tortured by rats. The Rat Man obsessively punished himself. Freud continues, "As a result, their neighbor is for them not only a potential helper or sexual object, but also someone who tempts them to satisfy their aggressiveness on him, to exploit his capacity for work without compensation, to use him sexually without his consent, to seize his possessions, to humiliate him, to cause him pain, to torture and to kill him."

During the nine months leading up to my son's birth in January 2011, I dreamed of rats. Rats lived throughout our house, in the attic and the walls. We were afraid to go into the garage. For months that summer the temperature in Texas didn't drop below one hundred. It was more than twenty degrees hotter in the crawlspace, twice that in the garage. The smell that soon thickened the blast furnace air made me gag. In three of the traps I set, what had once been boot-size rats became rotting clumps of furred blood, swarming with maggots and their lip-smacking song. In the dreams, rats carried away my not-yet-born son after gnawing away half his face.

C. G. Jung was arguably Freud's most important student. But instead of following precisely in his teacher's
footsteps, as Freud expected him to, Jung had a vision
of psychology that split from Freud's. Jung believed in
different analytic approaches to hysteria and neuroses
and wedded a compilation of research by Freud and
others with his own ideas on symbols and the collective
unconscious. Jung believed in reincarnation; *The Tibetan
Book of the Dead* greatly influenced him. As Jung aged he
became more interested in mythological and theological
symbols. "None of us stands outside humanity's black
collective shadow," writes Jung. "Whether the crime
occurred many generations back or happens today, it
remains the symptom of a disposition that is always and
everywhere present—and one would therefore do well to
possess some imagination for evil."

As the setting sun dropped its own mask over
Minneapolis, the bridge became cold. After rush hour
there were hardly any cars to wave and yell at, and in
just a few minutes the bridge would empty of protesters. In the exodus I'd scamper down the densely bram-
bled hill that led from River Road to the Mississippi.
I'd lie in the weeds until full night had settled in, and
then, gorilla mask still on, I'd emerge. I'd drift over
the bridge to Marshall Avenue, back toward Saint Paul,
chain-smoking, blistering the mask's vinyl, setting
myself on fire. When the moon was clouded over, I'd
watch the river, that heaving thrush of reflected light
and shadow. But when it was out, I couldn't help but
stare; through the mask, the moon lost all its moon-
ness. Always it seemed brighter, beautifully whittled,
the perfect edge of a knife. Through the gorilla eyes,

the moon seemed to fill the sky, covered by face after face on its vivid canvas.

Freud is also the name of a crater on the moon. It is 1.77 miles wide. Because the moon has no atmosphere, meteorites and asteroids pummel its surface, pounding in craters and highlands and maria. When Galileo first saw these dark spots through a telescope, he called them *maria*, or "seas."

Near the end of *The Big Lebowski*, Walter and the Dude stand on a cliff above the ocean with the cremains of their friend Donny. Walter opens the container and Donny's ashes swirl in the wind. Like fresh snow, the dust of Donny powders the Dude's sunglasses and goatee.

The Tibetan Book of the Dead is also known as *Bardo Thödol* or *Liberation through Hearing in the Intermediate State*. Filled with instructions and prayers for finding liberation from rebirth during the forty-nine days between death and reincarnation, it should be studied and read over the dying or dead.

I love the time before the world wakes. I loved it, reading Rilke this morning, and I will love it again tomorrow. In the dark there will be a few passing cars. A quiet perfect for reading, for all the explosions of our world. Birdsong from somewhere in the purple black. Everything glazed over. There will be no space to think about the shale and natural gas beneath me, how, in one life or another, this place where we live will become a massive crater or widening circles of fire. Slants of light tint the morning air pink. Knowledge is everywhere in the coming daylight.

That knowing—knowing that anyone who survives anything, ever, is nothing short of miraculous—is an emporium of collisions and adoration and it is everywhere in morning's blush. The soft snores of my baby boy, the sighs of my wife. Glint of tree bark. The tremoring leaves. It's always a comfortable burning, that knowing. It is a thousand matches erupting to life inside me.

MIGRANTS IN A FEVERLAND

The morning air is so wondrously crisp, so flesh tingling, that it covers the writer's body with love nibbles. It erases from him last night's nightmare, in which he sat cross-legged at the bottom of an empty swimming pool, paralyzed, while in front of him a German shepherd shredded a naked child. He leans out the second-story window, inhaling deeply. Every hollow and crack of him swells with a feeling of goodness. The summer sun is just beginning to rise. On the yard below, the farmhouse's shadow stretches like a landscape imagined by Dr. Seuss.

He can see every dip and curve of the mile-long dirt driveway, hundreds of acres of undulating pastures, all the way to the far-off woods that, as he stares, begin to grow slivered with light. A weather system of shadow and glow paint the colossal old barn.

He exhales, measuring and tasting. After another long inhalation he bowls his hands over his face and gently hisses, trapping the warm breath to his skin. It makes him think about the rich old men who paid, hundreds of years ago, to have virgin girls exhale into their rotten-toothed mouths, because they believed the unblemished breath would keep them young and healthy.

The new day comes to life in the warming air: a buzz

saw—loud insect hum, a bird singing from somewhere nearby and another answering with a barking staccato. A pair of fat rabbits zig after each other down the driveway, then vanish into the brush.

His friend isn't yet awake, so the writer moves quietly around the farmhouse, tiptoeing down the stairs and stepping into the kitchen like a burglar. He sets coffee to brewing, then powers on his laptop and sends a good-morning-and-I-love-you e-mail to his fiancée back in Minnesota. It is the first time he's written her in days, since his flight landed at JFK. He had promised to be better about staying in touch when he travels, and he's already fucking up. Sighing, he eases the computer shut.

He takes a mug of black coffee outside and sits on a wide tree stump. A sugar maple in the yard has been turned into an enormous chandelier of diamond shine. He looks at it and puzzles over his seemingly endless reservoir of unintentional cruelty. How each time—after the fact— when he sees what he's done, the wreckage on someone's face, he swears to himself *No more, never again*, but the next day or two later, here you go, my love: acerbic words, an arctic silence, another in a long line of broken promises.

He walks an expanding orbit around the home, listening to the waking woodland. Chittering in red oaks. A surround sound of birdsong in a grove of black locust. Crunches and snaps in the alders. Around him the fields flicker. And then he's standing on the shore of a pond, shivering in the near dark created by the steeply treed and overgrown hills rising around him. Mist hangs above the water. Moss-crusted limbs poke from the pond's surface like the knobbed knuckles of giants. He wonders how lost he is, and how long he's been wandering.

The writer swigs the mucked coffee congealing in the mug and instantly spits it out again. His bladder is throbbing. He hooks the mug with a finger and then pees steamingly into the brambles. Across the pond willows sigh. Sunlight filters through the birches that tower above, and the pond looks like molten glass, like he could walk across it with burning feet. He loves this kind of life-filled silence, especially after staying the previous week downstate in the bustle and clang of New York City. He turns away and, rubbing warmth into his arms and ankles, climbs up the hill and clambers through a grove of trees—hickory and beech and more sugar maples—that sweeps open to a field. Within a minute he's sweating.

A half hour and some false turns later, he reaches the farmhouse and sees his friend hopping out the doorway, jogging toward his hundred-year-old barn. The barn is two stories tall and so well built that it looks as if the decades have just made it stronger. The writer doesn't say anything, but slowly follows his friend, trying not to be noticed.

His friend's arms are loaded down with construction materials. A bucket of tools sags from the crook of his elbow, and more tools peek out from his backpack, which jingles and clinks like it's filled with fifty pounds of nails. He nearly drops a power drill barely clinging to the lip of the bucket. And he's oblivious to the drill bits falling from his pockets, scattering behind him like a trail of crumbs. But the writer doesn't shout or laugh at the mess his friend's making. He just walks behind, smiling.

He could be my father, he thinks. The thought catches in his chest. His friend is twenty-five years older than he is and in his struggles, in his sobriety, he feels a closer kinship to this man than to anyone. He sets down his mug on a log. Then, one by one, he picks up the fallen drill bits and occasional nail.

When the writer has nearly caught up, the friend stops, yells, "What might that be?" and turns. He grins, then snarls and shoots a finger gun. "Sneaking up on me, huh? I smelled you coming."

"Ambrosia and blood?" The writer takes some of the tools, lightens his friend's load.

"How are you on this fine morning? Are you ready for some hard labor?" His friend laughs. "Gonna be some back breaking today."

"I only came to help because I was worried, you know, about how old you are and shit," the writer says. "Any second you could break into a thousand pieces. My concern for your well-being compelled me."

His friend drops the tools, winds the handle on an invisible jack-in-the-box, and slowly raises his middle finger. "Come on," he grumbles. "We really have to get at it now. Fucker, you just wandered off like this is some goddamn fairy tale." The writer tells him about the pond as they arrange the tools around the entrance to the barn. "So much to do and you're off fucking around in the woods," his friend teases. "Now fun time is over. It's time to do work!"

For the next two days the writer will help him renovate the barn. It needs to be gutted and wired and plumbed and drywalled, remodeled clean and pristine to become a home for the friend and his growing family. The two men are happy to be spending the time together. They met four years ago at a writer's conference in Portland. Something clicked. They ended up spending most of the conference in a coffee shop, talking, telling stories. Now they see each other once or twice a year and their visits are hilarious and profane and filled with indecent joy. And also with their sadnesses and struggles. They speak in ways and about things the writer doesn't with anyone else. Even spending the briefest amount of time together is healing. They drink too much espresso and bullshit, watch movies and discuss literature and art, work through their beautiful monstrosities.

"Where do you want me to start?" the writer asks. He tosses a crowbar from hand to hand, ready to do some damage.

His friend shows the writer around the building, pointing out the finished parts and new rooms within. He flips the lights on and nods at the wiring and electrical run tightly up and down the inside of the drywall, the newly piped sink and shower, and the half-started toilet. They walk through what still needs to be done. The writer will start down below, sorting and cutting scrap metal and pipes to use in other parts of the renovation.

His friend puts a tool in the writer's hand and tells him to start with one-foot lengths. When he's got two dozen pieces cut, he should bring them up into the barn, and cut the same number of two-foot sections.

"Sure, of course," the writer says. "No problem. But what is this thing?" He holds up the pipe cutter.

His friend squints. "You're shitting me?"

"Nope." He smiles. "Serious. No fucking clue."

"Fucking fuck fuck." His friend shakes his head, and

then leads him to the piles of pipe in the basement and shows him how the tool works.

"Just like a can opener," the writer says, as his friend heads upstairs again. "I love tuna. Cat food, too."

A half hour later the writer walks upstairs, yelling for his friend. The pipe cutter is broken into pieces in his hands. He managed to cut three lengths before the tool started wrenching apart. Rather than asking for help, he decided to just apply more force, twist the tool harder, put his weight into each turn. It did not end well.

"What the fuck," his friend says, kindly, but also seeming confused and slightly pissed. "What did you do? That's our only one." He shakes his head. "What the hell am I going to do with you? Follow me." He walks to a toolbox, picks something up, and tells the writer to follow him outside, where he stands in front of the barn like a professor at a chalkboard.

"OK, this is a caulk gun," he says. "From this tip, caulk squirts out. You are going to use it to seal cracks between the boards in the barn wall." He shows the writer how to reload the gun, and says it will probably take half the caulk for one side and half for the other. "This is easy," he says, smiling grimly. "I know you can do it."

The writer doesn't say anything—he's embarrassed—and just starts working. He loads a caulk tube, knifes off its tip, and tightens it in the gun until a bead bubbles on the end. He focuses hard on the boards. He doesn't want to fuck up this job, too.

He can slip his fingers between the wide cracks in the

old boards. He empties tube after tube of caulk, flinging them into the tall grass and then hurrying to reload. He hums while he works from left to right, until the wall ends, and then down to the gap below and back right to left. He squeezes the trigger as many times as it takes, until the crack is crammed with caulk. He thinks about how cold winter must be up here and is meticulous about closing every opening he sees. The gaps are vanishing; everything is fine.

The sun scorches his shoulders and neck. He smears his face with caulk each time he swipes the sweat away.

He tries to concentrate on the work but his mind wanders: he imagines what his fiancée is doing at this exact moment, is mesmerized by flitting dragonflies and the chain of ants hefting bread crumbs from the barn doorway, wonders what kind of apples are growing in the trees and what his friend and his wife will do with them all.

Truly the writer is filled with happiness. Fields surround him and the distant woods beckon. He can get cell service only if he stands on the hill beside the barn. And the flex and squeeze of his tired body—doing something physical, working his hands calloused and raw—feels amazing. Beneath the caulk his fingers are dirty from the basement, the smell reminding him of being a kid, of rushing outside after rainstorms to gather night crawlers from the wet garden, of throwing bowls and teacups in the ceramic studio in college. The writer realizes this is first time he's labored like this since he was sick, since— for each second of the last eight years—he's been struggling to live in the body brain surgery left him.

The first twenty-one years of his life were all body, jubilations and outcries of the physical and of blood-pumping extremes. Then his body became a cage. After more than a hundred years of battering, the planks in front of the writer are more than sturdy—but his still-young body is a broken machine.

He is standing back from the wall, looking at the work he's done, when he hears his friend singing out his name inside the barn and asking in a too-sweet voice for the writer to come inside. It's at least fifteen degrees cooler inside the barn, and dim. It takes a minute to make out his friend standing on the other side of the wall.

"Oh, friend of mine," he says. "What in the fuck is going on?"

"What?" the writer asks, eyes still adjusting. "What did I do?"

His friend just nods down at the boards. Caulk is piled in globs on the floor where it's oozed through. Long strands droop from unsealed cracks. Blobs of it hang like half-filled water balloons. Light streams in from gaps, pearling the dust that drifts through the air.

"Shit," the writer mutters. "Shitty shit. Man, I was really trying." He doesn't know whether to laugh or cry. "I'm sorry," he says. "I'm so sorry. I thought . . . man, shit. I'm sorry."

"I'm going to take this back because you are a dangerous man," his friend says, delicately prying the caulk gun away and hiding it under a pile of old newspapers. "Let's see," he mumbles. He paces. He juts his jaw, feigning troubled thought. "What does the man who can do nothing do?"

He stops, smiles, and gently pats the writer's cheek.

Then he strides out the barn door with purpose, calling for the writer to grab a shovel and follow him down the hill. The writer scrambles to find one in a corner where dozens of tools lean, then sprints to catch up with his friend, the shovel banging against his thigh.

Fifteen yards downhill from the barn, his friend stabs a stick into the ground. "Sure you know how a shovel works?" He laughs, then squeezes the writer's shoulder. "There is the digging part, then the lifting, then the piling. Repeat until you collapse or the wolves come—whichever happens first." The writer drops the shovel and bear hugs his friend until he howls. "Too damn hard," the friend cries. He lifts a fist and mean-mugs. "Yer gonna get it."

"I'd have stopped after the first few bones snapped. So brittle, though. I'd be worried." He catches the shovel his friend tosses at him. The wet dirt says *shhhhh* every time he takes a step.

"You cannot fuck this one up," his friend says. "You dig. From this spot to that stick. Two feet deep. Two feet across. Dig, dig, dig. You are a digging animal."

The writer watches his friend jog back up the hill. Notices the oppressive heat, the silence, no birdsong, no symphony of bugs. "I'm sorry," he yells. He stares up at the old barn. "I really am."

At the top his friend turns and beams. "You're the best fuckup I know," he shouts. "And I'm happy you're here."

The writer dips the shovel into the dirt. He can do this. The table saw roars to life in the barn and his limbs are thrilled and alive and moving through the sunlight and he will do it. He will shovel and dig and shovel and dig until dusk makes him shiver in his sweat-drenched shirt and the trench is perfect and complete.

RABBIT HOLE MUSIC

I

It's a good day in California. For a week I've been pacing the living room because of my hemorrhoids, but now I can finally sit in the pillowy backyard grass. There ripening fruit droops the orange trees' limbs. The air smells like BBQ thanks to wildfires in the hills above Malibu. Ash flits down from the orange-gray sky.

Though I spent my time indoors trying to read, I often gave in, lay on my stomach, and watched the news Americanize Mother Nature. The firestorms have become celebrity. Air tankers swoop over the burning hills, and, briefly, everyone forgets Britney Spears's exposed crotch and Tom Cruise's wackiness. All day and night, reporters stand before the engulfed hillsides, interviewing weepy residents whose homes smolder and fold in on themselves in the background. Embers levitate around the residents' heads. Each TV station has at least one helicopter—the burring machines clog the sky. Below their cameras, yellow specks weave through the hillsides, firefighters switchbacking from the racing arc of fire.

There are so many layers in this instant: the distance between the fires and the reporter's lens, the flying machinery, the digital signals in the air, the anchorwoman's bobbing larynx, the dented satellite dish atop my home, the thousands of miles of power lines, the glass plate on which the images appear. In the living room I'm gifted the illusion of safety. All the danger is locked down within the TV. It's sterilized. Cellular. The firemen as antibodies. The glowing hot spots in the blackened hills as a growing malignancy.

The most titillating footage repeats every twenty minutes. A mansion raging with fire. Crackling cinders dropping from the sky like paratroopers. The supermarket manager on the roof with a garden hose. Commercials for Taco Bueno, Pechanga Resort and Casino, the Dodgers' Bobblehead Doll Night. The wall of fire is twenty feet tall. "We have to pull back," one of the firemen says into the camera. A boy cries about his lost toys. Burger King. Hustler Casino. Repeat.

When the TV's Novocain wears off, I start considering which vessels and veins in me are ballooning now that the ones in my ass are no longer painfully swollen. I'm dragged back into myself: equilibrium, balance. Pain has vanished in one part of me—so good money says it's working its way to another.

II

As a result of a bleeding vascular malformation in my brain stem, I had brain surgery on September 16, 1999. I was twenty-one years old. Before the aneurysms I'd never been sick. But then, at nineteen, there was a brain bleed. A two-year whiteout. And then more bleeding. More cutting. Physical rehabilitation and disability services. A wheelchair, walker, and cane.

Medical clinics and hospitals have become a second home. Panicked, I race to them every few weeks—I *must* see a neurologist because I'm *sure* my brain is bleeding again. Something is wrong inside me. So the days, the sleepless nights are endless. MRIs. X-rays. CAT scans. Blood and urine and skin and nerve tests. Swallowing is painful, so scopes are snaked through my nose and mouth. My face is aching and numb. I have tremors. Trigeminal neuralgia muscle tightness and cramping in my legs and back. Abnormal reactions to stimuli. The pins and needles of paresthesia. Chronic constipation. Ulcerated sores in my mouth and throat. Hypothyroidism. Double vision and nystagmus. Lisch nodules in my corneas. Panic attacks. Depression. Insomnia. Exhaustion. Genetic testing for neurofibromatosis. Therapists. Psychiatrists.

I grow convinced that there are lumps in my breast, armpit, neck, stomach, testicles. Annually I embrace my cancer. And each time, after the doctor reviews the test results, she says that nothing is wrong with me, nothing at all.

III

An unbuckled baby smashes into a windshield. Bricks drop on a foot. A face is slapped and blood rushes to the surface. This is acute pain. But many people don't experience the hurt until minutes, days, or even years later. A table saw slices three fingers off, but the carpenter doesn't feel anything for weeks. A city bus shears off a bicyclist's leg. Only later, and then for the rest of her life, there's an unbearable pain in the empty space where her leg was. It itches. It's on fire.

Beyond the explicit physical manifestations of pain—the cuts and blood and bruises—the more complex elements of pain can be confounding. In many cases a pain's source can't be found.

When someone wants or needs pain it's called psychogenic.

My self-hurt has always been delicate, veiled. An X-Acto knife sliced between the gums. Drumsticks banged against the knee. A rainbow of underarm bites. Vomiting in the shower. A black eye made midnight with my fist. And then the accepted, the "manly": tattoos and hours in the gym and muscle-building, fat-burning diets. Partying, sleepless weeks, and mile after mile of running. Wounds and wounding Trojan-horsed into daily life through violence and sports.

Ascetics, mystics, and martyrs have self-applied pain for thousands of years through rites of passage: symbolic deaths, rebirth through self-flagellation, beds of nails, starvation, and weeks without sleep. Freudian psychoanalytical theory views "holy" masochism as the ego's response to the guilt of the superego.

In *The Body in Pain: The Making and Unmaking of the World*, Elaine Scarry argues that chronic pain destroys its victim's ability to communicate, and, in the end, shatters their world, including the innermost self. In "Sacred Pain and the Phenomenal Self," Ariel Glucklich, a theology professor at Georgetown, writes, "Pain, in short, unmakes their profane world and leads the mystics to self- and world-transcendence."

IV

There's been no medical cause for the numbness in my extremities and face, the twists and knots in my gut, the tremoring in my hands and eyelids, the weight loss, or the surprise bruising. I'm in and out of MRI tubes and X-ray machines. Needles collapse my veins. The muscles on my right side are weaker; they have a different *tone*. My right leg is jammed up in the hip socket because I always fall in that direction. I'm in and out of the hospital. Pill bottles, herbal treatments, vitamins, and tinctures forest the bathroom sink. I stretch, meditate.

I get two digital rectal exams, by two separate doctors, on the same beautiful California Tuesday. To see if I can feel "normally," to see if my nerves and pain receptors are functioning properly, a neurologist has me undress and then uses a needle to scratch the flesh of my groin. He scrapes methodically, like he's drawing Van Gogh's *Sunflowers*, then looks up and asks what I feel.

That night, in the shower, I feel my thighs and groin, thickened with dashes and welts.

A week later the same neurologist attaches me to a computer. Working from foot to neck, he inserts an electrified needle into my nerves and shocks me. Three escalating pulses. The muscles between the needle and the electrode contract and the computer logs my body's reaction.

Exhausted, I sit in my car for an hour afterward. The stereo murmurs as if I'm underground.

For months every part of me hurts. I take handfuls of pills. I lie down. All day I am a zombie, lurching around my home. My wife sleeps in our new bed. Every bone in me feels like it's shattering when I lie on the mattress so I sleep on the floor, flat on the hard carpet or fitted into a homemade armature of cardboard.

V

People born with congenital analgesia do not feel pain. Often they bite chunks out of their tongues. They cut their fingertips off, pick up scalding pots with bare hands, and fall from jungle gyms, but don't realize something's wrong until someone points out the streaming blood, the furrows of blisters, the way a bone shard pierces forearm skin.

People with congenital analgesia sometimes develop Charcot joint from simple wear and tear. Normally pain prods one to protect a wounded area—by limping, for example—until it heals, but when pain isn't felt, the injury is worsened, and the area, especially in the joints, is ground down. This place of erosion is the perfect breeding ground for bacteria, and it can lead to life-threatening infection.

Jean-Martin Charcot (1825–1893) has been called the father of neurology. Freud and Alfred Binet studied under him in France. Charcot is credited with first identifying multiple sclerosis and Lou Gehrig's disease (or ALS, amyotrophic lateral sclerosis), and with modifying James Parkinson's findings and then granting a name to Parkinson's disease. Charcot also studied hysteria, which he believed was a mental disorder with physical manifestations. He tried to expand scientific and medical knowledge by adding hypnotism, magnetism, and electricity to his therapeutic detective work.

Charcot's work did not benefit me, however; I'm not lucky enough to have the terror of a nameable malady. They say it's not multiple sclerosis, ALS, or early-onset Parkinson's. My body is a backfiring car. Punch up the volume and it accelerates, in reverse. Turn on the dome light and the hood pops. For years pleasure came to me only in pain. I needed to hurt. A sweet caress was an aching jolt.

Now everything's on fire—it throbs and I am blissed out. I'm numb and my cuticles bleed when I wash up and I feel good and weep when someone says they love me and sometimes my wife's breath burns my cheek.

VI

So I make lists. On September 13, 1848, outside of Cavendish, Vermont, Phineas Gage and a group of rail workers were blasting rock, preparing a roadbed for a new train track. After a hole was drilled into the stone, Gage added gunpowder, a fuse, and sand, and then pounded all of it down with an iron rod. The rod was 1.25 inches in diameter. It was almost four feet long. When the powder exploded, the rod ripped through the side of his face, shattered his upper jaw, and passed behind his left eye before sprouting from and passing through the top of his head. Amazingly, Gage was speaking within minutes.

Frank Sinatra stars as Tony, a widower and wannabe playboy, in the 1959 Frank Capra film *A Hole in the Head*. Tony asks Mario, his wealthy brother, to finance his dream, a Disneyesque resort in Miami. Mario, sickened by Tony's lifestyle, agrees under the condition that Tony either marry and settle down or give Mario custody of his son, Ally.

Hole-in-the-head disease starts as sores above the eyes. If the sores are allowed to grow, they'll penetrate a tropical fish's skull.

In the British girl group Sugababes' music video for "Hole in the Head," a man licks a guitar. He is a bandleader, singing and strutting, gyrating and headbanging. The Sugababes, half-clad, glammed-out women, dance in the crowd. They fawn over the all-male band and caress the bandleader's bare chest. They trace fingertips through their cleavage and over their hips. By the song's finish, however, the three women have pushed the bandleader to the floor. They kick and stomp, destroying his band's equipment. Guitars are thrown. Mic stands topple.

A hole in the head. Versions and subversions of the cliché have been pervasive in music since the early twentieth century. Recently it's been used by Sting, Cypress Hill, the Dixie Chicks, Box Elders, Nickelback, and Andrew Bird.

The first time I saw the movie trailer for the documentary *A Hole in the Head*, I thought it would be about memory loss. It begins with grainy footage of an African tribe dancing and singing exuberantly, long spears like flagpoles. The voice-over—"Dawn in the uplands . . . the land of mystery"—sounds straight out of a middle school classroom. But the next image stunned me. Tightly framed: four hands in a bloody mess, weaving in and out of red muck. A grinding sound, like a nail scraping concrete. The next shot makes everything clear; a skull is at the center of the slick flurry of fingers. The scalp has been peeled away. A metal tool digs at the human head. The voice-over recedes. The scene changes to a woman cutting her hair in front of a mirror. The trailer begins rapidly cutting between four people explaining trepanation and footage of a human head being drilled into. The woman reappears, this time wearing a hair cap, with a gap across her forehead. The four explanatory voices continue in voice-over while she arranges her coverings. The scene jumps. Now her entire head is bandaged and bloody. She swabs her face. The scene changes again. The final time she appears is the missing scene, between the second and third appearances. Her hair cap is pulled back. The background music, trippy classic rock, gets louder and louder. It's rabbit hole music. A small power drill angles diagonally from her exposed forehead. It's held in her hand. Blood rivers from the hole she's drilling, down the bridge of her nose and into her mouth. She's wearing aviator sunglasses.

VII

Outside, the smoky California air smells like a diesel engine. The hummingbird feeders are filled with red sugar water, but there are no birds. The rat that's living in the aloe plant is gnawing on something in the shade. I'm not sure how many days now the world's been burning.

All our elderly neighbors have their TVs on. One stops by with a bag of fruit from her backyard trees—pomegranates, grapefruit, oranges, and lemons. She tells me that the book her eighty-year-old husband's been working on for decades, an academic tome on Lutheranism, has finally been accepted for publication. Teary eyed, she says she hopes it will be published before he dies. After she leaves, I halve a pomegranate, spoon out the magenta seeds, and eat sloppily. The TVs drone more endless news about the wildfires. Every five minutes the old guy who lives behind us shouts, "Awww fuck!" when the Dodgers game loses its signal and blips to static. Throttled by the wind, the sun-bleached prayer flags I purchased in Nepal tear loose from the porch columns. After scrambling over the fence, I chase them down the block. All afternoon I rehang them, listening to the neighbor cuss.

VIII

I bought the prayer flags outside Boudhanath Stupa, one of the holiest sites in Boudha, in Kathmandu, Nepal, in 2002. The building, a UNESCO World Heritage Site, used to be the focus of the neighborhood, but when I visited it was hidden by tall restaurants and thick clouds of exhaust. Beggars and the maimed moaned for coins, beating ramshackle drums. Trinket sellers and vendors— singing bowls, Vishnu, the North Face, the Nepalese flag—lined the narrow entrance to the temple.

But walking through the gate, I molted. Kathmandu's cacophony peeled away. The primary pilgrimage site for Tantric Buddhists, Boudhanath serenely bustles with monks and nuns in maroon and orange robes, Sherpas, Tibetans. The mandala-style structure is a hundred feet tall. Prayer flags arrow down from the golden spire. The sky is a flock of shifting colors. Enormous painted eyes gaze out from the tower. The unblinking eyes of God. Blue and red and yellow and black. Each stair represents a step on the path toward enlightenment. Pilgrims circumambulate the tower, chanting and spinning the 108 copper prayer wheels embedded in the structure's base. Everything goes clockwise. Everything has meaning. Juniper incense burns. The temple space is open to the sky, and unlike in the rest of Kathmandu, it is brilliant, blue.

The day after we visited, my girlfriend and I took a bus to the India-Nepal border. On a jungle walk we had to cross a river by walking over a fallen log. Our guide pointed out the alligators below us and smiled. I was the first to cross. Five steps out on the log, the world spun and blurred and I toppled. It had not even been a year and a half since my brain surgery. Two hands locked on my shoulders—and the Brit who was on the walk with us said, "Easy, mate, easy," and helped lower me to the log. I was ashamed, and though I only heard him lighting his cigarette, I knew all of them were giggling behind me.

I returned to Boudhanath a few nights after we got back to Kathmandu, and thousands of worshipers, monks and tourists, were crowded around the stupa. Everyone lit butter candles. In the dark their faces glowed.

IX

In 2004 I start seeing things. Streaks and lightning, something whiplashing past the corner of my eye. Sitting on a Manhattan bench, I look above the taxis and see tiny orbs of light, like will-o'-the-wisps. I adjust the eye patch my neuro-ophthalmologist has me wearing. I blink and furiously rub my eyes. The ghostly lights have vanished when I look again. But within a few minutes new bulbous flashes appear, bobbing and jerking through the autumn air. My vision is failing, so my walk to the Hudson is slow. I step cautiously off each curb. Walkers stream briskly around me like I'm a boulder in a creek. They are a haze. With the eye patch, I have no depth perception but at least my double vision is gone. My eye trembles each time I set my foot down. Above the Hudson I see fireflies lighting up the gray day.

The next day I do not leave the apartment where I'm staying. I cry to my host, ask him why this life can't be easier. I say it would be better if I cut out one of my eyes. He hugs me before leaving. Turning in the doorway, his face weighted by my sadness, he cracks a joke. Says it could be worse. Something about dog collars and Abu Ghraib.

In the middle of the night, I'd sent an e-mail to my doctors. I'd read it over and over before sending. I sounded crazy. Batshit crazy. "Vibrating rectangles of light." "Bulbs swinging in the air." By noon there are a number of responses in my in-box. I need to make an appointment. They tell me about Charles Bonnet syndrome. Occluding one eye with the patch has radically changed my vision, and it's possible that I might be hallucinating in ways similar to those who have CBS. I Google and read, Google and read—hallucinations after car accidents, hallucinations caused by torture, hallucinations due to sensory deprivation.

A person who hallucinates may see the faces of loved ones or objects in swirling carpets or in shadows. The hallucinations may take the form of concrete objects, like iron skillets or coffee mugs or knives, or they might be abstract:

spots of light, glittering spackle. CBS usually affects those
with damaged eyes or optic pathways, or who have developed visual impairments through aging. Macular degener-
ation. Glaucoma. Methyl alcohol poisoning.

Charles Bonnet, a Genevan naturalist, studied tree lice
and discovered that butterflies and caterpillars breathe
through pores called called *stigmata*. Bonnet's eyesight
began failing, but he continued working, fascinated by
plants' abilities to choose and feel. He believed that man's
mind is fueled by pleasure or pain, and that happiness is
the end of human existence. He first described CBS in
1769, when his grandfather, almost blind from cataracts,
began seeing people, birds, horses, homes, tapestries,
and floating patterns that weren't actually there.

In "Sacred Pain and the Phenomenal Self," Glucklich
describes hallucinations that are similar in nature to
CBS. He says that visual hallucinations are not caused by
psychopathology or impaired thinking, but "result from
the disruption of sensory input among patients suffering eye damage." When the eyes stop working correctly,
when they don't *see* properly, the lack of external stimuli
is overcome by hallucinations created and projected onto
the seen world by the brain.

X

A week after my thirtieth birthday I get a colonoscopy.
The last thing I remember is a nurse smiling as she flips
down a clear welding visor. Afterward, deep in the drug
fog, I lie in a hospital bed, drinking a juice box. The
gastrointestinal specialist is beside me when I look up,

pointing at pictures of slimy caves. Other than the hernia and ulcer and a few hemorrhoids, the doctor says that everything looks fine. I need to return in two weeks. A half hour later I sign a form and a nurse says I can change into my street clothes. At home I show Ariane, my wife, the images from the wormhole camera. The slick pink world of my insides.

XI

Ariane leaves me in a dream. I do not know why she goes, but the dream happens weekly. More of the narrative unfolds each time. I live in a mansion on an oak-topped hill. From the porch I can see a town with industrial smokestacks. Now and again I hear traffic, but there are no roads. There's no driveway. I hear trains. Fields of sunflowers stretch down the hill. A yellow sea surrounds the mansion except for a small grove of apple trees in the back. Seven monkeys live with me. Time passes—I know this because my toenails grow long and my hands wrinkle. I can no longer wear socks. I go barefoot. The apple orchard begins to smell sour, like whiskey. At night apples smack to the ground mushily. Four of the monkeys have babies. I take two of the babies away in Adidas shoeboxes. I give them food and water, but raise them in separate locked ballrooms on the third floor. The other monkeys, the seven adults and two additional babies, live together in a jungle in the basement. The jungle used to be a gym. Vines on the basketball hoops. Cracked bowling alley. A canopy of trees making the ceiling impossible to see. The temperature regulated to keep my monkeys happy. A thin mist spraying from above. In a greenhouse I grow orchids under expensive-looking lamps. Once a day I wheelbarrow bananas and leafy greens to a gazebo and unload. Hidden in the trees, I watch the monkeys eat. Years pass. My toenails are so long now. The baby monkeys grow up. The elder monkeys are gray around the mouth. The baby monkeys I'd kept secluded upstairs get large, but they spend all their time staring at the veins in leaves.

One morning I walk into the greenhouse and all the orchids are withered. All day I walk up and down the lanes of the bowling alley. The next morning I shoot all the monkeys with tranquilizer darts. I fit them with shock collars. While they are knocked out, I fill the feeding area with bananas. In the ballrooms upstairs I build desks out of dried sunflower stalks and planks of wood. Lit candles and bananas are arranged on the desks. When the monkeys wake up, I watch them gaze at the flames. Again and again their sausage-like fingers reach into the fire. One afternoon I walk out of my hiding spot toward one of the monkeys, flicking a lighter. The monkey looks up, puzzled, as I touch the flame to its bearded face, but it doesn't draw back. When I pull away the lighter, the monkey waves its hand over the flame. A week later the two monkeys in the ballrooms are lousy with weeping wounds, and I realize they've been biting themselves. I begin shocking the seven monkeys in the jungle. I push a button and they roar. I push it again and screams shake the trees. They tear at their necks. I walk toward them with my lighter and they sprint into the jungle. This goes on for dozens of weeks. My toenails snap off and bloody footprints begin layering the parquet lanes of the bowling alley. I no longer hide during feeding time. When I shock the monkeys, they lope hunchbacked out of the trees and look around, eyes glazed. Smoke from the collars rises above their heads like a foul halo. They saunter by me and sit at the gazebo. Lumpish hands curled in their groins, they wait.

XII

The Emergency Care doctor rests a stethoscope against my abdomen, my back, my spine. Deep breaths, she says. I haven't shit in a long time, four days, a week—I don't know. I'm so full. I'm brimming. She scribbles on a prescription pad, and tells Ariane to rush me to the emergency room.

Head wounds, chest pains, an old lady moaning about how she wants to die: the waiting room is purgatorial. After checking in, I leave my wife in the waiting room and stand outside. It hurts to sit. It hurts to move. After two hours I join Ariane, who's called her doctor father to ask his opinion. She smiles, comforts me, but the fear in her eyes is obvious.

A gaggle of teenagers stand in the doorway, peering around the waiting room. Two sit, and two others step up to the receptionist. One of the boys asks her, too loudly, if they have to give their names to be seen. Is there another way to get help for their friend? Shaking her head grimly, the receptionist says no. The boys back away from the desk as if she's flashed a pistol. Their fucked-up friend is sitting across from us. He's pale and skittery. They gather him up like a sodden duvet cover and leave. The old woman moans, asking her husband why it's taking so long. She can't wait any more, she wails. The husband tries to hush her. A man in a halo brace offers her a Vicodin. The husband gets a glass of water. He tips it into her mouth, and gently cradles her head while she swallows it down.

Dozens of people get called back. Paramedics roll people in on stretchers and wheelchairs. We wait. Next to us the elderly couple discusses whether it might be quicker to go home and call an ambulance. The woman says they don't have the money. The waiting room clears and night falls and then the waiting room fills again. I've been forgotten.

A woman in a wheelchair is pushed to a stop beside me. Her face is blue white, like a whale's belly. Her throat sounds as if it's filled with Jell-O. While she struggles to breathe, bright veins work up her chest, circling her neck like vines of licorice. As I stand, she turns the color of fresh snow. Her head slumps. People point and shout and a pair of nurses rush her into the ER.

It's almost one in the morning when I get called back. We've been here for almost seven hours. It takes another hour to see the ER doctor, and while Ariane watches, I receive a rectal exam. They take X-rays of my abdomen. When the doctor returns, she says that no physical obstructions appeared on the images, but my intestinal muscles have stopped working. I'm packed with shit. She tells me that people who've had surgery like mine sometimes lose digestive tract functioning, that I should supplement my diet with pills and vitamins. I tell her that I do. She hands me a list of tests for my doctor to perform. "Now we will fix you," she says. "We are going to get an enema." She says it as if we'll all be doing this together. Me, the doctor, the nurse, Ariane looking on from her chair.

The doctor is a Sarah Palin look-alike. She has me roll onto my side and open the back of the hospital gown. Ariane sits directly in front of me. The ER is lit green and outside my bay is a hive of commotion. I groan, try to laugh as the doctor nestles a bag of fluids onto a hooked pole. She pries her fingers inside me and snugs something hard into place, like she's just connected a hose to a spigot. I stare at the wall above my wife's head. The doctor says, "Here we go," and suddenly the fluids are cascading through me, swelling me like a manatee.

XIII

Like the windblown smoke from the wildfires, what I put inside me comes and goes—there are old drugs and new meds, doses change, I forget to or intentionally stop taking them. Blue-green algae, Vicodin, Neurontin, hydrocodone, calamine lotion, codeine, Amitiza, calcium, Lyrica, baclofen, flaxseed oil, Valtrex, Ambien, Flexeril, shark cartilage, Robitussin, Lunesta, clonazepam, chamomile, Ultram, Zantac, Vivarin, Xanax, Adderall, Tylenol with Codeine No. 4, Senokot, Ritalin, Carmex, Wellbutrin, saw palmetto, THC, Cymbalta, Mylanta, omeprazole, Soma, passionflower, Halcion, Celexa, Dexedrine, tea tree oil, vitamins A and B complex and C and D and E, Motrin, Cipro, garlic, Colace, magnesium, grape seed, iron, Saint-John's-wort, Claritin, licorice root, corticosteroids, green tea, Tylenol PM, prednisone,

ginger, B-12 injections, Advair, willow bark, inhaled
albuterol, fish oil, diazepam, ginkgo biloba, finasteride,
Diflucan, belladonna, milk of magnesia, cranberry,
ephedrine, a "magic mouthwash" of steroids and lido-
caine and antihistamines, Keep Alert, Darvocet, lysine,
oxycodone, beta-blockers, bilberry leaf, MiraLAX, chew-
able caffeine, Dulcolax, cocaine, witch hazel, naproxen,
goldenseal, amoxicillin, yohimbe bark, Klonopin, lemon
balm, amitriptyline, ma huang, Imodium, LSD, antihistamines, evening primrose, magnesium citrate.

One doctor gives me steroids. Another wants to insert
a baclofen pump into my abdomen, which I can press
when the pain gets too bad, madly pumping my belly
like I did my Reeboks in eighth grade. She gives me a
DVD that explains the benefits of the medical equipment
and details the surgical procedure. All the actors in the
DVD, the "patients," are at least twice my age. Older than
my dead grandparents. *They* look sick. On the cover of
the DVD an elderly, overweight woman strolls happily
beside a perfectly manufactured creek. I stop taking the
medicine, and decline the surgical pump. I prominently
display the DVD case on my coffee table, however. I tell
Ariane that it's funny; the woman's overzealous smile is
ironic. But really I like to see it there because it pisses me
off, and that hot fury feels good.

I am what I am. *Man is what man eats.*

What I receive and consume, even what I see, becomes
my blood. The blood is my anger and love and bewil-
derment. As I walk through my neighborhood before
sunup, morning birds beginning to squall, all of what
I've taken in, all of what's happened, all of what I'll never
know, feels engraved into my flesh. Words, whole stories,

are carved onto me like hearts on a birch's white bark. Pictographs chipped into stones. My litanies rise from every outward inch of my body. An ever-growing illuminated manuscript. I am turning and turning, a prayer wheel embedded in the breathing air.

XIV

The International Trepanation Advocacy Group— ITAG—says trepanation "favorably alters movement of blood through the brain and improves brain functions which are more important than ever before in history to adapt to an ever more rapidly changing world." Its website documents the transition from ITAG's first incarnation, an anthropological and medical database about trepanation, to what grew from it, the trepanning of fifteen volunteers by a medical professional between 2000 and 2004. No conclusions could be drawn from these cases. But the website states that in 2005 "an internationally known and widely published professor of cerebral circulation took up the investigation of trepanation and its effects on cerebral circulation for ITAG." ITAG looked at a small number of minor brain surgeries where the skull was left open for some months before being closed. After monitoring the brain's blood flow before, during, and after the procedures, ITAG reports that the blood flow in these patients' skulls reached youthful levels while open, and returned to preoperative levels when closed. The website claims that these studies are the impetus for eight medical and scientific papers that are being written and will be published.

Near the bottom of the page, there is a link where people who would like to become volunteers can send in their names. I fill out the form, press *Submit*.

XV

Under the smoke-thickened clouds, I lie in the backyard grass. The Dodgers game is back on the radio. Every few minutes the crack of a baseball bat flutters through the trees. Despite the clouds, the California sun is so strong my face is burning. Frank Sinatra records start playing next door. Teenage girls shriek and begin dancing in the cul-de-sac. Magic Mountain, Malibu, the Corral Fire. The air vibrates around me—the ways we drill and dance and sing. Ash somersaults on the hot breeze. The rumble of fire trucks. Helicopters. Sirens. All of it seems perfect. Oranges to be picked, the aloe plant about to bloom.

WAY UP HIGH WAY DOWN LOW

I

*G*od's entrails, I think, half-awake, staring out the airplane porthole. The hallucinatory sky is golden orange, rippling with clouds, snakes trying to swallow identical snakes. The airplane shifts and dips. I am looking almost straight down. I lean from my seat into the aisle, toward the window, where morning light blossoms inside a bed of clouds. *They are God's guts aglow.* I am still asleep, maybe, fever-dreaming. *Guts, guts, guts.* My watch is gone; probably someone in the Bangkok airport is wearing it. Having stayed up all night for my early-morning connection, I am wired and exhausted, trying to ride out my paranoia, a folded-paper boat flaming and spinning through gutter water. I've chewed my fingernails bloody. I am sick, too. I've been shitting at least once an hour since my first flight. Two days ago? Three? Kathmandu, Bangkok, Narita, and now we are on our way to Minneapolis. Home. Who knows how long it's been? I am raw and fetid. A silent stranger was sitting beside me when I fell asleep, but now the scabbed seat is empty. An old man dozes in the aisle seat across from me. The darkened cabin is hushed—everyone I see asleep—but the silence is hollowing. It feels like I am the only person on this plane, in the world, breathing raggedly, alive. For a few seconds I forget about the earthquake that bounced the cups across the table right before I left for the Kathmandu airport. The clouds fall away as the plane rights itself. The light of the sunrise swings through the cabin, kaleidoscopic, and beside me, suddenly, the sleeping man's arm, resting across his gut, is unshadowed. He's drooling. A heart-shaped gob of spit dangles from his chin. His hand is writhing slowly. Where his thumb should be, a nub dips and rears and shines.

II

Sometimes, lost in thought, I wander my home, picking up mugs or books. I stare at them as if I've never seen them before. I turn them in my hand and gape as I chew my thumbnails. My wife says that I spit the slivers out wherever I might be standing in our house: living room, kitchen, bedroom. "Like some little prince, you walk around, *patooo patooo*"—her lips pop the air—"not worried in the least about who will have to pick them up. Damn!" I try to laugh with her when she tells this story.

III

Apes, especially chimpanzees, have been subjects in experiments for decades. For scientists they are human substitutes: physiologically similar, but different enough that we can justify using them. Utilitarian and effective, but disposable—like paper plates.

But the posttraumatic stress these chimps suffer resembles that of people, at least as described by the American Psychiatric Association. In labs, apes are treated like murderers: violently controlled, deprived of their senses in isolation, maimed purposefully, wounded by side effects, knocked out by darts and stun guns. Recent studies report that these treatments can compromise "scientific inference," and question the legitimacy of experiments that use apes as test subjects. Many have concluded that the results are invalidated by the apes' trauma and stress.

IV

"To suffer is to find oneself mired in oneself. Pain then is the inner experience of one's own being as a weight, an affliction. . . . What wounds may be the instrument, but what pains is the sensuous element. In pain what oppresses is the light, the heat, the din, the density, the depth as such. In pain the sensuous is an oppression before it is a sense impression, impression of a sense."— Alphonso Lingis, *Phenomenological Explanations*

V

Many people say spitting is: *Disgusting. Gross. Crude. Repulsive. Dirty.* A disgust response makes a person want to turn away; it saves you from the inedible, the worse than rotten. "We don't do that," my wife tells our son when she catches him hawking up phlegm outside. "It's bad

manners." If this happens, I firm up my face with serious-
ness and nod—dutifully reinforcing her words—but find
myself looking at a spot directly over his head. Growing
up, I spit constantly: into the air as I pedaled my bike,
all over baseball and football fields, while mowing dirt-
patched lawns, out the rolled-down windows of Pontiacs.

Spitting can be seen an aggressive act. The lizard brain
needs to protect and help itself, to disguise uncomfortable emotions, to get a reaction. The boy hard-swallows
a handful of worms. A girl throws a used tampon on your
car's windshield. A guy asks the sky if it wants some and
then whips his T-shirt off. Today I catch myself before
spitting about half the time, and stop. The rest of the
time I go ahead with it, then feel guilty, even if no one's
watching. Each night, as soon as I step onto my porch,
I clear my throat like I am about to give a commence-
ment address, and then I spit into the bushes. Thousands
of wads of chewed gum are buried in their shadows.
Sometimes I see ribbons of saliva, tiny spit bulbs, gleam-
ing like diamonds in the darkness.

VI

I have always believed the worst was about to happen.
More than that, even—I've felt disaster, like smoldering
embers, always with me, always inside me, always waiting to burst into flame. One of my earliest memories is of
peering at my mother from the doorway of my bedroom.
It was hours past my bedtime. She didn't know I was
watching her. I was so worried that she would leave or
die that each night I cried. Now I have a four-year-old son

of my own. Often I find myself suddenly wide awake far past midnight. After tiptoeing into his bedroom, I press my face closer and closer to his, until his warm breath paints a mask over me.

VII

In the years after my brain surgery, I have a recurring dream in which I am a monkey. My head has been shaved, and I'm strapped to a metal massage chair, facing downward. A silver tray sits in front of my face. The restraints are so tight there is no possibility of movement. From above me there is the buzz of saws. And then I can feel my skull open, splitting with a crack like it's made of balsa wood, followed by a painless prodding, like the push and pull of a dentist working at a Novocained tooth. Sometimes a piece of me—a chunk of gristle, a worm of tissue—is laid atop the tray and comes to life, crawling off the metal edge and falling silently to the antiseptic floor. Always, before the dream goes black, I feel blood rushing down my back like a cape and trickling over my forehead, pooling in my eyes.

VIII

But deep within, I think that a part of me loves this, the fact that disaster is always with me. That my bones are somehow lined with cravings for doom, sharp-edged dread, self-immolation, and violence. They bubble up jubilant and unseat me from the world in the precise seconds that most demand I be present, that I pay attention.

I am twenty-eight: sleet glazing a midnight two-lane highway, my car buffeted by passing semis. Its wipers are embedded in the frosted windshield. I push the pedal to the floor instead of turning on the hazard lights and pulling over. I pass each truck I see. I flick my headlights on, off. I am eight: hundreds of feet in the air, high above Red Wing. I lean so far over the edge of the cliff that I wobble and my stomach churns. I am every age I have ever been: *This motherfucker*, I say, *I'm going to punch him in the face.* I am twenty-one: heading into the brain surgery that will save my life. The chrome gurney arms are ice cold. The nurse who pushes me into surgery asks the same questions I've already been asked over and over again. I lie to her, say I've never done that, nope, that's never happened, because I want to make the surgery fail, because I want to die. I am thirty: heading east on an overnight train, staying up all night to talk to a neo-Nazi drug dealer. I am thirty-four: asking myself how fast this hinged knife will flick open. It's the sharpest knife I've ever held. As I slice a cucumber into thin pale-green moons, the blade passes through the two hand towels beneath and cuts a surgical line in the Formica.

IX

Excessive nail biting is called onychophagia. Almost half of all teenagers do it. Many adults stop before their thirtieth birthdays, but some studies have reported that about 20 percent continue. More boys do it than girls. Stress, anxiety, boredom. Before your lie detector test, before your date's knuckles rap the door, with nine hours to kill before your flight departs. As a child you might have watched your mother gnaw at the edges of her fingers. Everyone has their technique: I start at the side of the thumb, then, delicately gripping the barely severed thumbnail between my teeth, slowly pull away, shearing the rest of it off. I suck it into my mouth, spit the perfect sickle into my palm, pop it back into my mouth. Then, I guess, wherever I am, I spit it out.

Freud argued that parental conflict (weaning a child from breastfeeding) can cause one of two oral fixations: aggressive or receptive. The receptive person loves to feast and reduces tension orally, by biting nails, eating, or drinking. They are sensitive and passive and needy. The aggressive personality is volatile. They speak over everyone at the dinner table. They will call you a worthless piece of shit, an ass clown, scream, *You motherfucker!* in your face. Today fingernail biting is categorized as a body-focused repetitive disorder. Chewing the inside of your cheek. Picking scabs. Pulling out hair. Prodding pimples and blemishes until the skin pocks and scars. Today everyone is anxious and over-medicated, and we know Freud was a coke fiend.

X

If spit is disgusting, it is also magical. In folktales from around the world, an object that is spit upon—or even the spit itself—will speak. Spit on that doorknob and it says howdy. Spit on the floor and it tells you where you must go. If you don't spit when you see a white horse it's bad luck. It was once believed that a person experiencing a seizure was being visited by something

superhuman, and therefore their froth and spittle contained essences of that visitation. Holy men pass their
baraka, their blessing, through their saliva. During ini-
tiation into most dervish orders, a sheikh would spit on
your hands and forehead, and into your mouth. Good
faith can be shown by spitting on a person's hand. A
priest spits on the foreheads of the kneeling couple
he is marrying, and on a newborn's head to bless it.
The spit of the gods can purify. Power is imbued in the
divining stick of a Zulu holy man when he spits on it.
Spit on as much straw as you can find, then place it
around your home to protect it from robbers. In certain
South American tribes, sacred herbs are hung in the
doorframes of newborns' rooms; each visitor must chew
some and spit at the child. All over the world, stones
are stacked into monuments—beside trails or roads, in
forest clearings, at the tops of hills—that show the way
for any wandering spirits. Each time a rock is added to
the armature, you must spit on it.

XI

Our kitchen table is retro: a glittery pink rectangle with
three inches of slate border around its perimeter. I look at
it and say, "Sock hop," sing "Great Balls of Fire," want a
roller-skating waitress to bring me a milkshake, for Buddy
Holly's airplane to crash into my lawn. The table would
seat four, but one of its long sides is tucked against the
picture window that looks out at the backyard. Because
of the tall Chinese mulberry and pecan trees there, the
table remains shadow dappled long after the sun rises.

Three puffy pink chairs are pressed beneath it. Each day its Formica top is covered with new monsters.

Outside, last night's rainwater drips from the hammock. An enormous green garbage bin is toppled on its side, the tiny lakes in its wheels imitating birdbaths. I have been up since six, when, still buried in a blanket covered in black-and-white monster silhouettes, my son told me that cold water does not "die" a cell phone. "All you do," he mumbled from under the covers, "is put boiling water on it and it will work." I asked where he learned this. "Dada, I just knowed," he said. "Let's get up." Now he sits at the table drawing monsters while I make him breakfast and pack his lunch.

In the elm tree directly outside the window, two squirrels are rolling around and flinging themselves at each other. Because one of the animals occasionally looks as if it's mounting the other, I am pretty sure this behavior is weirdly violent foreplay, but my son howls with laughter and chops his arms in the air, says it's squirrel kung fu. Then it's back to the page in front of him, which he focuses on like a surgeon. I have to remind him to eat. Each time he finishes a drawing he asks, "Dada, what is a new monster I can draw?" I throw out ideas. "String cheese–armed kung fu squirrel monster," I say. Looking up, he gives me the stink eye, a disappointed look too mature for his four-year-old face. "Dada," he says, "no more crazy stuff, remember?" We had a long talk last night about the "too-crazy" monsters I've drawn. He shook his head and referred to a chain-armed fire mummy I don't remember drawing, ever. "Oh, I got one," he says. I glance up from cutting cucumbers and he's hunched over the table, his face inches away from the page and the markers that cover it. He talks under his breath and his face grimaces, tightens, and smiles as he works. I love these mornings, watching him invest everything in what he does, answering the thousand and one rapid-fire questions he asks each hour. He amazes me—he wants to understand and know everything—and I imagine his brain as an inferno, sparking beautifully, growing exponentially. I'd do anything for him. "Tell me about the eggs again, Dada," he says without looking up. "The monkeys and the eggs and the old man that laughed."

XII

No one really understands why people litter, what their deeper motivations are. Maybe it is about power. Maybe it is about rage. People who litter feel disenfranchised elsewhere. The girl who throws an empty bottle out the car window is saying, *Hey, world, look at me—I am here and I matter.* The guy who spits his fingernails onto the carpet feels invisible. Others believe people litter because they've been socialized and cultured to believe that someone else will pick up their trash. Some theorize two types of littering: active and passive.

XIII

Sunshine, and I am soaring off the bike jump, leaving my blurring first-grade world, but suddenly there's laughter and it yokes me back to the Minnesota day and I'm drenched. A basketball court away, I skid into an arc and look back. Beside the jump, standing on the steps that lead to the steel back door of my elementary school, are a gang of boys. All of them are a few years older than I. Bullies and assholes. They're howling with laughter, wiping their mouths, zipping up their pants. As I turn to ride home, one of them throats up phlegm, lets it fly, and stares as it *splacks* right against my face.

XIV

In Kathmandu's still-dark morning, I clatter through the locked gate surrounding the house to go for a run. I want to get to Swayambhunath early, before the streets are most clotted. All the tuk-tuks and cabs and bikes and *you want smoke you want smoke?* and singing and heaps of trash, garbage piles that always seem to be shifting, sliding, something alive beneath them, and Maoists protesting or blowing things up and beggars without legs or arms or hands and whipping flags and butchered chickens or hogs and skinny bodies pushing against me in crowds, hands feeling my pockets, and squat fires or barrel ovens and some kind of meat cooking, all the time, and I must buy a skewer, I really want to taste, I am constantly told, so delicious, I must try, for very little I can have it all. Each time I go for a run, I hope to feel the wildness and beauty of Kathmandu come into being in the quiet. Crossing a bridge I glance down. Ankle deep on the shore of a creek, an old man is taking a shit. I run along and into the fields on the fringe of town before returning the way I came. This time, below the bridge, a woman dips a bowl into the water and holds it to the mouth of the baby boy toddling beneath her.

XV

But the story I tell my son over breakfast begins hours after I see the woman and boy drinking river water from the exact spot where I'd just seen the old man taking his morning shit.

XVI

Swayambhunath means "sublime trees" in Tibetan. It's a World Heritage Site, revered by both Buddhists and Hindus. With my eyes closed I sit near the bottom of a waterfall of steps, trying not to hear all the chaos and wonder. At the top of the temple, the domed white stupa is crowned with a golden spire that can be seen from all over the Kathmandu Valley. Huge, sleepy-looking eyes look out from each side of the spire's squared base. A series of narrowing gold discs is topped, somehow, by an enormous golden ornament shaped like a street cone. Prayer flags run to the ground. I am sure the iconography all means something, but I feel clueless and overwhelmed. At the stupa I joined a clockwise-circling herd of people, walked among the monks and Nepalese and foreigners fingering prayer beads and turning mandalas. I lost track of time and then, suddenly, I was weeping. I didn't know what was happening. Tear-blind, ashamed, I stopped walking and was run into by a monk.

Now, on the stairs and exhausted by all of it, I am starving. I peel shell from a hard-boiled egg and zone out, staring into the trees. I'm here and not here and wandering in the always-whispering world. I barely register the monkeys clambering around the walk, the bench, until *ZOINKS*—coming up from behind me, a monkey plucks the egg from my hand and sprints away, cackling, before bounding up a wall and into the woods. The monkeys hoot madly around me. On the nearest bench, an ancient-looking Nepalese man smiles big at me and shakes his head. He is toothless. Grinning, he rocks with silent laughter, until soon all his pruning and furrows split with guffaws: *GAA-GAA-GAA-GAA-GAA-GAA*.

Egg. Monkey. Old man.

XVII

The other recurring monkey dream I have had also has variations, related to the sexual abuse I suffered as a little boy. I am a monkey, trapped behind a smeary sheen of glass on a stage that is lit so brightly I can hardly see beyond its wooden edge. But I have human genitals. A small boy's penis, sometimes, or the vagina of an adult woman. Sometimes both, Frankensteined together from different bodies. Out in the blinding light I hear orders: to turn around, to pull and touch myself, to press my body to the glass. I can hear laughter and threats; someone must be punished, someone is going to die. I notice circles cut in the glass. Hands and forearms start stretching through them, penises and sucking mouths and hairless pudenda, too. There are hands holding knives. Hands curled in fists. An invisible force pushes me closer and closer to their slavering and fondling.

XVIII

My walk home from work takes twenty minutes, one parking lot, a right, a left, mostly following the same long power line. A half block of student apartments that transitions into live oak–shaded family ramblers. A landscape of cast-off energy drink cans and condom wrappers and chewed-up chicken wings on the curb, changing to one of dark-skinned men pushing lawn mowers and meticulously trimming hedges. My pockets and shoulder bag fill with the busted treasures of my walk. Cicada husks. A caved-in robin's egg. Wasps. An empty money clip with "$$$" printed on it. Baby shoe. Dice. A bolt large enough to fit over my thumb. Buttons. A dead crawdad that smells like a burning outhouse when I reveal him to my son. When I come in he's at the kitchen table drawing a new batch of monsters. My wife, home early from work, sits with him and writes down the "episodes" of his imaginary TV shows. *Circus Monsters & Zombie Bites. Monster Island. Spookiest Creatures. The Giant Beetle Season 2. Egypt Tomb Dead. Big Top Swim. Swimming Pool Creature. Piranha-Faced Go. Curse of the Park Monster. Where's My Tree? Swim Bite. Yucky Tales. Owie Deep.* She says NPR was on this morning, that most of the coverage focused on an earthquake in Nepal. Each time the reporters said, "Kathmandu," Felix would look up from his monsters for a moment and say, "Dada's been there. Monkey stole his egg."

XIX

"I have never seen greater monster or miracle in the world than myself," Montaigne writes in "Of Cripples." At its core, his is an essay about human stupidity—about our refusal to fully understand the nuances of the world and, more specifically, about our failure to understand other people. Because we understand so wrongly, what we see as monsters are as likely miracles; we love to deceive ourselves and to be deceived, will support our not knowing with lies and believe the lies of others, because we'd rather seem right to someone than know the truth. Montaigne's lines are armatured with quotes: Cicero. Livy. Saint Augustine. Seneca. Quintus Curtius. Tacitus. The world's cruelties, he says, are caused by our failure to acknowledge our not knowing. "Whoever will be cured of ignorance," Montaigne says, "must confess it."

XX

I am not sure I will ever be able to confess enough to temper my monstrousness. But here is one confession. Every time the phone rings, I fear something has happened: to my wife or my children, my parents, my brothers, any or all of the people I love. Someone has had a stroke, the results have come back and it doesn't look good, they've had a terrible fall, or, somehow, magically, all these people were in the same place, on the same plane, train, ship—and it crashed, went off the rails, sank—there are no survivors. The helicopter circling over the university

where I teach means there's been another school shooting, that there's a lockdown, that there have been many
fatalities.

For years I have thought that I am the source of disaster, that the suffering of those around me is, or will one
day be, caused by their proximity to me, by the way I
greet them or say good-bye, by the soft way I hold their
hand or kiss their lips. I have lived through my own
dying—through sexual abuse and self-hatred and a brain
that tried to bleed me to death—while the people I loved
committed suicide, died of cancer and of multiple sclerosis, did not come back from war, and miscarried every
pregnancy. I believe the places I go will cave in or burst
into flames because my feet have stepped there. Before
flying to Kathmandu, my girlfriend and I spent part of
a week on beaches in the south of Thailand, eating ram-
butans and the sweet cheek meat of fish. On December
26—the exact day we were there, but three years later, in
2004—an enormous earthquake off the coast of Sumatra
caused dozens of tsunamis that killed 230,000 people.
Huge swallowing waves erased each of the villages I'd
spent days in and each person I'd waved at, as if, instead
of saying hello, I'd been wishing them Godspeed a few
years early. The first day I lived in California there was an
earthquake, and there was another the day we finished
packing everything up, just an hour before we moved to
Texas. Each year the hills I ran outside Thousand Oaks
turn to infernos that confetti the air with ash. Bridges
I've driven over in Minnesota have crumpled, crushing
drivers and their cars. I've clambered over the shore of a
river that later took a boy and the father who tried to save
him. Skyscrapers I've elevatored up have had airplanes

explode through them, folded into themselves and down, gusting city blocks with toxic dust. I've walked over lawns and through parking lots where shootings would later occur, where exploding bombs would tear limbs from bodies, places that would soon be crowded with ghosts.

XXI

Montaigne's essay "Of Thumbs" is a different kind of beast altogether. Often an essay of his will begin periphrastically, before, like a grinning python, it measuredly, assuredly, constricts, sentence by sentence, into a narrowing vise of argument and story. But "Of Thumbs" is just a few paragraphs long, a brief list. A barbarian king sealed his oaths by sucking the blood from pinpricked thumbs. "The Romans exempted from war all such as were maimed in the thumbs, as having no more sufficient strength to hold their weapons." Emperors thumb-signaled for the life or death of gladiators. Ancient war dodgers cut off their own thumbs, or the thumbs of their children, so they wouldn't have to fight.

XXII

"I found ancestors, like Shakespeare, who said, in *Macbeth*, that the world is full of sound and fury, a tale told by an idiot, *signifying nothing*. Macbeth is a victim of fate. So is Oedipus. But what happens to them is not absurd in the eyes of destiny, because destiny, or fate, has its own norms, its own morality, its own laws, which

cannot be flouted with impunity. Oedipus sleeps with his
Mummy, kills his Daddy, and breaks the laws of fate. He
must pay for it by suffering. It is tragic and absurd, but
at the same time it's reassuring and comforting, since the
idea is that if we don't break destiny's laws, we should be
all right. Not so with our characters. They have no meta-
physics, no order, no law. They are miserable and they
don't know why. They are puppets, undone. In short,
they represent modern man. Their situation is not tragic,
since it has no relation to a higher order. Instead, it's
ridiculous, laughable, and derisory." —Eugène Ionesco

XXIII

People have always created monsters, from Beowulf to
Bigfoot, for so many reasons. We create monsters because
they are what we want to be; they are what we are told
we should hate, but secretly we love and desire. To live
forever with a power nearly impossible to overcome, to
hunt and kill and be sexy and sexed up without ever having to pay for our proclivities. They represent the anxi-
eties of our time: zombies as a metaphor for AIDS, for
example. They are manifestations of the "other," and give
shape to behaviors we find unconscionable, sinister, and
abhorrent: murder, Satanism, sexual abuse and rape. But
in the horror, the grotesque, we also find the fantastic.
We love stories of the monstrous, tales that enlarge the
possible, because they can help us understand our fears,
help us cope with the day-to-day horrors of our lives and
the historical catastrophes whose shadows we live in.

XXIV

The hour before I left for the airport in Kathmandu, on January 26, the earth shook. The doorways of the home I was staying in rocked, the floor bucked, lightbulbs swayed from the ceiling. On the cab drive to the airport I saw a few toppled motorcycles, a handful of broken windows, and lots of groups standing around rickshaws. The traffic was terrible, everything on the ramshackle roads pressed tightly together because of the earthquake. At the airport I gave the driver all the rupees I had in my pocket, shouldered my bags, and ran in to catch my flight. The Himalayas seemed just outside the window of the Thai Airways jet as we took off. For a while we flew below them, then rose so they seemed touchable, right beside us. Before falling asleep I heard the people in the seat in front of me saying there'd been a massive earthquake in Gujarat, India.

It was impossible to sleep, so I stayed up all night in Bangkok. On the flight from Kathmandu my stomach started to twist and catapult and I rushed to the lavatory. I thought I was turning inside out each time I threw up.

I'd just spent a month traveling Asia with a woman I thought I was in love with. It had been the only thing in my life I was looking forward to, the only thing I felt good about. Less than two years earlier the vascular malformation had been removed from my brain stem, and each morning I still woke with a line of crusty pus on the back of my head. I inhabited my new body well enough to walk and read and cook rice. I could take care of myself, had returned to Macalester College for my senior year, but I was a black hole. No matter how many times doctors and family and friends told me that I was doing amazingly well, I didn't feel like myself.

My new body fit like the most perfect cage. I was up from the wheelchair, the walker, not using a cane. The instability and stagger in my gait felt almost gone when I jogged. My eyes had stopped working together, but the exercises I'd learned in physical therapy had nearly returned them to center. *Aching for Beauty: Footbinding in China* was in my backpack along with *Sanctuary: The Path to Consciousness*, and it didn't matter that I sometimes had to wear an eye patch—I was once again a voracious reader. I could drive and my father had gotten me a new car. I was off the charts, a land-speed record for healing. But it was grueling. If I didn't actively work at not thinking about it, I obsessed about how strange and awful it felt, about how I'd probably never feel like myself again and whether that was something I could live with. Self-destructive and self-medicating before the trip to Nepal, I had been doom eyed with depression, rolling through my bleary days like an unexploded bomb. And now I was going back to Minneapolis and I had nothing.

Hollow with sickness and terrified I'd miss my flight to Japan, I paced the terminals of Don Muang International (now Don Mueang) all night. I obsessively listened to any news I could find about the earthquake in India. A 6.9 on the Richter scale, and probably tens of thousands killed, but it was too soon to know for sure. The few images that were replayed on the TVs were horrible. A half circle of squatting men, digging at a skinny arm growing out of a rubble pile. A woman slapping herself in the face, yowling. A white-haired, shawled woman kissing the blood-masked face of a little girl.

After chewing all the packets of betel nut that I'd been saving for home, I bought a carton of Thai cigarettes. All night I smoked with women whose every other word I understood, who pressed their tiny hands to my inner thigh. The longest hours of the night I spent with a sinister-faced Mediterranean man in military fatigues who, urging me more and more forcefully to join him in a room at the airport hotel, became so frothed that I held his hands, told him "I will, of course, I will, but I need to run to the bathroom first." I sprinted to a bathroom as far away as I could find, locked myself in a stall, and squatted on the closed lid of the toilet, trying not to breathe, until my flight number was called.

XXV

Almost a year before my trip to Nepal, after deep breathing in the Oldsmobile for ten minutes—I feel good, ready for the job interview—a pair of sliding doors swish open and I stutter into the supermarket. But the fluorescent light axes me immediately. Shoppers swarm around me, stomping snow from their boots. Those leaving jostle me with their grocery bags. I am not using the cane or eye patch anymore and the new hair on the back of my head makes the scar hard to notice, but I go out only if I have to. I am not sure what the brain surgery did to me. I don't want to see anyone. I am not sure what I am anymore. Bright lights or loud sounds can stun me, spin my head with vertigo, and I list to my right when I walk. When I close my eyes, things get crazy; it feels like my fingertips are hundreds of feet away and I can't tell up from down. But I am here. I am going to get this job. Visoring my hand over my eyes, I squint through the bustle—bakery, produce, juice bar, aisles stacked with cans, a counter and wall of all-natural remedies and cosmetics—before I finally notice the meat-department sign. It is small and looks mean and plain, and its arrow points to the back of the store.

All the beautiful people work up front, with their perfect skin and white teeth and dreadlocks and nose rings and sleeves rolled up, showing off rippling muscles or a Sanskrit or bright-purple treble clef tattoo, and their shaved heads and buttons undone and everything both rugged and soft and always sexy. Crisp air cushions through the sliding doors each time someone comes or goes. Fresh muffins and loaves of Ten Grain Delight are taken out of the oven every hour. Mangoes and blueberries are buzzed to pulp, and pineapple perfumes the air. The Minnesota sunlight stripes in from the big windows, glinting off their jewelry and their gorgeous smiles. But if the front of the store is an Apple commercial, we in the meat department are an antismoking ad. It is always winter in the meat department. We wear pants and long-sleeved shirts, adding long underwear and turtlenecks sometimes, and, if we are working in the freezer, gloves and supermarket-logo hats that cover our product-less bad haircuts, our bald heads and bruises and rashes and cuts and scars. The long jackets we button up over our warm layers are white—bleached each day—but a minute into a shift they become blistered with pink and streaked with red. By the end of the workday we look like enormous slabs of raw bacon. The chin-high display case we work behind has three tiers of meat products you might want for tonight's dinner: chicken breasts, honey-basil turkey sausages, long trays of free-range ground beef, varying in fat content and slight gradations in pinkness. A digital scale and label printer squats on each end of the case. The closest walk-in freezer is lined with meat-filled shelves—every two days, boxes the size of a child's red wagon are delivered. A Plexiglas window separates the case and meat counter from the room where the cutting happens. It is filled with meat saws, steel-topped tables for carving, hoses and buckets and great steel basins for washing knives. It is always wet with boiling water. Its tile floor, along with the window, must be power-washed clean at the end of each day. The room is soundproofed. Customers might look through the Plexiglas and see a butcher singing into a mop handle, veins corded out of his neck, but not hear a thing. But if you're standing in the room, AC/DC rattles the blood in your ears. Off this room is a smaller walk-in freezer. Huge plastic bags of beef are turned inside out here, poured into the bathtub-size meat grinder on the concrete floor. There are a thousand ways to lose a finger in this place.

XXVI

By the time the plane lands in Minneapolis, the sleep deprivation and sickness make me wonder if I've hallucinated the flight from Kathmandu. The Cambodian man sitting across from me is younger than I thought—in his fifties, maybe—his body was just crumpled and hammered down. Behind his dark sunglasses, he has bleached-out eyes. And so many scars. Splotched slices down his arms. A cashew-shaped patch of white skin along his neck. A puckered starburst on his chin. The missing thumb, and two fingers, index and pinkie, gone from his other hand. Each time I came back from the lavatory, when I was sure he wasn't looking my way, I stared. The man assigned to the seat next to me never returned. Perhaps he, too, was afflicted and we missed each other in our rotating lavatory visits. Or maybe he never existed at all. Trying hard not to think about the thumb-less man, about how lonely I felt—I do not want the life I am returning to, I am not sure I want to keep going—I imagined all the ways people might have died in the earthquake. The flight seemed to take a week and I died and was reborn a dozen times. My belly is wrecked. At first I thought it was food poisoning, but I can feel the parasites somersaulting through my insides.

Waiting for my roommate at the airport, I read about the Gujarat earthquake. Hundreds of thousands devastated, whole cities destroyed. It will take weeks to unbury all the dead. When Brian honks and I run outside, it's frigid and gray and I'm a mess.

I ramble to him about not feeling well, about how I spent five hours in the airplane lavatory. Suddenly, just out of the Humphrey terminal roundabout and on the highway between Minneapolis and Saint Paul, the urge to defecate powers through me like a bulldozer. I hammer my fist on the dashboard and shriek obscenities. I sing as loudly as I can. Saint Paul's streets are lined with piles of dirty snow and I am going to shit myself. Brian whips the car into the parking lot of the first SuperAmerica we

reach. Before the Blazer comes to a full stop, I am sprinting from it, the door swinging open behind me. Fever
eyed, I burst into the gas station, sight the restroom sign,
and power walk toward it. Every muscle in my body is
bolted down. The clerk asks if she can help with anything—and there are so many things on the list of my
troubles that I want to tell her about—but there's so little
time—and I open my mouth to speak but all that comes
out is a hiss of spit as I speed past her.

MIGRANTS IN A FEVERLAND

From trapezius to calf, the husband's muscles are cramped. Baseball-size knots up and down his spine, hamstrings and calves like concrete. His back is unmovable. Everything hurts from sitting so long. He unshoulders his backpack onto a chair, then stumbles through the kitchen. In the living room he falls flat on the carpet and lies there like a dead man.

The drive from Gallup, New Mexico, to his in-laws' home in southern Colorado took almost ten hours. There were a series of speed traps west of Albuquerque, a turned-over semi that turned the freeway into a parking lot, and the hypnotizing desert haze of I40 followed by snow in the mountains on I25. Glowing swirls of falling snow mirror-balled the sky, blinding him. As he came down Ratón Pass his knuckles were bone white.

His wife squats beside him, wreathes his forehead in kisses, and stands. "Can I do anything for you? Water or soda? A burrito?" she asks kindly. Through his pinched eyelids, he can see her smiling. "There's leftover lasagna."

"No, no, no. Thank you," he groans. "I snacked the whole way, too much. Shitty me." Thanks to the Corn Nuts and beef jerky and cashews and dehydrated pineapple and can after can of Mountain Dew, his guts are twisting.

The husband is also dazed from focusing on the free-way while alert to all the strangeness blurring the road-side: a hitchhiking family, each adult holding a baby in their arms; a homeless man clambering out of a lean-to built in the brush; lava rock frozen in raised waves; dozens of tumbledown shrines at wreck sites; animals smeared unidentifiable across the road; other creatures, still alive, streaking past, never—he's sure—an innocent rabbit or deer or marmot. Each one a ghost.

He tried to read each message written on the roadside memorials, but the speeding car made shards of them: "It's Not the Same"; "RIP You Will Always"; "In Loving Mem"; "Forever in Our."

With Pueblo's old mining and smelting factories dotting the horizon, he leaned his head out the car window and held his hot, blinded eyes open to the wind, his cheeks sopping with weeping. He was sure to smile at the drivers of the smudgy cars he sped past, and only now does he realize how insane he must have looked. He presses his palms into his eye sockets and listens to his wife pad away. Moaning, half-laughing, he stretches his arms and legs out.

He grins up at his wife when she returns. "I feel like one of those pig ears that dogs chew on."

"That's nasty," she says. "Try not to touch them. Just blink." She sets a ramekin of almonds on his chest. "That's the best way to make them feel better." He pretends not to hear her and rubs his eyes fiercely.

The carpet still smells like his in-laws' two dogs, a little white one named Andy and an even smaller black one named Jack, both dead now. Neither of them liked the husband. They'd yip at him whenever he entered a room. He liked to take a lunging step at them to see them scamper backward.

Years before, on his first visit to meet her parents, Andy pissed in front of his bedroom door every single day. One morning he accidently left the door open, and the dogs sneaked in and urinated all over his clothes and bags. The gifts he'd brought for her parents were soaked through. There was an actual puddle on one bag. He seriously considered pissing long and hard in the dogs' own cozy little beds. He stared at the ceiling for hours at night, letting the rage drain out, remembering that he was a guest in this home, realizing that he was thinking like a psychopath.

His mother-in-law walks into the living room and stops short. Worriedly, she asks if something happened on the drive. "Is everything OK?" The husband doesn't answer. He just closes his eyes and breathes deeply. His wife says that the roads were bad, and his mother-in-law hurries away.

Outside the wind is picking up, gusting down from the mountain range. Because he's terrible about calling, he asks his wife what she's been up to these past few days. She tells him about having lunch with a childhood friend and her daughter. He vines a hand around her ankle, waiting until she's finished talking about how great it was to see Lisa and Erin before saying gloomily, "I got eaten up by fire ants." He doesn't mean to crush her good mood, but she steps back from his grip. "Finished a run, sat in the dirt to stretch, and realized I was smashing down an anthill when my legs and ass erupted into a thousand tiny stabs." He slips his shoes off. "Look at those fuckers. Ugly, right?" His feet are red and puffy.

He can't stop himself from scratching them even though they burn and start to bleed.

"Oh, baby," his wife says. "Stop. Stop. Stop. Let's put something on them."

His mother-in-law comes back into the room with a platter of steaming food. She sees his feet, says, "Oh my," and starts telling a story about one of her friends from Puerto Rico who had to have his foot amputated. "When the doctors were removing the foot, they found enormous mold balls in his lungs," she says gravely. "Cancer, too, I think."

"Mom!" his wife says loudly. She stares. "Not now, OK? Do we have anything to put on his feet?"

"Oh," his mother-in-law says, taken aback. "I'm sorry." She tells the husband that she cooked a steak for him, arranging the mounded plate and napkin and silverware on the coffee table. His wife is a vegetarian, so when they visit Pueblo he's always fed huge amounts of meat. As his wife and mother-in-law leave the room, he says that he'll be up in a minute, that he'll come sit in the kitchen and eat at the table.

Floating on the carpet, the room silent except for the soft-hammering wind, he thinks about the gas station in Albuquerque. The husband was inside the store, paying, when he saw a man and woman sprint to his Subaru and try to yank the doors open, slamming their elbows against the windows. He left his wallet on the counter and ran outside. The man and woman speed-walked away from the car, and the husband shouted after them, "Where the fuck are you going?!"

The woman quickly crossed the street—but the man stopped. He turned slowly; stared hard, and pulled a forearm-long knife from the hip of his track pants. His face was caved in and too white for Albuquerque's blistering sun, like he'd been living underground. He didn't smile, didn't blink his huge eyes, just raised the knife so no one but the husband could see the tip of it reaching almost to his Adam's apple.

The husband froze. He had always had a taste for blood, but he wasn't as stupid as he once had been. He bit his tongue and choked down whatever he'd been about to say. The man glared for a few long seconds, then tucked the knife away and jogged after the woman across the street. As the husband watched, the two walked slowly down the block, side by side, swinging their joined hands. They didn't look back. Then they turned onto a side street and vanished from sight.

His last stop before Pueblo was a rest area near Las Vegas, New Mexico, for an emergency bathroom break. It was turning cold. The setting sun looked like it was being gnawed apart by the Sangre de Cristos.

Only one other car was parked in the rest area, a chromed-out white pickup with monster-truck tires. The husband parked on the far side of the lot, to force himself to walk. Slipping into a hoodie, he felt a pang of longing.

When he was away from his wife, he lived an imagined life, where his actual life receded into the shadows. He couldn't make himself call home. He might, on a rare occasion, send an e-mail or a text, but even then only a few words, his arrival time or flight number. But he was so close now. Pueblo was on the other side of the mountains, a hundred miles away, and his wife was waiting for him in a house that looked out over the Arkansas River, where one could watch Pikes Peak gleam in each sunset. So close he couldn't ignore how much missed her.

Hoping to uncoil his body, he walked draggingly slow. But his legs locked when he passed the pickup. In the truck bed a twentysomething man with a boulder-like belly sat cross-legged. His shaved head shone above a long beard, and black wraparound sunglasses hid his eyes. Neatly arranged on a quilt beside him sat an end times armory of rifles and handguns. Quickly the husband looked away, but a second later he was staring again, at a sawed-off shotgun being methodically polished by the man. He sputtered out a hello, nodded, benign and polite and harmless. The man ignored him and kept working a bandanna around the barrel.

His bladder was about to burst so he hurried to the bathroom, trying to not to look as if he was fleeing. Inside, the air was dense with the reek of urinal cakes. After splashing water on his face and rubbing his burning eyes, he looked at himself in the mirror: his sunburn, the bags beneath his eyes. He suddenly remembered the way his college roommate used to clean his white Nikes each day with a toothbrush. The man in the truck wore the same loving focus on his face while he worked.

Next to the humming pop machines inside the building, he waited for another car to exit the freeway, but no cars passed. The afternoon sun was falling and everything outside the finger-smeared window glowed a deepening orange. The dropping temperature made his bones feel fragile.

When he finally passed the pickup on his way to the Subaru, the husband wished the man a good day. He was syrupy with fear, but wouldn't let it stop him from that small kindness. Before merging back onto the north-bound freeway, he had to pass the truck again. The man was standing upright in the bed. The gun was like a rod of sunlight tucked into his armpit as he waved and gave the husband a thumbs-up.

He doesn't tell his wife or mother-in-law about the fucked-up things that happened on his trip. He thinks it's because he doesn't want to burden them with fear and worry, but in truth, a part of him wants to keep all the pumping blood and oddness for himself. When his wife returns to the living room, he's still pinwheeled on the floor and the food is still on the table.

As he stretches he tells his wife about the changing colors of the mountains as the sun arced across the sky. Sunrise in the desert. Snow in the hills. How the snow-caps of the Sangre de Cristos looked like porcelain.

While he talks, his mother-in-law returns with a package, a gift from his wife's aunt. He watches his wife delicately unpack fine dinnerware from the box, Portmeirion bowls and assorted plates to add to the cabinet full they already have. He shakes his head and sighs and laughs harshly as the bowls and plates stack up.

"Oh man, I guess I'll have to take all this to the Goodwill when we get home," he says, half-jokingly. His wife shakes her head. His mother-in-law looks shocked, like he said he was going to take a shit on the floor.

"Oh, you can't," she pleads. "These are so beautiful." The large salad bowl in her hands is laced with roses and lilies and a kaleidoscope of butterflies. "These are very expensive, too. You really can't give them away."

His wife shoots him a look that tells him to shut it, but he can't help himself.

"I don't know," he says, pretending to be resigned to taking it all to the thrift shop. "We have so much already. Way more than we need." His wife slaps at his hand, but he dodges her. "I'm sure the Goodwill would . . ."

His wife puts up with his complaints about owning nice stuff, the disdain of someone who grew up poor. She listens when he says that instead of buying single-serving cups of flavored yogurt, they should buy big vats of plain yogurt and stir in strawberry jam. And she doesn't say anything about the junk he hoards. Like the tall glass bottles lining the windows of his office, each one stuffed with chewed bubble gum or rusty nails or the gray and white fur brushed from Catface.

One side of their garage is stacked with cardboard. Moldy magazines. Glass. Twine and rope. Canisters of yet more chewed gum. Construction-grade staples. Screens ripped from windows, and window frames without screens. Mesh. Rubber gloves. Boxes of the wood scrap, old gutter metal, wire, and wrenched coat hangers he twists around glass bottles filled with colored water—orange, blue, green, red. He stretches and bends more wire, builds steeples above the bottles, adds another object: a railroad spike, an empty hot sauce bottle. He arranges these wobbly-crowned "sculptures" in corners of the yard and along the fence.

For years an enormous five-gallon lemonade dispenser sat on their back porch. It was half-filled with yellow water and a life-size plastic brain bobbed in it whenever anyone stepped on the deck.

His wife puts up with a lot, but they both know that he's just being an asshole to his mother-in-law now. She slaps at him again, and holds on to his hand this time, until he flushes and feels guilty. His mother-in-law looks forlorn and confused.

"I'm just kidding," he says softly, apologetically, and forces himself to look up at her, to smile genuinely and show her he's being honest. He turns his wife's hand in his so he can rub his thumb over her palm with love. "I wouldn't do anything like that. I won't. Promise. I was joking."

His mother-in-law says, "OK," as if she doesn't know whether to believe him or not, and the three of them carry the forgotten food to the kitchen and sit at the table. The trees in the backyard shake in the wind and rain begins pelting the windows. A questioning look passes between his mother-in-law and his wife.

The husband watches them. "I'm so happy to be here," he says. "I've missed you guys." He spoons up some of the food, but before taking a bite, thanks his mother-in-law again. He wishes he could erase the sad look from her face. "This is delicious," he says with a full mouth. "Super good."

"Oh, thank you." She smiles. "Thank you."

"Really," he says, and he means it. He takes up one bite, and another, and another. "It's so so good."

BECOMING ANIMAL: A HISTORY

Note: Italicized sections are excerpts from Aristotle's *History of Animals*.

Of the parts of animals some are simple: to wit I am sun-damaged skin rotting on deepening layers of flesh and ligaments, organs and bones. *Cutis* is Latin for "skin," which, for the most animal animal, the human, consists, from outside in, of the epidermis, the dermis, and the hypodermis. Because of skin I am a water balloon, an oven mitt, a furred-hide rug; I am *come closer*, I am *too hot*, I am *get the fuck away*.

All those parts that do not subdivide into parts uniform with themselves are composed of parts that do so subdivide, for instance, hand is composed of flesh, sinews, and bones

These ribs will never again fit right. But I can't hear the voice that articulates what, deep inside, I already know. I can't stop myself from trying. I work until my legs give out beneath me and then I work harder, until my heart bleeds all over.

For many animals have identical organs that differ in position; for instance, some have teats in the breast, others close to the thighs

The souvenir baseball bat cracks the snapping Doberman's head. No yelp, no last heave; it slumps at my feet, head lowered into the dirt as if it is begging. I feel my son turn away behind me. Another dog backs up, growling, and prances a tight circle in front of me. It maintains eye contact. "Can we go to school now?" my son asks. I glance over my shoulder at him. His face is a blank, fleshy canvas. "Can we just go?" We are still a block away from his school and the other dog doesn't look like it cares about the pool of blood growing at my feet. My son peeks out from behind me. Even without a face I know who he is. The sleek-ribbed Doberman dances harder around us, a knife-footed ballet.

The soft and moist are such either absolutely or so long as they are in their natural conditions, as, for instance, blood, serum, lard, suet, marrow, sperm, gall, milk in such as have it, flesh and the like; and also, in a different way, the superfluities, as phlegm and the excretions of the belly and the bladder

A full-grown electric eel—six and a half feet long, over forty pounds—can generate a six-hundred-volt shock. It must rise to the water's surface every ten minutes for a breath of air before it returns to the muddy bottoms of the rivers and lakes it lives in. A male eel will use its spit to make a nest for the female eel to lay eggs in. An eel can produce intermittent shocks for over an hour without tiring. *Electrophorus electricus* is an electric fish. In truth, an eel is not an eel.

The dry and solid are such as sinew, skin, vein, hair, bone, gristle, nail, horn (a term which as applied to the

*part involves an ambiguity, since the whole also by virtue
of its form is designated horn), and such parts as present
an analogy to these*

All I have is imperfection. My bleeding. I know this. Each
day it gets harder and harder to face the reality of myself.
To be real about what I am. I know this, too. But I can't
keep myself from wanting more, to be better, to be whole.

*Animals differ from one another in their modes of subsis-
tence, in their actions, in their habits, and in their parts*

My eyes do not work together. Individually they focus
and spin; separately their pupils dilate and shrink. With
one eye I can almost see in the blackest night. With the
other I can never adjust to the darkness of a room. I have
to close one eye to focus on a placard or read a page of
a book. I see two of you and you are vibrating. Always.

*Many of these creatures are furnished with feet, as the
otter, the beaver, and the crocodile; some are furnished
with wings, as the diver and the grebe; some are destitute
of feet, as the water-snake*

The neurologist thinks I have multiple sclerosis. He says
"might," that I "might have MS," but I can see it in the way
his face stiffens each time I answer a question. "We also
need to rule out regrowth," he says. "What?" I gawp. "If
it wasn't totally resected," he says, "it is possible." I don't
remember anyone's ever telling me this was a possibility
before.

As it is, I have good days and bad days. It's always

hard to see, and the sadness is ever present. But lately—
in my last months in Minneapolis and in almost all the
time I have lived in southern California—the numbness
in my face and down my limbs seems worse. The muscles
and bones from my back into my butt and legs smolder.
My hamstrings lock up when I walk and my thighs go
tight when I sit. They are impossible to loosen no matter
how long I stretch or what stretches I do. I am taking
so many pills I can't keep them straight. In our backyard we have tomatoes and slugs and a monstrous aloe
plant. Mornings, when it's too painful to go walking, I
crawl into the thick grass. Until the sun droops and sets
fire to the hills on the way to Camarillo and Ventura,
I watch the golden rat that lives in the aloe as it scurries through the plant's spiny alcoves. The neurologist
wants tests done, including an MRI, and he scribbles a
prescription for another muscle relaxer before walking
out of the room. Each day I hate California more.

*And of creatures that live in the water some live in the sea,
some in rivers, some in lakes, and some in marshes, as the
frog and the newt*

When the first throb races through the electrodes, I forget
all about the MRI I am supposed to get this afternoon.
In fact I forget everything. My shoulders spasm, and the
neurologist tells me to relax, that each muscle needs a
number of pulses, that it'll be over soon. Beside me a
machine graphs nerve conductivity. I think Richter scale,
that my body is crumbling to the bottom of the ocean.
But this is what I have to do. This is the only way to get
better. For the next forty minutes the neurologist makes a

map of the broken land of my body, shuffling electrodes: one electric tentacle on the nerve, others sprawling over the muscle. A to B. C to D. E to F. The machine scribbles. My body jerks.

And by "insects" I mean such creatures as have nicks or notches on their bodies, either on their bellies or on both backs and bellies

That night I am rabid, thinking about the neurologist's words. *It is possible.* I took the films from the MRI home, ready for my neurology appointment tomorrow, but having them so close to me—knowing that the answer to my anxiety is somewhere inside them—makes my insides feel flea bitten. At dinner I tap my bowl with a fork until my fiancée, as gently as possible, tells me to knock it off. After we finish the dishes there's a message on my phone from the imaging clinic. The man says to call him right back. I try to smile when I tell my fiancée who it was, but she still has to hold me close while I weep. "It's all happening again," I tell her between sobs. My breath catches in my throat. With shaky fingers I dial the number. He isn't available. The MRI must have shown something cataclysmic, something that could not wait, something that was life or death: that my brain is bleeding again. I am going to throw up. I am about to be dead, I think, and then the phone rings.

And of land animals many, as has been said, derive their subsistence from the water; but of creatures that live in and inhale water not a single one derives its subsistence from dry land

Ten minutes after the call, the man's knocking on my
front door. He's come to deliver two MRI films that were
somehow omitted from the folder I was given earlier. He
apologizes profusely, says, "Have a good night," but the
mix-up doesn't turn into something to laugh at, a crazy
accident that fucked with my mind for a little bit. Nearly
gasping, I hold each film up to the dining room light,
staring intently into the plastic as if trying harder will
help me understand what I am looking at, to magically
see in it a better version of myself.

Some animals at first live in water, and by and by change
their shape and live out of water, as is the case with river
worms, for out of these the gadfly develops

My daughter does not have a face when she looks up at
me. "It's OK," I tell her, "we're almost there." I squeeze her
hand. She nods. Ahead of us the snowdrifts seem to go on
forever. The day is dreary and gray shawled. We should
have frozen to death long ago. My little girl's sleeveless
dress is tattered. My T-shirt has long tears across its midsection. But I am warm, almost too hot. I have no idea
where we are. My daughter is gripping the even smaller
hand of a cloth doll in her other hand, but its arm is floppy
and it hangs to the ground, dragging through the iced-
over mud. I have no idea where we are going. We walk
on without talking. Her doll bloats with moisture. I try to
breathe slow and steady, step after step, but each time my
foot lands I'm afraid of collapsing. She starts to hum. The
snow is so incredibly bright. As in the other dream, with
the faceless son—two encounters with children I do not
yet have—I am nearly crippled by panic blossoming up.

*In the water are many creatures that live in close adhesion
to an external object, as is the case with several kinds of
oyster*

I watch Los Angeles dissolve. Union Station and the city's
concrete sprawl flatten into the desert and then it is night
and the overnight train to New Mexico quiets. Sporadic
lights flare and wheel outside, but mostly there's nothing, and so I stare at my ghostly reflection. Past midnight my seatmate, a hulking Latino teenager, asks if I
want to smoke up and I laugh, tell him that I am too old,
that those days are long gone. He calls me a veteran and
walks down the aisle to the lavatory. He is taking trains
all the way to Virginia to live with a cousin because his
preacher father kicked him out of the house. He's sixteen,
a sweet kid. He says he's going to miss his mom and sister. A minute later the entire train car smells like pot. I
listen to the soft snores and muted movies being watched
around me. When he plops beside me again, floss eyed,
he says I am missing out. Moments later a train conduc-
tor rushes past, huffing.

Before the kid falls asleep, I slip out of my seat and
walk to an observation car. I won't sleep all night; I hav-
en't slept a full night in months. I shuffle like there's a
teeming load of shit in my shorts. Not too long ago this
body felt as homelike as it had in years, but now there
are so many doctor's visits and new meds piling up that
I feel like I am floating above the wreckage of myself.
A man with a cowboy hat pulled down over his face is
stretched out on a ragged couch. On a lounge seat a couple mutter wetly and press their faces together. Sitting on
another couch, I stare up through the glass ceiling at the

sky. A few hours after sunrise, I'll step off the train into a landscape wholly different from the bustling glass-and-concrete one I left. I'll spend the next week wandering through red-rocked canyons and cliffs and piñon-furred hills. I will be able to breathe, deeply. Every few months I've been coming to the desert. I have to. Tonight I left a rabid America, ridiculously sprinting after its own loveliness. Anything but perfection is deemed inadequate there. My brokenness, my maladies, make me feel radioactive. When eyes pass through me as if my hurt is invisible, hot blood pounds in my face.

"Hey," a guy standing above me says. I don't know how long he's been there or how long I've been sitting on the couch. His upper lip and eyebrows are pierced. A cobweb tattoo grows from his elbow up into his shirtsleeve. He folds his backward ball cap off and rubs his shaved head. "Mind if I sit?" he asks, pointing his cap at the open space next to me. His words are unexpectedly soft. Past the sharp edges of his face I see that he's just another kid. I want to drift into nothingness for the rest of the night, but after I welcome him to sit, he hems and haws and yawns. He taps his feet and talks to himself while scrolling on his phone. When I look out the glass, I see him glancing around twitchingly.

He is fucked up—I am sure of it—but the more he thumbs his phone and whispers and groans and peeks over, the more I feel his nervousness and fear. That he just wants to talk to someone. "What's up, man?" I ask, turning to him. "Where you going?"

"Oh man," he laughs, half-crazed. "Who knows?" But he does. He's from a desert town north of LA, but he had to move away. Some people he knows hurt someone and he got blamed for it and he can't be around anymore. He pulls down his collar and a Woody Woodpecker tattoo peeks out. He's one of the Peckerwoods, he says, which I learn is a gang of white supremacists. Already, he says, he misses home. And so he shows me pictures. A family photo. An elevated pickup. Him shooting a big gun I've seen only in war movies, with a number of close-ups. He glows. Then a gorgeous Latina. "That's my girl," he says. "Beautiful, right?" I nod. After he shows me a dozen more photos of her I ask, finally, if that, if she, isn't against the rules for him or something. He keeps flicking through pictures. "Well, it's not really like that," he says. "We're gonna get married." And then it's more photos of the machine gun. Then bullet-riddled signs, a half-exploded mannequin. The phone vibrates and switches to a portrait of the girl. "Gotta take this," he says, "see you," and then he leaps up, answering as he walks out of the car.

And, by the way, the sponge appears to be endowed with a certain sensibility: as a proof of which it is alleged that the difficulty in detaching it from its moorings is increased if the movement to detach it be not covertly applied

The neurologist I visit after we move to Texas rules out multiple sclerosis and a handful of other diseases, but she can't pinpoint the source of my constant pain. Fibromyalgia or chronic fatigue syndrome, she says, or maybe Lyme disease. But these diagnoses seem amorphous and unhelpful. I don't believe anyone. I am prescribed more pharmaceuticals. On the new MRI images I am shown an abnormal spot, which could be a regrowth or just scar tissue. Without actually going in, without surgery, there is no definitive way to tell.

Other creatures adhere at one time to an object and detach themselves from it at other times, as is the case with a species of the so-called sea-nettle; for some of these creatures seek their food in the night-time loose and unattached

I am my un-daughter's doll, overflowing with pills, stuffing more pebbles in my mouth. I am bloated with mud and sickness.

Some can swim, as, for instance, fishes, molluscs, and crustaceans, such as the crawfish. But some of these last move by walking, as the crab, for it is the nature of the creature, though it lives in water, to move by walking

There are so many pill bottles. From CVS and Walgreens and delivered in the mail. Orange with white lids. White with pink lids. Foil packs, gels, a nasal spray. Pills to gulp with food, pills on which I should not drive or operate heavy machinery.

Of land animals some are furnished with wings, such as birds and bees, and these are so furnished in different ways one from another; others are furnished with feet

The blaring TV wakes my wife. In the living room she sees the screen and a sockless foot hanging over the back of the sofa. She tries to wake me but I am totally out of it. A baby, or a drunk, or a drunk baby. There's an empty jar of Nutella in my lap. A slice of bread falls to the carpet when she shakes me awake. She tells me I have to come to bed. I stand and stagger, ask if she liked the movie. I tell her that I have to go to the bathroom. A few minutes later she finds me sitting on the toilet, trying to put her contact lenses into my eyes. In the morning she asks what I remember about the night. Nothing, I say. She tells me I have to stop taking sleeping pills.

Of the animals that are furnished with feet some walk, some creep, and some wriggle

I never thought I would or could become a parent. Most of the time this seemed like a good thing. I didn't think I would live through my brain surgery, and a large part of me didn't want to. After I woke up I could hardly take care of myself, so it seemed inconceivable that I would ever be able to take care of someone else. And what would I pass on, medically, emotionally, to my offspring? Sexual violence and medical hardship and chronic pain and depression: that these horrors could happen to my own child froze me. No way. Never.

But then, a decade into the twenty-first century, my son was born.

But no creature is able only to move by flying, as the fish is able only to swim, for the animals with leathern wings can walk; the bat has feet and the seal has imperfect feet

In addition to my gorilla mask, I now own cardinal and owl masks. Each stares with bulbous black eyes. Each is terrifying. On Halloween, when my wife answers the doorbell, I walk slowly into the room behind her. From my owl mask I silently watch as she doles out candy to Spider-Man and Batman and Queen Elsa.

Furthermore, the following differences are manifest in their modes of living and in their actions

After cracking the door to the baby's room open, I lean into the green-tinged dark. Felix is ten months old, and it's two in the morning. Minutes before, I startled out of sleep. Wide awake, I lay beside my wife and over the monitor listened to Felix's horse-clopping snores. The more I tried to fall back asleep, the more my head felt as if it were on fire, and when the snores stopped, a hot wire shot up my chest. And so, as I do almost every night these days, I slunk out of the bed's warmth and tiptoed to Felix's room. The plastic turtle on the floor projects dozens of stars and planets onto the walls and ceiling. I walk through the hazy galaxy and stand beside the crib. Since I can't see anything, I lean over the railing, levering my face down until his scrunched face sharpens. I inch nearer, close enough to kiss him, close enough to feel his warm breath on my face, close enough to assure myself that everything here is indeed real.

Some are gregarious, some are solitary, whether they be furnished with feet or wings or be fitted for a life in the water; and some partake of both characters, the solitary and the gregarious

What do I consist of? I was born with 270 bones, and now have 206. Busted and bruised and sheared. Nearly seven hundred skeletal muscles, not including my cardiac muscles or organs. Around nine pounds of skin, and a hundred thousand miles of blood vessels. I hold within me the potential for hundreds of gallons of tears. Yet I have so little courage. I am bluster and blubber, confused and unsure. I am sick. I am tired and weak. I am scared. At the very top of my closet there is a shoebox. The Adidas that came in it are long gone, dropped off at the Goodwill in a white garbage bag filled with khaki pants and T-shirts. Inside the box now are hundreds of pills. All prescriptions I've stashed from early Rx refills and multiple doctors prescribing me the same painkillers. The box is full. Enough there to help me do whatever I might want with myself.

Gregarious creatures are, among birds, such as the pigeon, the crane, and the swan; and, by the way, no bird furnished with crooked talons is gregarious

Bird-watchers in Brazil observed a harpy eagle flying away from a dead black-bearded saki monkey. The monkey had two sets of puncture wounds, left by the bird's claws: one across the head and neck, the other on the lower body. When it returns to a dead monkey, a harpy eagle will pluck its kill's hair, making a pile of it next to the carcass. You may scare the bird off again, but the next time you pass by, the body will be gone.

Such social creatures are man, the bee, the wasp, the ant, and the crane

The acupuncturist taps needles into me and connects each to a power source. He slowly modulates the electricity, asks if I can feel it, turns it up, asks if it is too much, turns it down, before moving on. When he delicately closes the door behind him, needles are bobbing in my skin like metronomes and I feel as if I am watching the tick-tocking flesh of a stranger.

And again, both of gregarious and of solitary animals, some are attached to a fixed home and others are erratic or nomad

A cheap plastic Olympic medal hangs from a red-white-and-blue ribbon wrapped around a curtain rod on the other side of the room. If I lock my eyes on its glint, I can stay upright, balancing on just my right leg, for *one one thousand, two one thousand, three one thousand.* Then *boom*, the room tilts, the bookshelves spin, the floor rushes up, and I have to plant both my feet. Over my resting breaths I hear Felix maniacally pedaling his tiny bike through the kitchen. He whips around the corner of the living room in a sliding skid—he's buck naked and red cheeked—and starts pistoning his bare legs, steering the Rocket right at me before jarring to a stop. I swing his sweaty body into the air and he laughs and tells me to stop. As soon as I perch him back on the bike he's off. My gentle swat at his butt hardly touches him.

I try the other leg and don't feel the earth swoop out from under me for six seconds, then eight. For over twelve years I have been doing this exercise, practicing with wobble boards and TheraBands and plyometric balls. I go back to the right leg. Two seconds. Again, two seconds. Again, two seconds, and then I have to drop my foot. From somewhere in the house my wife hollers, asks what that noise was and if I am OK. "Totally cool," I shout, but it's not. My life is full, teeming with everything anyone could want, but in moments like this, hearing Felix rumbling around the house and my wife saying he should think about slowing down, I am utterly, hopelessly alone.

Also, some are carnivorous, some graminivorous, some omnivorous: whilst some feed on a peculiar diet, as for instance the bees and the spiders, for the bee lives on honey and certain other sweets, and the spider lives by catching flies; and some creatures live on fish

The immortal jellyfish begins its life as a planula. This larva of *Turritopsis dohrnii* attaches to the sea bottom and sprouts a mob of polyps. Over the next few days, each polyp produces an eight-tentacled medusa, and each medusa buds off on its own, floating the oceans, maturing into an adult jellyfish that feeds on other jellyfish. Under stress—environmental or social, or even just old age and illness—the immortal jellyfish can reverse the biotic cycle, decaying its bell and tentacle cells, and— *alakazam!*—turning back into a polyp. It becomes again what it once was and lives forever.

Again, some creatures catch their food, others treasure it up

Slowly, as if they're the tiniest, impossible bones of people I love, I slip the molted exoskeletons of two cicadas out of my pocket. The brittle shells drop to the bottom of an empty pickled-okra jar with a dull *plonk*. Cicadas are cryptic. At night male cicadas flex the tymbals—

ribbed membranes, with the lined look of radiators or
the mouths of humpback whales—on each side of their
abdomen to sing to females. A click sounds every time
the tymbal tightens inward, and again when it relaxes.
It is amplified by echo chambers in the cicada's trachea.
I shake the skins back out into my palm like dice. I am
wonderstruck by how alive they feel.

*Some creatures provide themselves with a dwelling, others
go without one*

My headlamp illuminates specks in the morning dark.
They zoom past like krill in submersible footage. The
sound of my shoes on the dirt path is a ratchet and shake.
I push harder, heaving, but I cannot catch myself.

*Further, in respect to locality of dwelling place, some crea-
tures dwell under ground, as the lizard and the snake; others
live on the surface of the ground, as the horse and the dog*

Loa loa, a parasitic river worm that causes fugitive swelling,
is found in rivers in India and Africa. A person is infected
with *Loa loa* filariasis when they are bitten by a vector
deerfly, and larvae crawl into the broken flesh. The larvae
mature in a person's lowermost layer of skin. Sometimes
an adult eye worm will move from the subcutaneous to the
subconjunctival tissue, where it can easily be seen working
its way across your sclera, the white part of your eyeball.
Loa loa can cause itchy red Calabar swellings.

*Some are nocturnal, as the owl and the bat; others live in
the daylight*

"We are marine iguanas today, Dada," Felix says from beneath the blanket. "We must dive deep to get our food." I peek my head under and ask him what we are eating. When he wakes in the morning, he yells "Mama! Dada! Mama! Dada!" until one of us comes to his room. Lying on my back in the living room at five a.m. today, I heard him, and hurried in so he wouldn't wake my wife. The air is hot under the blanket and he whispers that we eat gold and dinosaur bones.

Moreover, some creatures are tame and some are wild: some are at all times tame, as man and the mule; others are at all times savage, as the leopard and the wolf; and some creatures can be rapidly tamed, as the elephant

The Norway rats use the pecan tree to get into the house, dropping to the roof shingles and scurrying about until they find a way in. The reinforced traps set in the garage look like open jaws and are called T-Rex traps. They snap down with such force that when one goes off in the middle of the night I am shocked awake, certain, until I hear another one go off, that someone is trying to break in.

For, whenever a race of animals is found domesticated, the same is always to be found in a wild condition; as we find to be the case with horses, kine, swine, (men), sheep, goats, and dogs

Lying in bed with my eyes closed, I feel as if I'm falling off the world. The vertigo has gotten worse. In the dark my sense of self is skewed. A hand feels sprouted directly from my shoulder. My feet are miles away. I have to open my eyes and see my stretched-out limbs to really know anything—hands: one right there on my chest, the other atop my wife's hip, slowly opening and closing, like an octopus undulating away.

Furthermore, some are combative under offence; others are provident for defence

We live in "Panther City," a nickname taken from an apocryphal story in which a late nineteenth-century visitor reported it was so quiet that he saw a panther asleep on Main Street.

Further, some are crafty and mischievous, as the fox; some are spirited and affectionate and fawning, as the dog; others are easy-tempered and easily domesticated, as the elephant; others are cautious and watchful, as the goose; others are jealous and self-conceited, as the peacock

At thirteen inches long, quetzals are fairly large birds. *Quetzal* comes from the Nahuatl, an Aztec language that has been spoken since at least the seventh century. Numerous words have been passed down from Aztec through Spanish into English—*avocado, chili, tomato.* One study found the male quetzal delivered almost all food to the nest, alternating meals of tree frogs and fruit. There are six species of quetzal: crested, eared, golden-headed, pavonine, resplendent, and white-tipped.

One sense, and one alone, is common to all animals—the sense of touch

"I am a roadrunner," Felix shouts, sprinting across the stretch of grass where we play soccer with the neighbor boys and their father. One of his shin guards has flopped loose, and he runs gangly, trying to keep the ball in front of him as he zigzags toward the open goal. It's the Bigs versus the Littles (dads versus kids, who are six, four, and three) and the Bigs are doing their best not to win by too much. But I sprint to get between Felix and the goal, yelling, "Here comes the freight train" as I come up behind him. As I pass, we collide and his small body sprawls forward. "Why did you knock me down?" he wails from the dirt, his face streaked with tears. "You did it on purpose, I know it." And part of me thinks he's right. I hug him and feel the growing knot on the back of his head, and then suddenly—still crying—he laughs and points at the soccer ball he somehow managed to kick into the goal even as he fell.

Every animal is supplied with moisture, and, if the animal be deprived of the same by natural causes or artificial means, death ensues: further, every animal has another part in which the moisture is contained

I stand in the bathroom with the lights off, listening to the house sleep around me. My wife curled up with a body pillow. The baby monitor rattling. My eyes begin adjusting to the dark. I see the contours of a cup on the sink edge and an Uglydoll timbered on top of the toilet. I close my left eye and the room goes black. When I blink the right the entire room—the blue tiles, a postcard tucked into the cabinet door—is brighter than when I have both eyes open. A spider hovers below the faucet's silver glow. In the mirror I stare where I know my face will appear and then I flip the switch. One of my pupils is huge, celestial. The other is a pinprick. I blink and blink and brace my arms on the sink. There is no spider. Maybe there never was. Who knows what I really see. The room wobbles and I knock the cup to the floor.

These parts are blood and vein, and in other animals there is something to correspond; but in these latter the parts are imperfect, being merely fibre and serum or lymph

The white tiger is a Bengal tiger that is missing the pigment pheomelanin. Its stripes are like fingerprints, which is true for all tigers—no two tigers have the same stripes—and are caused by skin pigmentation. If you shaved a tiger's fur off, you'd see striped skin. In humans there are at least three types of naturally occurring pigment melanins: eumelanin, pheomelanin, and neuromelanin. They influence the color of eyes, hair, and skin. White tigers grow faster and larger than the normal Bengal tiger; they are often ten feet long and weigh over five hundred pounds. For a white tiger to be born, both parents must carry the rare gene that causes the pigmentation variant. Only one in ten thousand tigers does.

The chief parts into which the body as a whole is subdivided, are the head, the neck, the trunk (extending from the neck to the privy parts), which is called the thorax, two arms and two legs

The uakaris are of the Pitheciidae family, one of five families of primates that comprise the New World monkeys.

They have shorter tails than most monkeys and are covered in long shaggy hair that makes their bald heads look
emaciated by comparison, like miniature red skulls.

The skull consists entirely of thin bone, rounded in shape,
and contained within a wrapper of fleshless skin

I have been a saddlebag, and the most delicate pages of
an illuminated manuscript. Broil me and my blister will
crackle. This body is a travelogue of cuttings.

When men have large foreheads, they are slow to move;
when they have small ones, they are fickle; when they have
broad ones, they are apt to be distraught; when they have
foreheads rounded or bulging out, they are quick-tempered

Another bald-headed animal, the turkey vulture, or buz-
zard, finds carrion to eat using both its vision and smell.
To defend itself, it vomits up stomach acid so full of bacteria that consuming it could kill a person.

A part common to the upper and lower eyelid is a pair of
nicks or corners, one in the direction of the nose, and the
other in the direction of the temples. When these are long
they are a sign of bad disposition; if the side toward the nos-
tril be fleshy and comb-like, they are a sign of dishonesty

Swimming laps in the university's outdoor pool, I feel
the left side of my body pull smoothly through the water.
But my right side feels a half second behind, fatigued or
weaker. I veer to the right and bump into the wall. Stop.
Walk to the end. Start over. Halfway down I slam into the

side again. To make sure my anger doesn't ruin my day with Felix, I stop swimming, walk into the shallow end, and use the wall to stretch the muscles in my arms and shoulders and back. It's summer and the pool is almost empty. Felix is taking a break from our races and our dives to the bottom to pick up rings. He sits at an umbrella-covered table, chewing a nubby carrot, goggles pulled up onto his crown. The red indentions around his eyes going purple as he cools. He waves, runs over, and gives me a handful of almonds. I kiss his forehead when he bends down. "Dada, look at all the bugs," Felix says. He points to the water around me. "What are they doing, Dada?" I'm surrounded by tens of dozens of insects. It's like a plague dropped out of the sky. I cup a dead cricket and swoop it up in a gush that splashes the concrete. "Going swimming, I guess," I say. "What do you think?" He shrugs and crunches a piece of seaweed into his mouth. I bowl my hands around another speck, but shout and throw them above my head when it feels like my finger is cut. I notice that half the bugs around me are wasps. My middle finger is bright pink. The growing orbit of the sting swells. "Yowzer." I show Felix my finger. "I've been got!" He grins. I pop out of the water and sit on the deck and Felix climbs on my back while I try to stretch my hamstrings.

The part that is sensible of taste is the tongue

I lie in our backyard hammock, shadow-splotched by the oak overhead. Felix sleeps curled beside me. Inside, my wife is reading in the air-conditioning—she is pregnant with our second child. I fall into a fitful, dream-thick nap. When I wake, all I remember is kneeling in front of

Felix, trying to explain that there is a little girl growing in his mother, that in a few months he will be a brother. I try to get him to laugh by telling him that the house will smell of dirty diapers but he bristles, seems not to care, and asks if he can hit Wiffle balls. The first ball I lob at him he smashes right back. When I fall, a split grows down my neck and through my belly and chest, and out stream thousands of Xerces blue butterflies.

In betwixt the two openings comes the so-called epiglottis, an organ capable of being drawn over and covering the orifice of the windpipe communicating with the mouth; the end of the tongue is attached to the epiglottis

The average yak will live to be only twenty years old.

Such are the properties of the windpipe, and it takes in and throws out air only, and takes in nothing else either dry or liquid, or else it causes you pain until you shall have coughed up whatever may have gone down

Every fifty days I am newly fleshed. Ask me who I am today and I will say a saint. Ask me in two months and I will say I have always been a sinner.

The heart is not large, and in its general shape it is not elongated; in fact, it is somewhat round in form: only, be it remembered, it is sharp-pointed at the bottom

Out into this morning's Texas dark. Sweat beads and then spits from me because it's already eighty-five degrees

and humid. Up Stadium Drive and for two miles down
the bike lane of Trail Lake Drive. When I run there are
flames in my bloodstream. By the time I get to the park
by Westcliff Elementary the sky is pinking. Down the
path and into the woods, I chase my old self. The one just
ahead, always ahead. The one I will never again be—but
my legs will not stop.

Those who imagine it to be empty are altogether mistaken;
and they are led into their error by their observation of
lungs removed from animals under dissection, out of
which organs the blood had all escaped immediately after
death

Almost every morning over breakfast, my wife and I play
a game with Felix about favorites—"What's your favorite
nocturnal creature?" one of us might ask, or "What's your
favorite canine?"—and the three of us will each answer.
Today I started talking about hybrids, about ligers and
zebroids and wholphins, and his face opened big eyed.
As he pedals the two blocks toward his preschool he asks
again and again, "For real? For real? Are you teasing,
Dada?" Walking beside him, I tell him about zedonks,
too. Watching his happiness surges some incapacitating
kind of love through me, so I don't stop him from riding
into the busy, strictly forbidden parking lot instead of up
on the sidewalk.

Felix churns ahead, behind a row of parked cars, and
I see an enormous pickup start to back up, reversing right
toward him. I cannot move. There is numbness in me, as
if everything I am has died and I cannot shout *stop* or

hold up or *wait* or *watch out*. So it's from a distance that I watch myself sprint and lift him off the bike and into the air—as right behind us the truck crushes his bike and, holding him tight, I keep running.

HOW LONG BEFORE YOU GO DRY

> The past is not closed, it receives meaning from our present actions.
> —CZESŁAW MIŁOSZ

I

When I'm whipped awake, stripped from my dreaming, it is 2:11 a.m., deep in the humming of the Texas night. I'm wonderfully tangled around my wife in our bed, starfishing her slumbering body, one leg aimed out of the sheets so I don't overheat. Ariane is a mummy under the blankets. Catface on her feet. A second passes and I hear my boy shriek from his bedroom. It is a still-dreaming squawk, one that shatters the dark. A low moan burbles, gets louder and louder, and then Felix's howling finds shape: "Mama! Dada! Mama! Dada!"

Call me old school, but I still believe that dreams can be been seen as portents. Throughout history dreams have been associated with prophecy. The answers to scientific puzzles have appeared in the beautifully strange worlds

that blossom when we close our eyes—the secrets of neu-
rotransmitters, benzene, Descartes's scientific method,
the logic behind Mendeleev's periodic table. Montaigne
argued that our true thoughts open in dreams, reveal-
ing all the darkness we'd rather hide. Freud believed that
during dreams the ego's defenses are lowered, allowing
fragments of repressed memories to surface. In my sleep
I experience again and again the terrible things that have
happened to me.

Behind my shuddering eyelids I see so much: A half-finished chess game, the pieces alive, the knight rearing
and the queen bowing, or the pieces replaced by fingertips, eyeballs, nipples. An enormous octagonal tent
woven from striped neckties and panties. A floating cake
adorned by a baby's hand. The sister of one of my best
friends, topless, sprinting right at and then whooshing
through me. Packs of gum that I cannot lift from the
boxes they're stacked in, a gas station attendant just
shrugging when I look to him for help. A handful of nails
thrown into the air, turned into tooth after tooth floating
to the ground. The number eleven. A row of bodiless
heads being shaved. A baseball unstitching itself in my
hand. A steel rake tangled with snakes. A nurse, extending a silver flash of metal toward my mouth, and then my
brain surgeon's hot breath growing closer. A whitewall
tire rolling down a dark street. An overturned gas can,
an endless parade of mice slinking out of it. Our post-
man—waving as he walks up Stadium Drive—wearing
nothing but his satchel of letters. An orchid, ablaze. I

dream about my past lives. I dream about lives I have not lived. I dream about lives I will never be able to live.

Smoke crows up from each of the temple's ghats, the cremation platforms raised a dozen feet above the Bagmati River. Inside them I see bodies curling smaller and smaller. It is 2001 and I am twenty-three, and for the third day in a row I am at Pashupatinath, one of the most important Hindu temples in Kathmandu. I squat on the stone steps across the river from the burning bodies, crouched like a catcher behind home plate, until my legs go numb. Then I walk down to the wall at the river's edge. I want to see the caves the sadhus—Hindu holy men—live in, where hordes of screaming monkeys swing in the rock outcroppings. I want to get closer to the burning.

II

Tonight Felix and Ariane and I spent the hours leading up to bedtime—from a bath to teeth brushing and jammies—coming up with a guest list for his fourth birthday party. Finn, Owen, Lilly, Jax, Sutton, Smith, Laila . . . The list didn't stop until I said no more, we're done, there isn't enough room to invite anyone else. The party will take place in two Saturdays at Pump It Up, located in one half of a gutted strip mall. Each cavernous room contains a bouncy castle, two-story slides, or an inflated obstacle course. In the last year Felix has grown eight inches and gained only eight pounds.

I am often and easily made sad, so I constantly look for new ways to understand it. For thousands of years a degree of sadness—more specifically melancholy—has been linked to powers of divination. So: Aristotle, in his *Problems*, looked at the numerous heroes and artists of a melancholic disposition, and diagnosed the melancholy as resulting from an excess of black bile. So: overheated, the black bile causes an outbreak of sores, anger, and madness. So: the black bile could also cause a person to push beyond themselves, to grow out of their consciousness, to become sibyls, soothsayers, and inspired persons. So: Plato thought that the craziness created by black bile had a spiritual dimension.

On September 1, 1953, at the age of twenty-seven, Henry Gustav Molaison underwent a medial temporal lobectomy intended to cure his epilepsy. This surgery meant cutting away almost all of his two hippocampi and his amygdala. Tucked beneath the cerebral cortex—what a child would picture if asked to draw a "brain"—the hippocampi are shaped like (and named after) sea horses, and are essential to memory consolidation. Molaison's surgery was a success only in helping his epilepsy; afterward he suffered severe retrograde amnesia and couldn't create new memories. For the remaining fifty-five years of his life he lived with his parents and then caregivers, a prisoner in the solitary confinement of the present tense.

I point two fingertips to the sides of my head, where I imagine holes were drilled into Molaison, then run an index finger up and down the back of my skull. I can't perfectly remember what life was like before my brain surgery, what that old body felt like. What, if anything at all, about my memories of that presurgery time is real?

On one of the burning ghats, a man uses a wide broom to sweep ash into the filthy, foaming river below. Around each pyre people wail and reach out for one another. Inside the flames the body folds in on itself until the stoked inferno is barely a campfire. The man with the broom shows up. The mourners hurry away. Slowly I unzip my backpack and bring out a handful of peanuts. I chew them to mush, but when I swallow I still feel like I am choking. Every other peanut I toss to the monkeys that cartwheel around me. Each one hops forward, lunges, dances back, fucking with me, trying to see what it will take for me to hand over all my peanuts.

III

One of the first books I read to Felix was Eric Carle's *Mister Seahorse*. In it Mrs. Seahorse lays her eggs in Mr. Seahorse's belly before he adventures away from her company. During his ocean journey Mr. Seahorse meets five other fish dads: Mr. Bullhead, a catfish; Mr. Pipe, a pipefish; Mr. Kurtus, a nurseryfish; Mr. Tilapia; and Mr. Stickleback, who hatches the stickleback eggs. To Mr.

Stickleback, Mr. Seahorse says, "Keep up the good work." This was my all-time favorite book. Each time Felix sat on my lap for a story I'd prod him toward picking it. At first he ran his fingers over Carle's drawings—the lionfish, the trumpetfish—but after a few months he was bringing me books about fire trucks and construction, and then, for a year, it was all Richard Scarry's *Busy, Busy Town*.

When I cry the lacrimal gland, which sits on the upper outside of the eye, releases a tear—a fluid thick with protein and mucus and oil—which slides across the surface of my eye until it rolls over my eyelid and down my cheek. I do not dab it with a tissue. I let it drop from my jawline. But there are three types of tears: basal tears, reflex tears, and emotional tears. Basal tears are constant, an all-the-time crying that keeps the eye from drying out. If my Marlboro's smoke blows into my eyes, the sensory nerves in my cornea send signals to my maybe-working brain stem and I cry reflex tears. When, over the phone, I learn about a death, and with a shaking hand can barely write down the info—date, funeral home, where to send flowers—the sadness I feel lights up my cerebrum and triggers my endocrine system to release hormones into the ocular area, and suddenly I am weeping emotional tears.

After Molaison's surgery, scientists researching memory formation and related disorders studied him constantly.

He could remember only facts he'd learned before the
surgery. Slowly he lost more of his memory—first from
the two years previous to the surgery, then from the
eleven years before. But in giving up the experiences that
make us who we are, the events that make us fully alive in
this lovely and blistering world, Molaison radically influenced neuroscience. He expanded our understanding of
epilepsy and amnesia and brain pathology—why that
part does what it does—and revolutionized knowledge
about human memory.

I cannot find a way to remember what I felt like before
my head was cut open. For hours each day, I'm confused.
The near and distant past both elude me—and I am
unsure if what I think happened actually took place, or if
something inside me has made it all up into a nightmare.
When I lived in Minnesota, were there three rooms
upstairs, or just one? Was there a sea horse toy glued to
the toilet in my apartment? Did I really push a shopping
cart off a bridge, into the river, on the Halloween of my
senior year of high school? Who kissed me in the dark
that night, whom did I kiss? Which of my friends died
jumping off the bridge and which ones overdosed? Did I
take my medicine today? Where are my pills? Have I hidden them away? Felix shows me a marker-scrawled treasure map, and tells me that I drew a real good one, that
he loves it. I say thanks and nod, but I don't remember
drawing the map for him. *What*, I ask myself, *who am I?*

Watching another round of cremations, I sliver apart
a hunk of cheese and pick out the hairs of the animal

the milk came from. I stick my pocketknife upright in
the hard dirt. Far below, the cesspool of the Bagmati—
the sacred Bagmati—sluggishly eddies and flows. The
water is putrid and packed with garbage. It's terribly
awesome, like photos of after-tornado devastation.
Miles south of the temple it flows into the Ganges,
the holiest of rivers to the Hindus. Pashupati is built
up on both sides of the river, ancient and ramshackle
and gorgeous with statues and color and carvings. A
stone bridge connects the two sides. Each time I've visited, the temple has been packed, but I'm mostly alone
on my hilltop perch. At the temple entrance men and
women hawk everything: deep-fried snacks plucked
from boiling oil with bare fingers, steaming blobs
stabbed with the end of a whittled stick, necklaces of
marigolds, statues of Shiva, thousands of trinkets and
offerings. Right in front of the entrance sits a wagon
housing dozens of trays of pigment, vibrant, a cosmos
of colors—oxblood red, yellow, blue, sunset-on-the-
ocean red, orange, pomegranate red, and every other
bird-of-paradise shade I can imagine.

For hours I have been watching the bodies burn.

Ten feet below each burning ghat, standing knee
deep in the sewage, are shirtless boys who constantly
dip into the muck and pull up their finds: a ring, a jewel,
a gold tooth. Each of the boys has a great balloon head
above a hunger-sharpened body. They stand in groups
of two or three, passing their treasures around, wet ribs
shining like the first rays of sunlight slicing through a
stormy sky.

IV

I adore all of Eric Carle's children's books: the one-of-a-kind collages, the sweet stories about love and nature. But *Mister Seahorse* is different. And my connection to the book is deeper than its broader message, deeper than how it allowed me to show Felix, or anyone else who saw me reading it, that dads can be nurturing, that fathers can do the work of childrearing, what it really means to be a man.

I read it to instill the belief that I, personally, will always be around, always protecting. That there will never come a day of slit wrists or a mouth swallowing a gun barrel; that there will never be a bottle of Bombay Sapphire in the too-high-to-reach cabinet, never rails snorted each morning to fire up the day, never a handful of pills to help curl me up at night. I read it to show that within me there is boundless love.

I read *Mister Seahorse* to show my wife and Felix that I am a good man. That I look for goodness in good places. To convince myself of that fact, too. To feel that even after brain surgery took everything, there still remained within me gifts the world might want.

Long after Felix stopped wanting to hear *Mister Seahorse*, I found myself thumbing through it late at night. Before the sun was up. In the middle of the day.

I read it for myself.

I read it to hear Mr. Seahorse say—not to Mr. Stickleback, but to *me*, over and over again—"Keep up the good work."

When I was an infant I cried to stay alive, to get food and milk, and to be warmly robed. But at ten months manipulative crying starts. I, like you, like him or her, like all little sociopaths, cried to get this and that. Up until puberty, boys and girls cry with about the same frequency, but then skyrocketing testosterone levels in boys make them cry less. Some scientists see crying as a safety mechanism, a release of stress-related toxins. And most psychologists believe that keeping your emotions locked deep inside can cause long-term damage. Holding back emotional tears elevates your risk of heart disease and hypertension.

But medical professionals still list crying as a symptom of many afflictions.

Beckett: My words are my tears. Voltaire: Tears are the silent language of grief. Plath: I didn't want my picture taken because I was going to cry. Saint-Exupéry: It is such a secret place, the land of tears. Rumi: You left and I cried tears of blood. Gibran: Keep me away from the wisdom which does not cry. Dahl: The fine line between roaring with laughter and crying because it's a disaster is a very, very fine line. Timberlake: Cry me a river.

A number of studies have shown that women cry four times as much as men. Some theorize that this is because young men sweat more, releasing through their armpits and ankles and groin chemicals involved in the makeup of emotional tears. But in middle age, when we all lose testosterone and estrogen, this reverses: men cry more and get angry less. Still, many believe that a man who cries is weak.

So: I am a man and my father dies and I cannot stop weeping for weeks. So: I am a man and the orange tabby I've named Biggie cannot be found—he probably has run off or been killed by a car—but whatever happened, I'm pissed, clenching my fists, gritting my teeth, and I say good riddance, that motherfucking animal better not come back. So: I am a man and my entire body is crying, but let's call it sweat so no one knows. So: I am a man, and the dryness of my eyes fills me with rage. So: I am a man and I punch and kick and tear and scream, *Fuck you, what are you looking at?* So: I am a man, so old that sometimes I cannot remember why I am crying. So: there are all these tears. So: and there are more. So: there will always be more. So: I am a man who cries and cries and cries—and if a man who cries is weak, what am I?

In the 1960s Molaison learned figure drawing by working from his reflection in a mirror. He could develop new motor skills—but couldn't remember the process of doing so. *How* was wired into one part of the brain; *when* was wired in another. In a 2002 experiment, scientists explored the complex neural structures that underpin spatial memory: Molaison was able to draw a detailed map of his home, even though he'd moved in five years after his surgery. One of the last studies performed with Molaison as a subject occurred in 2007. He was shown a number. The number was taken away. He was asked to recall it and could.

Each day I think about my deterioration. My tumble-down insides.

If tomorrow I do something that I already did today, the only promise I can make about it is that it will be done more shittily. With every passing second my disabilities grind me down a bit more. Blunt me. Make me mushy.

Yesterday it took all my concentration to see and then catch the Wiffle ball Felix lobbed at me. This morning it took all my concentration to miss the white blur as it bounced off my cheek. Felix guffawed, thinking I did it on purpose. I forced a smile before zinging it back at him.

Today my vision is terrible. It looks as if the world is tipping over. Streetlights and trees nod and headbang and bow down to me. The leaves on the spring oaks are an emerald slurry.

I walk with a rightward lean, and I stumbled over a curb on my way to work this morning. I dropped to a knee and buried my knuckles in the wet grass of the boulevard on University Avenue. The drivers whizzing by must have thought *Heart attack, how sad,* or *Poor thing, terrible, terrible,* or *Goofy fuck can't even walk.* But no one stopped to check and I jogged the rest of the way to campus.

In the parking lot I catch a glimpse of myself in a parked car's window and I'm shocked at what I see. Blood rushes my head woozy as I wonder what could have happened to the person staring back at me.

Each day I remember less about what has happened

to me. Each day I grow more puzzled about what is and what is not—when that, what is, what's not, why now?

Talk therapy is used to help survivors of trauma cope with anxiety, depression, and suicidal tendencies. Say that you were repeatedly molested as a child. Say that you hated your body, were sure that it was worth nothing, that in it there was no pleasure. Say that you did not know how to love yourself. Say that you felt this way for a long, long time. Say that after this long time your body failed you. Say that to stay alive you had to abandon that sick body and let the surgeons cut part of it away. Say that you try to live in your new body but it doesn't work right. Say that each day feels slightly off, that the strangeness of this body fills every second with panic. Say it is all an uncomfortable dream in which nothing happens but that you can't wake from. Say it is a nightmare. Say it every day.

Talk about it, think about it, relive it again and again through exposure and somatic therapies. Tell the therapist that you wish you were dead. And in talking so much, learn—maybe—to deal with your sadness.

In a waiting room I read about the future. Neuroscientists have learned that our memories aren't forever stored on hard drives in our brains. They aren't static. Each time we remember something the act of remembering—the circuitry of neurons, and the proteins and chemical compounds that connect them—changes the memory itself. I think about the dying man I heard screaming in the intensive care unit after my surgery. I glance around the waiting room, but no one is looking at me. The article goes on: pharmacology is using advances in the science of memory to influence what we remember, creating pills that inhibit recall, pills that destroy memories, pills that make us forget, permanently.

V

Felix has started having night terrors, so I learned as much as I could about them. While sleeping, we usually move through five phases—stages 1, 2, 3, and 4, and rapid eye movement (REM)—before cycling back through. During stage 1, light sleep, you drift in and out; you might sit up in bed after hearing a door close loudly or someone shouting a few streets away. In stage 2 the eyes do not move. Less electrical activity occurs in the brain, except for the occasional sleep spindle, a burst that is often followed by muscle twitching. Combined, stages 3 and 4 are called deep sleep. It is hard to wake someone from this part of the cycle. During deep sleep kids might wet the bed or sleepwalk. In Felix's case, as he transitions to REM sleep, night terrors set in.

Sweat lacquering his pajamas to his body, he sits up in bed and shouts, "Someone stop them" or "Keep them away" or "But they are right there." He thrashes in his blankets as if drowning. Putting my palm against his heaving chest, I can feel his thoroughbred heart.

He alone can see these horrors, and while we try to comfort him, he starts to cry as if he is the only boy left in the world. He does not hear me or know that my wife and I are holding him. It seems impossible to wake him, and many pediatricians say you shouldn't even try to. A few minutes later he might plant his head back on his pillow or wake, say he's got to use the restroom, and scamper off. He has no memory of his horror show journey.

Because I can do nothing about what haunts him but wait his terrors out, I have never felt so powerless.

Almost fifty other people lived in the elder care center where Molaison stayed after his parents died. It was also home to three cats, four birds, a number of fish, a rabbit, and a dog named Sadie. Molaison spent most of his hours in the center's courtyard, sitting in his wheelchair, the rabbit in his lap and Sadie next to him. A few times a day, from the window of his room, he could watch trains rumble by.

In the 1970s Suzanne Corkin, a neuroscientist at the Massachusetts Institute of Technology, legally took control of Molaison and all access to him. She decided whether or not a scientist could "use" him as a subject and required a presentation on their proposed research, at MIT, first. Corkin refused the requests of most scientists; barely one hundred were able to study Molaison during his lifetime. Corkin, however, made her career studying him. Between 1966 and 2000, Molaison visited Corkin's laboratory fifty-five times, staying for weeks on every trip. She told the staff at the elder care center to neither confirm nor deny his presence there, to refuse anyone who wanted to see him. Corkin was the only contact—no friends, no family—listed in the facility's files. If Molaison died, the staff was to immediately get in touch with her.

Becoming a memory-less father in a wheelchair—a shell of a man, with a rabbit in my lap—is one of my biggest fears. I do not want my family to feel pressured to visit someone who doesn't remember them. I do not want to be kept alive like a sick dog. I do not want to be shepherded through my delusions and fantasies and dementia. I would rather be nothing at all than not have anything to give, not be able to help my son on his path to becoming a good man, not have love or warmth to cradle around my wife and daughter.

Before landing in Kathmandu I spent a week in the southernmost part of Thailand. Because it was Ramadan I barely ate during the day, but when the sun went down, I enjoyed huge meals with the village's Muslims. Laughing over teeming plates late into the night. Long after my girlfriend went back to our mosquito-netted cabana, I walked to a starlit beach. A tiny man with black, damaged teeth tugged at my shoulder. With an unnerving casualness he urged me to buy drugs from him. He wanted to know what kind of girl I wanted, how young; he assured me that anything I wanted to do was totally fine. The glass-edged waves rolled onto the white sand, and for as much as a latte would cost back in Minnesota, I bought a bag of weed the size of a kindergartner.

The night before, our first on the small island, the daughter of the man renting us our cottage sat in the sand next to me while I watched the early slope of the sunset. Looking straight out at the ocean, without a word, she squeezed her hand into my board shorts, leaned into me, and bit my ear.

A week earlier, in the elevator of my hotel in Bangkok, a woman pressed back into me, puzzle-piecing her ass against my dick before reaching behind to squeeze once, twice, then long and firm until beneath us the floor jerked to a stop. There were three other people in the elevator with us. The door slid open with a *bing* and like magic the woman untangled herself from me and was gone. When I stepped from the hotel lobby into the smoke of Bangkok, there she was. Without any acknowledgment that she'd done the same thing the day before—or that she'd also seen me walking out of the hotel with my girl-friend—she smiled and asked what I'd come to Bangkok to find.

I went looking for food. In the span of two blocks, I saw four horrifically disfigured children. One had no legs, and wheeled after me on a rotten board on wheels. While they begged, each massaged a stump—an arm rounded off at the bicep, a leg chopped off at the thigh— or picked the hollow gnarl where an eye should have been.

Jostling through the multitudes in a food market, I felt a hand slipping into my pocket and grabbed it, pulling up quick. I turned and stared down at the skinniest kid I'd ever seen. No one stopped. The crowd flowed around us like water. Before the kid wrenched out of my grasp and sprinted into the masses, I wanted badly to break the bones I held in my hand.

In Kathmandu, I've also been groped and fondled each day, offered sex or drugs or both, always anything I might wish for. My skin buzzes each time. I've never felt such a huge surging in me: of want and shame; of a need to inflict damage, to destroy myself, to feel someone's love, to pray for forgiveness; of a yearning for cruelty; of promises to do it all again, to do anything at least once.

Now, back at Pashupatinath, watching another day's worth of bodies being burned across the Bagmati, I feel light-headed and feverish with knowing: I do not love anyone. Not the girlfriend I've flown across half the world to visit, the one who for a year back home I've hardly thought about. And certainly not myself.

VI

Walking into Felix's room, bedtime ready with a water bottle for his nightstand, I see him peeking out of his blankets, staring into the mirror on his dresser. Slowly his hand creeps out of the covers as he squints, aims a finger gun at whatever he sees, and blasts it, his hand recoiling. "What do you think you're up to, buster?" I ask, the words rushing out, my voice going high pitched as it does whenever I'm trying to mask the sharp edges inside me. My face is hot. Felix jumps, then jerks the blanket over himself and flops onto his belly. Quiet. Still. Holding his breath. "That can't be a gun, right?" Felix's shape—like a mound of earth piled over something just buried—doesn't move.

I grew up in a household that did not tolerate guns or violence, including the imaginary: toys, sticks aimed like rifles, and even just talk of such things. If I returned from a weekend at my dad's with a new G.I. Joe or a tiny green man kneeling with a plastic bazooka, it was instantly confiscated. Of course I resented these rules. I didn't understand them, didn't know why I felt guilty or what I'd done wrong. I just saw toys, my toys, being tossed in the trash. So I stockpiled contraband at my dad's house like a paranoid survivalist. There, one weekend a month, I'd chase my stepbrothers around the yard in fatigues. I'd roll behind the elm tree for cover, my father's metal helmet from Vietnam bonging on my head, spent shell casings strapping an X across my chest. One of my brothers would belly crawl for the garage. Rocky, the German shepherd, might lean toward me, baring his canines. I'd shoot thousands of pellets at them from the shotguns I held under each arm. If Rocky snarled or stepped closer, I'd let him have the *pop pop pop* of a cap gun. I'd take deep breaths of the sweet-and-sour blue smoke before machine-gunning my brother as he streaked for the bushes, then tossing a firecracker overhand into his hiding spot.

But somehow I've grown up and become a father who lives by those same rules.

"What did we talk about the other day, bud?"

For a year Felix has been coming home from visits to his friends' homes, where he plays army, war, or cops and robbers, and birthday parties where—like all the other boys—he receives in his gift bag an army man, weaponized robot, plastic knife, or water gun. Ariane and I started seeing him rolling around the house, ducking behind the furniture, pretending to shoot at Catface or at couples walking by in the street. We had family meetings. Sit-downs. Spent hours before bed talking about it. We did our best to explain to him that we are a family that does not own guns and does not pretend to have them or to imagine shooting other people. We do not want to hurt anyone else no matter what. Again and again we told him and again and again his face grew puzzled, and he'd ask why—why was it wrong to have toy guns, to play shoot 'em, when it was totally fine for all his friends? Why not him?

Two weeks ago Felix and I were out in the backyard. The day was gorgeous, the Texas sun leavened by a gusting breeze. While I turned the dirt in the garden he played in his "Bear Cave," a grotto between the fence and some trees that grow shoulder high before slumping over, making the perfect canopy. Taking a break from the shovel, between gulps of water, I shouted to ask Felix if he wanted some Goldfish. I looked at the grotto, and there he was: one open eye tightly regarding me from the far side of a long stick he held up like a rifle. "Felix! Get over here. Now." He sprinted to me and stood grinning. "How many times do we have to talk about this, little man?" The pleading in my voice sounded caustic. His smile dissolved. "I don't know," he said, staring at his shoes. "Come on, guy!" I blurted. "You know better." And before I could stop myself—before seeing that he was just as I had been as a little boy, confused and feeling guilty, scorched by my anger—I ripped the stick out of his hands, snapped it over my knee, and hurled the pieces over the fence.

Standing beside his bed now, his motionless shape beneath the blanket, I take a deep breath. I set his water by his pirate-ship lamp, then ask the room where Felix might have gone. "Is he in the sewer with the raccoons again? Is he in a dinosaur's belly? Where did he go?" I laugh goofily, then bend over, press my mouth to the blanket, groan forlornly, and say, "Well, I guess I'll just jump on his bed until he comes back," before toppling onto the bed and tickling him.

Whatever else I might be, I have always been a crier. Worried that my mother would die, I cried myself to sleep, thinking that she might be gone in the morning. At recess my friend Jesse stomped on a bug after I'd begged him not to and I bawled. Slumped in a snow fort I'd built, I wept for a dead deer I saw hanging from a tree below the bluff. I'd ride my bike as fast as my little legs could make it go and sometimes, for no reason at all, a fist would form in my throat and tears would wing from my cheeks.

And as I've grown older, it's only gotten worse.

Anything can set me off: commercials for insurance, commercials that feature babies or the elderly. Apple commercials, Coke commercials, commercials for beer or fabric or bubble gum. I cry when I hear songs: Beck, Elliott Smith, Sam Cooke, and Nina Simone. Books, poems: Gabriel García Márquez, *Lord of the Flies*, "If I stepped out of my body I would break / into blossom."

Every kind of movie: ones that star The Rock, Jason Statham, Jack Black, Will Ferrell, or Forest Whitaker; ones with superheroes, aliens, zombies, or nurses who torture their mentally ill patients; ones where nude, all-male knife fights break out in saunas; one where a man, to make sure he won't forget what he's found out, what he might be making up, gets tattoos up and down his body. Children's movies especially rip the heart from my chest: *How to Train Your Dragon*, *Cloudy with a Chance of Meatballs*, *Despicable Me*. Felix, curled next to me on the couch, will pat my hand and, his face scrunched with worry, ask if I'm OK.

My crying is triggered by so much: by video game arcades, batting cages, roller-skating rinks, Sunday Night Football, boxing matches, and comic books; by yard work, gardening, strip malls, and casinos.

Without my constant tears, I would not be *me*.

And so today I grin and give the double-barreled finger to the driver who barely misses me as I cross University Avenue on my way home. I skip the rest of the way across the street, hop onto the sidewalk, and, halfway down Odessa, am laughing so hard I can barely breathe. Chest heaving, I stop and sit in a ragged and stained papasan chair set on the curb for bulk trash pickup. It is sodden with beer. I stretch, reaching for invisible rungs in the air. Hot light filters through the chinaberry tree above, burnishing me. Orange pinwheels glow when I close my eyes. Sharply the laughter dies in my throat and I can breathe again, but now I can't remember what was so hilarious. My collarbones rise and fall as I inhale deep and slow, deep and slow, and suddenly I'm incredibly tired, sinking deeper into the swampy cushions. The tears come hard.

Long minutes later I blink back into the Texas day as a can-you-believe-it conversation and footsteps approach. Three pretty blonde students in matching sorority T-shirts are trudging to the university. One of them is in my morning class, so, still crying, I wave. They stop speaking to each other and look away from my side of the street. From the fetid chair I say loudly, "Have a good day," and when they turn back, I smile and wave again. I tell the woman from my class that I will see her on Thursday morning, that she better be ready for some fun.

Imagine being able to remember the kid who pedaled his bike right at you, running you down before a tumbling crash that made everything go black, but not whether your parents are alive or dead. Imagine that for fifty-five years each time you see the Stars and Stripes you think about how difficult it must be for Harry Truman to be president, though he hasn't lived in the White House for decades. Imagine never finishing *Adventures of Huckleberry Finn* because the pages you read are erased every time you set it down. Imagine that after being asked how old you are and not coming up with an answer, just a sick feeling in your gut, you are told that you are forty-five years old, that you love sliced mangoes and the way they make your fingertips smell. Imagine asking then what a mango is; imagine that when you are next presented with glistening slices of fruit—like slivers of sunlight—they're a delicacy you can't wait to taste for the first time; imagine afterward, how amazing your fingertips smell! Imagine asking the young woman who brings you dinner about your parents because she seems harmless, and after stumbling over her words she says that they aren't around anymore. Imagine asking where they went. Imagine the woman saying, "No, no, I'm sorry, not that kind of not around," before she starts to cry and rushes out of the room. Imagine that morning comes the next day with a sensation that something is wrong; imagine feeling fine that afternoon; imagine that you ask the first person you see about your parents. Imagine the silence of his open mouth and you hoping you'll get popcorn when your family goes to the movies this weekend.

I shoo away the monkeys rioting around me and close my eyes. I listen until all I can hear are the fires of the ghats. For an hour the flames whoosh, sputter, snap, hiss, and *pop pop pop.* I'm half here, half nowhere. I am myself and nothing at all. And then I am suddenly shocked erect and open eyed by an impossibly loud cracking noise, like an oak being felled or a Louisville Slugger crushing a baseball. But looking up and down the temple steps—at the bodies being cremated, the sadhus begging, the monkeys scrambling on the rooftop, the crowds of mourners and tourists—I can't find the source.

Something in that sound changes me. I've never slept a full night since. My hearing is too good. When my wife was pregnant, I woke each time she wheezed or curled a finger. Any sound in the night has me up on my feet, ready to chop and kick and punch, before I go plodding through the house's dark rooms, eyeing the yard from behind a curtain. Branches brushing the roof. The barely audible shriek of a train braking miles away. On the opposite side of the house, a solitary cockroach bumping over the kitchen tiles.

VII

"I bet he cut so many people's heads off," Felix says. "I bet it was awesome. An infinity of them!" We've just read *The Birds of Texas* and stacked the glow-in-the-dark rocks on his bedside table. We listed all the things that made us happy today and then I did my floundering best to answer each of his rapid-fire questions—*Why is there night? Where do the lizards go? Why do we have to sleep? Where do the zombies live? Why can't I walk across the street by myself? When can we get a komodo dragon?* "An infinity," he says again. Like a mannequin, I stand above him, one arm halfway to turning out the lamp. I have to lick my lips before I can speak.

"What?" I try to look confused. I know exactly what he's thinking about but I am buying time, thinking about how much I hate this conversation, how much it hurts, what to say this time.

"Grandpa. He was a . . . what do you call it? A fighter guy?"

I sit on the bed and brush the curls back from his forehead. "Wow, guy, you have such a great memory. Yep. Grandpa was a marine. He fought in a war called Vietnam."

Maybe a month before we'd been looking at a book of historical pictures—Martin Luther King Jr., the Pope, Mother Teresa, the Dalai Lama, Malcolm X, Princess Diana, and Lincoln, among hundreds of others. A handful were famous war photographs: Nazis marching in a packed stadium; the mushroom cloud growing from Nagasaki; a trio of hollow-faced soldiers in Vietnam, grinning, hands hung over the ends of the M16s resting behind their necks, like angels, like they were about to be crucified.

"Man, you know so much. Do you ever forget any- thing?" Felix smiles hugely, proud for remembering, and I can see the hope in his eyes. He wants me to be proud of him, too.

"So he probably did, right? Heads and stuff. He was a fighter. When I grow up I want to be a fighter, too."

I hold Felix's small skull in my hands and tell him to look at me. "Buddy, I'm amazed by you each day, by how much you know, by how nice you are, but I can't tell you. I am not sure what Grandpa did in Vietnam. It's not something we talk about. I think maybe it's not something he wants to talk about." Felix blinks and props himself up on an elbow as a question builds in his face. He asks why. "I don't know, little man. Probably because it was scarier than anything ever and maybe remembering it, talking about it, makes him sad or angry or both. I bet just thinking about it is really hard."

I can see Felix's brain whirring. A few seconds later, again, he asks why.

"Well, wars and fighting, like whatever Grandpa went through in Vietnam, are not fun. They are horrible and lots of people never come home. And everyone hurts because of it." Felix blinks at me, then looks at the floor. None of this is what he expected tonight. "I hope you never ever ever ever become a soldier," I say, holding back the tears I feel coming. "Never."

Felix fidgets with his mummy doll. "OK," he says quietly, picking up a plush fishman and focusing on it. "I don't want to be a fighter anymore."

I gently pry the mummy and the fishman from his hands, then ask if he can keep looking at me. He nods and forces himself to look up. "Lots of people get hurt and lots of people die in wars and the people that get hurt or die are someone's best friend or daddy or brother. Each one is someone who is loved. They get hurt. They die."

Felix tries to look away but I tell him to keep looking

at me. I squeeze his hand. "And that is really terrible, really sad. It doesn't matter whether they are your friend or maybe you don't like them or whatever, when anyone gets hurt or dies it's a sad thing. That's why we don't laugh about hurting people, or think it's cool when something bad happens to someone." I give his hand another squeeze, then kiss his cheek. "Got me, buddy?"

Felix starts sliding out of bed toward the lamp on his nightstand and the Legos that surround it: a pig farmer, a pharaoh, and a janitor surrounded by skeletons.

"Felix? Make sense?"

He drops the Legos to the floor and turns. A thoughtful look softens his tanned face. I'm nearly overwhelmed by my love for him—by his unlimited reservoirs of kindness, by how he is amazed by, interested in, and concerned about all the world around him.

He starts to speak, then stops and smiles. I am sure he sees through me, sees how lost I feel trying to talk about this, how I want to show my pride in him though I'm so incredibly tired. He keeps looking at me and I'm sure he knows me better than I know myself.

"Yeah, I think so," he says. "Like when those boys were stomping beetles and I didn't know why they thought it was funny and I wanted them to stop?"

"Kinda," I answer, and then tell him that we'll talk about it more tomorrow.

After he's in bed and the pirate ship has winked off, I hear him burrowing beneath the covers. He stills, and as my eyes adjust I see that he is looking out from the blankets. He asks if I will tell him stories. I do, until he sits up fifteen minutes later.

"But then someday after they die they might come

back as anything, right?" His face glows in the light that slats in through the blinds. "Like a snake or a tree or a worm or maybe even a ladybug. Right, Dada?"

I press my face into the side of his head and inhale as his hair soaks up my tears.

"Dada," he says, pulling away from me, falling back into bed. "I really want to be a squirrel."

Mythology is wonderfully drenched with tears. Tears turn into blood, tears turn into honey, tears turn into diamonds, tears turn into gold. The tears of a bird cure blindness. Tears fall from a mourner's chin and a speaking tree, which can reveal only the truth, grows from the wet spot on the ground. Fallen tears expand into lakes and seas and rivers. Tears turn into pearls and make a poor man rich, until, overcome by greed, he's lost everything he loves. A phoenix's tears can heal mortal wounds. Tears wake a man thought to be dead. Tears are a sign of wonder. Tears are a sign of grace.

On December 2, 2008, immediately after his death, Molaison's brain was removed from his skull and flown from Connecticut to the University of California, San Diego. Over the next two and a half days, his brain was frozen solid, then cut into 2,401 histological sections. Each one seventy microns thick, stained with dye. Images were taken of each slice and uploaded to the Internet for researchers across the world to study.

In Felix's bedroom closet I keep thousands of pictures of my brain, almost twenty years' worth of MRIs.
Each yard-long image is sheathed with the other scans
taken on the same date. The first folder: when I learned
I had a vascular malformation in my brain stem. The
most recent one: the scans that made the neurologist say
another brain surgery was the only true way to distin-
guish between a regrown malformation and simple scar
tissue.

Sometimes, when my family is out of the house, I
grab a stack of folders, dump out the scans, and scatter
them around me on the floor. The color slides look like
crosscuts of an oak tree or jellyfishing clouds of ink in a
sink. They are litanies of all the shit I've done, my cruelties and kindnesses, my guilt and shame, my joys and
loves, everything that has happened and will happen to
me before my life ends. They are treasure maps that go
nowhere at all. They are Hieronymus Bosch. They are
Mark Rothko. They are labyrinths for fire ants. They are
shards of a mirror that reveal nothing. They are unread-
able pages from the book of me.

Wide awake and upright like a vampire in my bed, I listen to Felix's lawn mower cry. Listen as he clambers from
his bed and thuds to the floor. Listen as his bedroom
door bangs open and his feet staccato across the carpet's
tight weaves, the beautiful telegraph of his coming. He
sprints into our room as if no obstacle can stop him. The
humidifier's soft blue light blushes his wet cheeks. The
fireflies on his pajamas glow in the dark. Ariane soothes,

and I whisper, "Hey, bud, what's up? What's going on?" Without answering, Felix raises his arms, wordlessly asking for me to lift him into bed. He is still crying hard as I tuck him beneath the comforter Ariane pulled back. He's a furnace, heart skittering beneath my palm, and his pajamas are soaked. Ariane says that she loves us both so much, so much, more than anything, while we cradle him tightly and over and over he gasps and blankly says, "I think I had a bad dream, a bad dream." He looks up at me with unseeing eyes. "Nothing was coming to help me. There was no one. It was a bad dream." I press my lips to his slick face, kiss and kiss and kiss until he's taking full breaths, before I exhale a whisper, my promise: "It's OK everything is fine it's all gonna be OK."

ALL NIGHT THE COCKROACHES

"It's your birthday present!" Felix shouts, pointing at me. "What?" I ask from an armchair. "What are you talking about, little man?" He jabs his finger again and laughs maniacally until I realize that he's pointing above me. I look over my shoulder and see a three-inch-long cockroach leisurely scaling the living room wall. "Look, it's for you!" The insect log-rides over the framed edge of a cockeyed David Hockney print of the California desert. Ariane shrieks, "Kill it!" and I'm torn. When my wife sees a cockroach she wants to burn the entire house down, but to my son they are amazing.

The cockroach must realize that something has gone terribly wrong, it must smell death—I'm already jumping up with a junk mail envelope I'd been writing on—because it scurries over the print as if the glass is inferno hot. I slap the air and knock the cockroach to the floor. As soon as it hits the carpet it's tearing ass away. The first time I try to scoop it up, it flips through the air like a Ping-Pong ball. Felix laughs louder. Ariane screams again. The second time I cup and crush it in the same instant. I smell its guts as they wet the inside of my fist. Ariane has run out of the room. Later she will tell me that I have to kill all these motherfucking things, every single one. But right now, when Felix asks to see it, I hold out my hand.

Cockroaches are over 320 million years old. If you went back 320 million years you would be in the Carboniferous period, famous for the highest oxygen levels Earth has ever known. Reptiles first evolved during this period, and plants grew and died so quickly that tremendous amounts of coal material were produced. The Carboniferous started off hot, but the temperature began to drop and an ice age that lasted millions of years fell over the poles.

Three plus two plus zero equals five. Five is the third prime number. A polygon with five sides is a pentagram. Five is the first good prime and a congruent number. (A good prime is a prime number whose square is greater than the product of any two primes at the same number of positions before and after it in the sequence of prime numbers; a congruent number is a positive integer that is the area of a right triangle with three rational number sides.) It is also the only prime number that is the sum of two consecutive primes. Five is the atomic number of boron. It is the number of appendages starfish usually have. If everything went well in utero and beyond, you have five fingers on each hand, five toes on each foot. This is true for most reptiles and amphibians and mammals. Hopefully, you have five senses with which you take in as much of the world as you can. The most destructive hurricanes and tornadoes are fives. According to Aristotle the universe is comprised of five elements: air, earth, ether, fire, and water. Members of the Nation of God and Earth, a movement founded by a former student of Malcolm X's in 1964, call themselves Five Percenters because they believe only 5 percent of mankind is enlightened. But three times two times zero equals zero. And 320 million years from now, enlightened or not, we will all be darkness.

Every cockroach has eyes, a mouth, salivary glands, antennae, a brain, a heart, a colon, a reproductive system, midguts, legs, an esophagus, gastric ceca, fat bodies, and Malpighian tubules. Their eyes contain more than a thousand lenses, so they can see more than one thing at a time—you over there, and me right here, and our kid standing on the kitchen table eating a Popsicle. Their legs are incredibly sensitive and they smell with their antennae. They have two small appendages on their abdomens called cerci, which sense even the slightest movements in the air around them. A cockroach's mouth can move from side to side.

Researchers at North Carolina State University have steered cockroaches through mazes with remote controls. They attached wires to the insects' antennae, sending small charges that trick the roaches into thinking they've run into a barrier. These scientists plan to equip roaches with other sensors, too—microphones, cameras, heat-detecting sensors, biological fuel cells—and imagine using them to explore and map disaster sites, finding and saving victims there, in ways humans can't because of size and physical limitations.

Cockroaches are insects of the order Blattodea, which includes almost ten thousand different species of termites and cockroaches. They have chewing mouthparts and the ability to flex their wings over their abdomens. They are communal insects, living in groups of up to a million.

Chewing mouthparts is a monstrous phrase, and makes me think of the wet-snapping face of the alien in

the movie *Predator*. But I'm grateful for my monstrousness and the pleasure, even the pain, of my chewing
mouthparts: lips, gums, palates, uvula, tonsils, papillae,
tongue, and teeth. We're more like cockroaches than
we might readily admit; like them, we rarely spend long
stretches of time alone. We need to be together.

Cockroaches are nocturnal, foraging for food and
water at night. After heavy rains come a few weeks in
Texas when they invade our home in hordes—up through
the crawl space; out the air vents; through the tiniest fis-
sures, the dark inch beneath the dishwasher or the oven.
They are supernatural, crawling through solid walls,
dropping down from a leak-free roof.

A few months after we moved into our first home in
Texas, Ariane turned on the kitchen light one morning,
saw the black streak of a cockroach racing across the
tiles, and, swearing, climbed atop a chair, and for the
first time I realized how deathly afraid of them she is. A
half hour later I had made an appointment with a pest
control company, and that afternoon two men in matching red polo shirts arrived. I walked with them as they
treated the outside perimeter. One left for another job,
and I tagged along with the other as he worked inside
the house, spraying in the crawl space, laying out traps
beneath the sink and oven and refrigerator. Slowly our
talk moved from cockroaches—or "water bugs," as he
liked to call them—to how we both ended up in Texas.
Before finding God, he told me, before moving to Dallas,
he'd lived in Europe and New York and worked as a slave
in sex dungeons.

There are so many criminals living inside the cockroach, as there are in each of us: the attacker, the thief,

the terrorist. The cockroach is the burglar who slips into your home and seems not to have taken anything, but is sure to let you know it has been there. A bag of rice on its side. A broken-off leg like a comma on the tile. Or there it is, whole—on its back, legs churning in slow motion— never ready to give up.

I hate the cockroach. I love the cockroach.

Cockroaches like to live in warm, dark, wet places and often enter homes through pipes and sewers and cracks in the foundation. And they are amazing and horrific. They can live a month without food or a week without their head, and almost two weeks without water. They can hold their breath for forty minutes and, at top speed, scurry three miles per hour. They can cause asthma attacks in children and spread thirty-two different kinds of bacteria. They will eat almost anything, including plants and other insects.

When I wake in the dark after a nightmare, I'm flushed, sweaty, the sheets sodden. I had no legs. A riot of children screamed as I rolled around their playground. A sniper was shooting from some invisible place beyond the fence. Tiny bodies fell all around me. I yelled out for my son, but no one answered me.

Cockroaches are predisposed to move away from light. But after living with cockroach-like robots for extended periods, real cockroaches will start to follow the robots wherever they might go, including into the light.

A few times a week, hours before he has to eat breakfast, Felix calls out from his room. He hides under his blankets, a potato-sack lump near the bottom of his bed. "Come on, Dada!" His muffled yell sounds as if it's coming from the bottom of a well. "Dada! Get in!" In the cloistered heat under the covers he leans close, says, "What are we today, Dada?" I wrap him in my arms and tell him we are whatever he wants us to be. "Armadillos?" he asks himself. "No. Cockroaches! Come on! We are cockroaches!" Then he's wiggling all his limbs, rolling out of my grasp, and as I laugh he's gently clawing me and mawing his mouth open and closed.

Because of the cockroach, I'm torn. I want to do right by everyone, to fully love both my wife and my child in the ways each wants.

Of the almost five thousand species of cockroaches, most people know only about the thirty that are pests. An inch long, reddish-brown, that noise in the dark, that scuttling in the pantry. I am one of those people. But some cockroaches are as beautiful as butterflies: cherry-red heads and metallic-green backs, wings orange speckled like ladybugs' and evolved to fold origami-like beneath their domed backs. The males of other species grow horns and fight, bashing their heads together like mountain rams. In Australia the rhinoceros cockroach can weigh as much as a mouse does, and is sometimes mistaken for a turtle. Instead of laying and leaving their egg sacs like many insect mothers, some cockroach moms carry their developing embryos in an internal brood sac sustained by a kind of mother's milk. Others shelter their young beneath their bodies, attached to the mother with their developing mouthparts.

Felix's homemade cockroach costume is built from cardboard, scissored oblong in front and back, topped with paper wings. Pipette antennae reach up from his headband. He sniffs and hisses, his hands held up to his chest, fingers fluttering. It is so much better than my best-ever costume—the Halloween I wrapped myself in tinfoil and responded to people only if they called me Space Junk—but I do not tell him this. Nor do I tell him that some of what I see in the cockroach, what I know my wife wants dead, I also see in myself. On that Halloween, I went out of my mind with booze and drugs, couldn't find my way home, and ended up sleeping in someone's yard. Instead I tell him only that I love his costume and that I love him. In the way he adores cockroaches, I see a boundless compassion. An equanimity I dream of someday having. An empathy that makes me feel lucky for each second I get to spend with him.

MIGRANTS IN A FEVERLAND

Three kids scramble down a hill, tumbling through tall lashes of dry grass toward the edge of the Trinity River. On the concrete trail above them, the boys' fathers—a professor and a doctor—stare at the other side of the river, where the drought-brown fields are being built up into a chic development: wine bars and yoga studios, an REI, and, any day now, a Whole Foods. It's barely ten o'clock on a blinding blue Sunday. Every week these five come down to this spot. To dig in the mud, hammer fossils out of the limestone, and wade slowly through the river muck.

With one eye on the boys, the two men listen to the live alternative country drifting across the water and joke that the world must be ending, the reverb of guitars and the singer's crooning seeming illicit on the day everyone is supposed to be pew-bound.

"So how soon before a meteorite blasts us into oblivion?" the professor says. He can't remember the last time he stepped into a church. The boys start roughhousing and he calls, "You better stop or there'll be trouble."

"Wait for us!" the doctor yells. The boys are seven, five, and four, working together through a stage of childhood in which they ignore, talk back, and fight. They don't look up at their dads, continuing to push each other down the hillside as they laugh and laugh. One of them—probably the littlest—will be crying soon. It happens on each outing. It's not a good time until someone starts crying, the fathers say.

"Or maybe some kind of skin funk that will rot off our limbs?" the professor says. He's a writer, and spends his time imagining dystopian worlds. "You're the doctor," he continues. "Break me off some knowledge."

There's a pause. The doctor is dragging ass this morning, after an overnight shift in the emergency room. The professor is amazed that he can work like that and still be an amazing dad at home. Pancakes and bacon. Bike rides. Soccer and basketball games. Piano lessons. Snake hunting at the river. All on an hour of sleep.

"Shit," he answers. "Ebola. West Nile. Zika. I'm sure there'll be something new next year and that won't work, either. There'll still be too many people. Everyone freaking out about that stuff—about the mosquitoes!—when they should be thinking about diabetes getting them."

At the bottom of the path the river is walled by limestone and concrete. But despite the city engineers' plans, it seems to always be flooding somewhere in the Metroplex. This morning the water is muddy and rushing because of the past week's heavy rain, so the fathers begin herding the kids down to a concrete bridge.

The professor's boy is already shirtless. The littlest one pees off the bridge into the roiling water, then starts crying when his big brother pushes him down before he's pulled his shorts back up. "Let the games begin," the doctor laughs before he kneels to hug his son.

The fathers say to have fun but be careful, then the boys sprint away. They drop their stuff as they run, leaving a wake for their fathers to gather as they walk across the bridge. Their fossil-digging tools spill out of their buckets. A juice box falls. Two fig bar wrappers flap across the concrete. The littlest boy loses his net but keeps jogging, screaming for the older boys to wait up. On the far side he falls and starts crying again. The professor's boy is already dunking his head in the algae-thick water along the shore. He splashes again and again.

The fathers unpack their bags as the boys scatter along the shoreline. It's inevitable: the boys will go rabid and feral at some point in the morning. They laugh about it, though they'll still have to yell. Last Sunday they looked to see the three stripped to nothing, flopping around in the rank water, while joggers and walkers and bikers looked down from the bridge with pity. When they saw the two men downriver they judgmentally shook their heads. But the boys need it, their fathers know. Their days are so regimented and watched over that the fathers imagine they must feel like prisoners.

"How filthy is this shit?" the professor asks. He points to a still pool of water behind a sandbar. A floating can. Ripped clothes hung on a stick, twisting in the current. A torn condom wrapper. He tears a small leech from his ankle.

"Oh, we're gonna die. For sure," the doctor says. "We're fucked, but it's good to see you've been using protection when you come down here."

For an hour they talk, their conversation thick with swear words because the boys are out of earshot. They point out ducks and the cranes that dig their beaks into the mud, and talk about all the strange shit found in the Trinity—gigantic goldfish, bodies, alligators—and how sick and crazy they'll soon be thanks to the toxic runoff and sewage. "Our poor boys," the doctor says.

They talk about books, about sports, about their long-ago lives. The professor discusses teaching and writing, the doctor the crazy shit he sees in the ER. The flashlights he removes from anuses, the drug seekers, and the testicular abscesses he has to drain. But he also speaks about the times—each day, it seems—he has to tell a healthy-seeming young person that something is going to kill them, probably very soon. Two kids, a new house, and now two months due to an untreatable cancer. These anecdotes make the morning go quiet. Minnows whisk the muddy bottom around their feet. A mallard surfaces and disappears on the river.

With one of the boys' nets the doctor catches a crawfish the size of a human hand. He holds it up so they can see its machinelike workings. When they let it go, it whips its fat pincers and flashes away.

"I couldn't do it. Couldn't do what you do," the professor says. "It'd kill me. You are a better man than I."

The doctor stares at the boys, who are scooping algae from the water. He says a man came into the ER the other night so amped up on drugs that the staff had to give him twenty-five milligrams of Ativan to slow his heart. Still the man was bouncing off the walls, so they gave him a shot of something else. The professor is incredulous. He once had an Rx for half a milligram of Ativan to settle prereading jitters, and even that small dose made him sleepy.

"Twenty-five?" He shakes his head. "I'd never wake up."

"Then get this," the doctor says. "The next day, he's at the ER again. Pulls up at the doors and drops off an unconscious girl about half his age. Just slumps her in a wheelchair and says hello to the staff that gave him all the Ativan the night before. He was totally fine. He acted like nothing at all had happened." The doctor sighs. "Crazy days."

"Oh, what fun I would have had back in the day," the professor laughs, "with that man as my best friend." He's told the doctor about his brutal, addled youth, about his pain and post-brain-surgery disabilities, about the whiplash of his decade of sobriety. "Oh, to be the body dropped off at the ER."

After the better part of an hour they begin cleaning up the piles of fossils and skipping stones stacked on the shore, the tools, the lost shoes. None of the boys are wearing their swim shirts.

Then they get snacks out and the boys sit beneath the scorching sun and eat, taking long pulls from the water bottles.

When they're done and have packed away all their trash, the five hold hands and step into the river. The dads point out the spots to avoid, where the water is too deep and the current is fast enough to whisk a child away. As they're walking gingerly through a sandbar, avoiding the old cans and dead fish, a foot of snake rises from behind a half-submerged log. It must be six feet long in total. It sways, and the five watch, barely moving. Water sweeps around their legs. The fathers squeeze the boys' hands even tighter.

The boys ask if they can catch it and grab for the nets. "No way," the professor whispers. "Look."

Another snake pops up and dances next to the first one. But then they vanish, as if they've been reeled back into the muddy river. The boys strain forward. The fathers let themselves be pulled closer, closer, until the log is a handshake away.

Suddenly both snakes leer up out of the water.

Everyone jumps back. The five grip each other and carefully walk backward. The snakes lean and bob in the sunlight.

"Back to the other side," the doctor says. "Let's go."

The boys complain. They try to move toward the log again and have to be yanked back.

"If anyone takes another step," the professor says, as sternly as he can, "it's time-outs for everyone."

Slowly they churn back through the current, glancing over their shoulders as they go.

Everyone is overheated, tired and cranky, sunburned. The kids need a real lunch. They're draping dreadlocks of algae over each others' heads. Showing their asses off, shaking them from side to side like hilarious little idiots. And then the roughhousing turns into fighting and the boys are pushing one another down into the poky weeds and sharp rocks.

"OK," the doctor says. "That's it!" His sons get a time-out. They're ordered to sit far away from each other until they learn to keep their hands to themselves. The professor's son steps into the water again to look for "treasure," and begins dredging the bottom.

"Look, look, look!" he screams. Instantly the professor is flooded with the fear that a snake has bitten his son. "Look over here!" The fathers sprint into the shallows toward the boy. But they stop when they see that he's grinning. The professor tastes his heart in his mouth.

His son is holding out what looks like a moss-covered rock. A huge one.

"How'd you get strong enough to pick that up?" the professor asks, because the rock is big, heavier than anything he thinks his five-year-old should be able to lift.

The doctor says, "Wow," loudly, and then tells his boys to come down to take a look.

"Dada! Don't you know?" the boy shouts joyously, just as his father sees the enormous rock winking at him. It's no rock at all. His son smiles as he strains to hold it up. The pride that rushes through the professor is molten, stopping the quivering in his gut. His son shouts, jubilant, "Look! Look! It's huge. It's the biggest turtle ever!"

FUCK THE ALAMO; OR, NEVER FORGET: A MIXTAPE

1. "Hot Coals" by Cold War Kids

My body lies loose and almost comfy, but my head is caged in place on the plastic tray. The MRI technician slides me into the machine, which is thrumming like the belly of some great beast. The ceiling is inches from my face. My shoulders squeeze together. I clutch a remote control in my fist.

I'm somewhere deep in the complex of University of Minnesota medical buildings. The sterile rooms I walked through to get here were half-lit, stacked with equipment and screens, but empty of people. Exactly like every other place I've gotten an MRI.

Built into my head cage is a mirror and in it I can see my socked feet and the midsection of the young woman as she explains what's going to happen. The headphones I'm wearing muffle her voice, as if she's speaking to me from the moon, but I'd be deafened by the machine's clicks, barks, and rat-a-tat-tats without them. She says I must stay as still as possible for the next hour, but that she'll be just beyond my feet. I grunt an OK. "I'll start the CD you picked out," she continues. "If you need anything at all, press the button."

This is the sixth MRI I've gotten, and a few years before my life will fall into ruins. I haven't yet had brain surgery; the neurologists are still telling me that my brain will not bleed again. I still believe them. I still think I will live forever.

In two years the machine will become a death-box, but today it hums with pleasure. My doctor's visits, MRIs, and blood tests are fodder for fantasies and daydreams cast with medical professionals and, once, the parrot fish from a waiting room. In moments like this half of me shouts down an erection as the other half prepares for the sex that could, I imagine, begin any minute— the technician appearing at my feet, the barely visible band of naked flesh in the mirror, my bottom half sliding slowly and sensuously out of the box.

I can feel the MRI in my bones when it starts. At the same time, the CD I picked fires up.

When I made my selection before entering the machine, the technician gave me a funny look. Was I sure? she asked. Johnny Cash? I wouldn't prefer Marcy Playground? But all semester I've been blasting Cash in my dorm, captivated by his fuck-you swagger and the way he can shitstomp the heart and the fact that none of my friends listen to him yet. "Folsom Prison Blues." "I Walk the Line." "Jackson," his duet with June Carter. I grow happy and sleepy.

The MRI is glugging peristaltic around me when I wake. The first lines of "A Boy Named Sue." *My daddy left home.* I look into the mirror, see my feet, the tech's outline. *Now I don't blame him 'cause he run and hid* and I am thinking about Keenan Sue, a freshman at Macalester, our best baseball player, balletically smooth in the field, blasting ball after ball deep into the gaps from the plate. He is better than any of us can dream of being.

I have no idea why he left Hawaii for Minnesota, but our rambling and serious talks make me happy. He's becoming a good friend—will become one of my best—so I'm grateful that he's at Mac. Wearing flip-flops, sharing dried seaweed, shaking his head when the weather turns, saying, "Brah, this shit is cold." He's magnetic, cool but so kind and caring that everyone loves him and so handsome he hooks up with any girl he wants.

I'm wide awake and ready to be done. The pornographic visions are long gone. My calves are cramping. I'm so exhausted from trying to stay motionless that I itch all over. To dodge the closing-in feeling that's making it hard to breathe I listen more closely to the Cash blasting over the headphones. This recording, from one of Cash's prison shows, is different from the one I know. Cash sings about busting heads and how rough life is for a boy named Sue, and promises that he'll find the man who cursed him. The shouting from his audience grows louder, sparking with laughter.

I feel panic rising up my throat. An MRI has never done this to me before.

Cash sings about confronting his father, the dirty mangy dog, and gets even louder: *My name is Sue, how do you do?* And then, above the hollering, Cash screams, *NOW YOU GONNA DIE!*

Sure that he's howling at me, I squeeze the remote

control so hard and fast it makes crackling pops and I push the button over and over as the technician rushes to let me out.

2. "Down to Earth" by Peter Gabriel

Rito hitches his gait and bends his eighty-year-old bones toward me to better hold my hand. The dirt road we walk is rutted and muddy. We go slow. Rito says that we must stick to the side of the road, close to the sugarcane. The morning is still dim, and a driver who isn't awake yet might not see us.

I don't remember seeing more than a car or two on this road in the whole few months my mom and I have lived in Hawaii, but I don't say anything. I'm barely two years old. My hand seems to melt into Rito's. The sticky pineapple his wife, Julia, sliced for me drips from the other. I have two bananas in my pocket. Rito and Julia are kind to me. We live in their dirt-floored basement. I want to tell Rito that these are my favorite mornings, the best I've ever had, but I'm shy and what I feel for Rito—awe and admiration and love—I won't be able to under-stand or articulate until long after we've moved back to the mainland.

Over the next half hour Rito hums, occasionally point-ing out a flower or standing still to listen to something chirping before telling me its name and asking me to repeat the word back to him. I love the words he gives me.

Eventually he nudges me toward a thin, shadowy path through the sugarcane. He lays a palm on my shoulder and I watch for bugs and frogs and snakes. I am scared; so much is happening in the surrounding cane, but I can't see anything beyond the path's edges. Behind me I hear a tinkle as Rito searches his shirt pocket for his first fishhook. I've seen him work before. Next he'll take from his hip pocket an arm's length of fishing line, and when his humming becomes muffled, I know he's holding the line with his lips and threading it one-handedly through the eye of the hook. His hand lifts from my shoulder to tie the knot.

Rito takes us to a new spot each time, prophesying the best hole of the day by listening to the thousand-voiced breeze sing through the field, or by cupping a handful of soil and grinding it out of his fist as we walk. A lifetime of work is carved in his face but his eyes are young. They are so focused I grow sure the sky is speaking to him, whispering secrets that I am not allowed to hear.

By the time the sugarcane widens in front of us, uncurtaining the shallow pond, Rito has slivered apart the banana I handed to him and run a hook through each slice. All the lines are draped over his shoulders, bouncing off his shirt as he circles the mucky pool. If the sugarcane hasn't grown too tall and it hasn't rained too much, Rito will sigh happily when he stops, crouches in the mud, and fins a thumb through the water.

Deliberately, almost sacredly, he holds out to me three fishing lines. In the slanting light of dawn they look like ribbons of sunshine. He helps me fling the hooks into the standing water. He watches the way I cradle the lines in my hands for a minute before casting his own.

But a second later I'm yelping because I've got one on, and within a minute two more are hooked on the other lines, and I am laughing and whimpering, asking Rito to bring them in. The three boot-size frogs are almost jerking me off my feet, toward the dark canebrake, which is surely filled with monsters and the bodies of boys not strong enough to pull in their catch.

In one graceful arc of his arm, Rito yanks the lines in and the enormous frogs appear at our feet, blinking dazedly, toppling punch-drunk from side to side. It is a magic trick that Rito will repeat all morning, until the bananas are gone and frogs are spilling out of the teeming bag that—joy soaked, sun sweaty, and right in time for lunch—we lug back home.

3. "Crazy Train" by Ozzy Osbourne

My head is mummified with gauze and athletic tape to cover the ringworm that started on the back of my skull and spread to my right bicep and forearm. My arm has to be totally covered, too, so the referee will allow me to wrestle in the meet. It itches worse than anything I've ever known. I stare into the long locker room mirror. I look like I escaped a house fire. When I'm sure no one can see, I flex and turn to see my profile. I imagine how, in an hour, everyone in the packed gym will be watching me tangle with another half-naked kid.

I think I'm going to throw up.

Which wouldn't be surprising because to make weight this morning—to hit less than 152 pounds rather than the 170 pounds I try to stay at the rest of the week—I ran sprints around the wrestling room wearing four layers of sweat suits and a stocking hat, stopping only when I could taste vomit in the back of my mouth. I ducked into the bathroom, heaved, and went back to sprinting. When I took the bottom layer off, a gallon of sweat poured out of it.

I dried myself, stepped on the scale for the official, and weighed exactly 152. An hour later, after stuffing myself at the breakfast buffet at Hy-Vee, I was sick and then fell asleep in the high school parking lot, the air in my car thick with my foul breath.

All the guys I know have been wrestling since they were five or six. I've wrestled for two years. I don't execute the moves—the fireman's carry, single-leg takedowns, and trips—with the exactness of the others. Because my muscles never look big enough, I lift weights for hours and try to lose every ounce of fat.

I will lose this wrestling match, but I'll lose like everyone's favorite maniac. I become a rabid thing, frantic with fear and shame from everyone watching in the stands. I make sure my opponent is gulping down his own blood when the referee raises his victorious arm.

4. "Banshee" by Santigold

I giddily call Mari to explain that her dress might have torn somewhat. I promise to shake everything I've got if she lets me take it off just for her. I look down at the slinky black material. The dress barely covers my body. I can't remember slipping it on or how it fit over me, stretching until it's almost transparent. My nipples headlight between its shoulder straps. It rides so high up my thighs that my penis peeks from beneath it if I don't yank it down again and again.

Music is playing so loudly from all the dorms that I

can't hear Mari's response and I don't really care anyway so I say I'll see her soon and hang up.

The QU Dance is one of the best nights of the year at Macalester. The Queer Union—the biggest student group on campus—hosts a dance that everyone attends in costume or cross-dressed or in barely anything at all. The dance ends at an hour enforced by campus security, but without fail we go all night. House parties in the neighborhood around campus. More intimate dorm gatherings when morning starts coming on, when there are only a few of us left. For weeks we will laugh about who hooked up with whom. Girls will kiss girls and boys will kiss boys. Enemies spend a sweaty night together. Anything can happen. I try to be there for it all.

Tonight I want everyone and everything.

I let the dress ride up to my waist and run into my dorm's shared living room. I roll my hips, flopping my penis seductively at the guys getting wasted on the couches. They hoot and spit beer on the carpet, then hand me a joint. Casey, my roommate, claps his hands above his head, says it's time to go and make some magic happen.

"Not yet, damn it!" I happily yell. "I have to finish my makeup!" I flutter my fingers at the room as I back out the door.

I head for the bathroom with a backpack of beer and a purse of borrowed makeup. Two couples are making out in the hallway: the guy who lives next door and the cute blond boy from across the quad—stopping for a second so one of them can pinch my ass—and the inseparable couple who speak to no one but each other, who eat every meal together in a corner booth in the dining hall.

In front of the bathroom mirror, I chug and pout and line my eyes and smoke cigarettes and paint my lips and settle a tab of acid on my tongue and think about what will happen tonight and cherry my cheeks with blush.

5. "I'll Be Your Man" by the Black Keys

I meet Nico at a basketball game at the University of St. Thomas. My friends have convinced me to go; it is the first time I've left my apartment for anything other than graduate school classes or teaching at the University of Minnesota. I have been sober for a month, a month of staying in my bedroom, reading books and listening to the silence.

Nico graduated from Mac before I started my first year. She tells silly-ass jokes and is taller than me and model gorgeous and, most surprisingly, the first woman I've found it easy to talk to without being wasted. For some reason, because of good fortune I in no way deserve, the day after the game, there's a message from her on my answering machine. She asks if I'd like to go to a movie.

Within a week we are inseparable, spending every minute outside of her work and my graduate school and therapy appointments together. At night we stir-fry and read poems to each other and watch movies. We talk about what we want out of our lives.

It is domestic and slow. A niceness I've never known, to be filled with hope, to feel safe and be vulnerable. I tell her how painful it is some days just to be alive and she holds me while I cry. She tells me about California, her divorced parents, and how much she wants to help other people. Her heart is huge; I imagine it fills every inch of her body, that I see it shuddering through the soft skin of her chest.

When she tells me that she loves me the first time, saying it back to her is as natural as breathing.

I help her pack and move to a new apartment a few miles away. I kiss her each time we pass on the steps or bump into each other at her car. I ring the buzzer downstairs and when she answers I tell her that she has a delivery. When I make it upstairs she's already getting undressed, and I hand her the books I brought as housewarming gifts.

So I can't excuse what happens a week later.

To this day I don't fully understand it. I think about how scared all that safety and niceness must have made me. The sobriety. The normalcy. How fast everything became good; emotional whiplash. How a healthy intimacy—in which I asked for us to pace ourselves, to wait sometimes, for a delicate pleasure—was totally foreign to me.

And I couldn't take it.

It is one of the things in my life that cannot be undone. I call Nico the night before I leave on a trip to Boston and say that I don't want to see her again.

6. "Nobody Speak" by DJ Shadow

Leota loves it when I stop by so every day I do, even if it's just to say hi. I'm not sure how old she is—eighty? Eight hundred?—or why she likes the company of a second grader, but she's in a wheelchair and needs help with stuff around the house and it feels good to see her smile. I make us snacks, sandwiches or bowls of crackers and slices of cheese, and then we play checkers or Go Fish or just sit with the TV blaring while she tells me stories. She rambles and doesn't make sense sometimes, but I don't say anything. She glows when she talks, even when spittle or crumbs lodge in the corner of her mouth. And afterward, if she needs something done, I take care of it.

But today I'm meeting my pals so I don't have much time.

I tell Leota that I am going riding with my friends and can't stay. Instead of acknowledging her droopy sadness, I wonder at the thinning whiteness around her head. I promise to come for the entire morning tomorrow, then ask if I can help with anything before I go.

I take out the trash and fix her something to eat while she sits in the sun-soaked living room, watching TV. Before I pour a glass of water, I quietly slide open a kitchen drawer where a few weeks ago I found two boxes stuffed with money, including Ziploc bags of rubber-banded bills. But I ignore these. Below them are hundreds of rolls of coins, mostly pennies. Every few days I've slipped a couple into my pocket before saying good-bye.

I arrange a bowl of snack mix and her water on a dinner tray beside her wheelchair. Before leaving I kiss her cheek. She tells me to have fun with my friends, to be careful, that maybe we'll play a new card game tomorrow.

I drop my bike in David's front yard next to Jamie's nice BMX. Paul skids to a stop behind me, screams *yip yip yip*, and then crashes his bike down on mine.

"Hey," I groan. "What's that for?"

He gives me the finger.

It is the summer before third grade and the trees above us are exploding with green.

David's parents sell tchotchkes. Their garage and a retrofitted school bus are filled with hundreds of thousands of them: ceramic cherubs and gnomes and clowns; wind chimes and wall hangings painted with Hallmark greetings; pencil sharpeners shaped like dogs and cats and owls and eagles and howling wolves and animals I haven't seen in any zoo and fairies and aliens and Uncle Sam's hat. There are bigger boxes that we are not allowed to touch. I don't know whom they sell these things to, but someone must be buying them. David has the nicest house of any of us, with new clothes and toys.

When asked to, we unpack them from their bubble-wrapped boxes and arrange them on display—at least until we start crashing them into each other and dropping them on the concrete floor, and David's parents tell us that we've been enough help. They give us treats for our work and tell us to go.

Sometime Paul steals one or two little things but I never tell.

David's parents won't let him ride with us—they never

do—so Jamie, Paul, and I wave good-bye, give him the finger when his parents turn away, and tear off down the street. At the corner we sail into the air off a ramp built from bricks and a plywood board. In the middle of the road, we see who can skid the longest. When a car comes we pedal glacially so it has to brake, then gradually make our way to the shoulder. The drivers always shake their heads at us as they pass.

Our front tires huddled, I look to make sure no one is around, then show Jamie and Paul the two rolls of pennies. "You know how much this is?" I ask. "You know what we can get?" I refuse to tell them where it came from though they ask and ask. "SuperValu!" I shout. "On your marks. Go!"

I take off a second before my friends and pedal as hard as I can to the grocery store.

"Whooooooeeeee!" I yell over my shoulder. "Eat my dust!"

We blow through stop signs. We jump curbs and tear through yards. I pop a wheelie in the parking lot because my friends are so far behind me. Outside the sliding doors, Paul and I slam our bikes into the wall and let them crash to the sidewalk. Jamie angles his precisely upright. We sprint into the store.

Tomorrow I will change the channel for Leota when she asks, playing board games or cards. If she's hungry I'll make her what she wants with all the love I have. I'll contentedly listen to her talk about when she was young. But today, before we raid the Dumpsters in downtown Red Wing for awesome junk for our forts in the woods, I will be a small and benevolent god, pressing penny after penny into my friends' dirt-smeared palms.

Paul will buy a pack of baseball cards—hopefully Topps—and a soda for us to share. He will, hilariously, ask for a bag. Then, one penny at a time, we'll feed the gumball machine coins. Slide the metal hook back and forth and open the plastic catch until the full machine grows almost empty. Until the two hundred pennies are gone and syrupy strings of spit are hanging from Jamie's chin and the fist-size gobs of gum are cramping our jaws and it is impossible to speak.

7. "Stay in My Corner" by the Arcs

Eliot uses his entire fifty or sixty pounds to inch the wagon I'm sitting in over the grass tufting up from the sidewalk's cracks. He steps, huffs, steps, huffs, steps, huffs, until he's got momentum and is sprinting. We race down the sidewalk. Eliot strains while, knees curled up, I use a hand to keep the too-small sombrero he's asked me to wear from blowing off my head. I'm laughing, yelling, "Go go go!"

He releases the handle, flips it back toward me, and sprints a few yards ahead. But abruptly he stops and turns and pushes his glasses up his sweaty nose to look at me. And the wagon is not slowing. I shout at him to get out of the way. He does not move.

Leaning all my weight to the right, I grasp at the side-walk and yank hard on the metal lip of the wagon, until, just before crashing into the smiling Eliot, the wagon veers off the sidewalk, flipping sideways and toppling me into the grass. I roll over the curb into the Minneapolis street. "Motherfuck!" On my skinned hands and knees, I try to gather my wits. Standing, I wipe the bloody gravel away.

I look up and see that Eliot is still standing in the same spot, but he's sniffling and behind his smudged glasses his eyes are going watery. He looks away when I catch his eye.

Eliot is eight years old, has Down syndrome, and requires after-school care. The work actually came to me through Nico, who called six months after I broke up with her. She told me she was moving, going back to school, and that she'd recommended to his parents that I take her place. Now I watch Eliot as many times a week as his parents ask me to, scheduling my graduate course work and obligations at the University of Minnesota around my hours with him. But it doesn't feel like a job, not one bit. Hanging out with Eliot makes me happier than I've been in a long, long time.

Last week we went to the Mall of America and spent two hours in Macy's, trying on every pair of Velcro shoes they had in Eliot's size. I asked if each pair was good, better than the one before it. The saleswoman huffed each time I sweetly asked if we might be able to see another. Shoeboxes piled around us. Finally Eliot made a decision. He held my hand as the cashier looked at me warily and wordlessly rung us up.

I knew we didn't look good. With my shaved and scarred head, tattooed arms and neck, and cut-up face, I looked like a recent release from prison. And holding my hand was a lovely, smiling, obviously handicapped boy.

After looking the cashier right in the eye, I thanked him and grabbed the bag. Then, with Eliot wearing his new shoes, we went to get ice cream from the food court.

Yesterday we didn't leave the yard. We lay on our backs in the grass, waiting to see jets landing at the nearby airport. When they passed overhead they seemed impossibly low, their roaring engines rattling our bones and making it impossible to talk. But whenever I turned to make sure Eliot was OK, a huge smile was waiting.

"Oh, buddy," I say, still pecking the gravel from my hands. "I'm not mad. Everything is fine." I fold him in my arms. "Everything is fine, buddy," I repeat. "No problem."

But already he's crying. He stands unmoving as I hug him. His glasses drop to the concrete. I pick them up, clean them on my shirt, and tenderly settle them back on his face. He leans into me for a second and starts crying harder, then pulls away but doesn't let go of my hand. We walk to the wagon together. I ask for his help getting it upright and pretend to strain, as if he does all the work to get it back on its wheels.

"Look, it's totally great." Explaining what each part of the wagon does, I show Eliot that nothing is broken. "It's perfect. The hat is good, too," I say. "Probably my all-time favorite." He weakly flails as I lift him into the wagon. I wipe his nose with my shirt and he drops his eyes to the ground. "I love it but—you or me?" I ask, holding the sombrero out.

His breathing slows. He looks up at me and the

sadness vanishes from his blotchy face. He grins beautifully and points at me.

"Help me," I say, and he stuffs it down on my head.

8. "The End" by the Doors

It's a fuzzy night in Marshalltown when they spur me
on, tell me to kick his ass, churn me into a froth, assure
me that I can take him, after the old guy pushes me to
the ground. Everyone seems to know him, but to me he's
just another drunk asshole—though years later I'll learn
that he soon robbed another gas station and spent a second stretch in prison. It is the third day of RAGBRAI,
the annual weeklong bike race across Iowa, each night
in a new town with a bacchanal of thousands. I didn't
bike; I drank and smoked the whole drive here, ready for
the festivities, saying stupid shit to make the guys laugh.
I'm underage but somehow they snuck me into the beer
garden.

I'll do anything to impress the seniors and the older
men they hang out with, the ones who stuck around
town, roofing houses and throwing parties, after grad-
uating or dropping out. For hours they cruise through
our town, over the bridge and onto the highway and
back around to Pizza Hut. They ride chromed-out
motorcycles slowly down Main Street, staring down
anyone who happens to look at them the wrong way.
If they even think you've slighted them, you are dead
meat.

I feel like the coolest kid in school because they
want *me* to be around: to chill at apartments I've been

forbidden to go to; to hang out at bonfire parties in the country, where they shoot holes in the sky with pistols pulled from leather vests; to cruise through town in the backseat of their hot-rodding Malibus or sparkling Novas. If they are road-tripping, they even ask me to go along.

I dodge the hook he throws, but he wallops me in the gut twice just as I get my feet under me. I guppy for air and then he's coming right at me and somehow I slam my hand up into his nose. The sound is like a walnut cracking. He staggers back, bleeding from both nostrils. The guys around us holler at me to get him quick. Someone else yells about the cops coming, and behind the old man I see the crowds parting.

I also see the sister of one of my best friends, a girl I'm totally in love with.

I fly a choking arm around his neck, drag him to the ground, and punch him in the face until someone pulls me off. Then I start walking away because the cops are everywhere. But now everyone is fighting and cussing. I slip around one of the police officers and charge the old man and head-butt him twice. He falls over the beer garden fence. I dive headfirst after him and jump to my feet.

I sprint far away from the stage where a band is playing Eagles covers, so far I can't see the lights of the beer garden anymore, to where the fields are choked with the tents of sleeping bikers. Among locked bikes and fading campfire embers, I lie belly-down on the warm grass and hide.

9. "First Song" by Andrew Bird

I've been on campus at the University of Minnesota, where I'm in my second year of graduate school, all day. Snow has been dumping from the sky since last night. It's up to my knees and still coming down as I trudge to the bus stop. To stay warm I hunker into myself like a turtle and hop beneath the heat lamps. By the time the next bus slides to the curb, plowing a wave of dingy snow, I can't feel my cheeks.

The brightly lit windows of the bus are packed with people. I knock my boots against each step. With the shitty weather, the bus is going to creep along, stopping at every block along the route to my apartment in Saint Paul.

And there's only one seat open on the entire bus. Right beside someone I know: Ariane, the woman I met in the graduate student lounge a few months ago, so gorgeous and intimidatingly smart that when we were introduced I sputtered idiotically and darted away. It seems as if I've bumped into her every day since. I can't stop thinking about her. But I've also never been so unsettled by a woman, so I've politely said hello or done my best to avoid her.

I walk up and ask her if I can sit. She smiles. She pulls off her headphones, sniffs, and tells me not to be daft, that she wouldn't mind at all.

Her teeth are perfect and white. Her gray wool hat is pearled with snowmelt. The enormous silver hoop earrings she always wears glint in the fluorescent light. They brush her puffy black coat—*snick snick snick*—each time the bus sways or jerks to a stop. Her cheeks are flushed red as her lipstick. She must have taught today, because I can see she's dressed up. I know her teaching outfit by now. Red turtleneck. Skirt. Knee-high black boots.

I mumble my thanks and sit on the seat's edge, forcing myself to stare straight ahead. Because the front and back doors of the bus open every few minutes, the driver is blasting the heat. There is a vent directly above me.

The bus stops and we tumble against the seat in front of us. We smile at each other. The bus turns up Washington Avenue and our bodies press together once again.

I hear a Modest Mouse song still playing tinnily from the headphones she took off and before my shyness can silence me I blurt that I just got the album at Cheapo Records. "It's great. Don't you think?" I say, each word getting quieter. "Do you know the Shins?"

Ariane says she does. And then, because my love for music—from Bach to Beanie Sigel—is suddenly more powerful than my inhibition, my rambling can't be stopped. By the time the bus winds up University Avenue we're laughing and she's letting me listen to the mixtape she made last night. It's amazing—from Nina Simone to T. Rex—and I'm even more smitten and *holy shit how is this happening we are talking so much.* I have to use my stocking hat to sop up the sweat pouring down my face, but instead of embarrassment I feel joy.

She says her stop is coming up and starts to put her gloves on.

In that moment, the bus careening through Minnesota's snowy dark, I don't know anything about anything. I'm still lost in myself, wayward in the world;

self-destructive and suicidal half the time. I'm years away from finding a sobriety that sticks or a therapist who helps me take the first baby steps toward being a better person. I don't know that Ariane and I will move in together next year. That she will take me to the ER after finding me blood soaked at the bottom of the basement stairs. That once, after getting blitzed out of my mind, I will call her in Las Vegas to let her know that I won't be able to pick her up at the airport—there's no way, it's totally impossible—and she will kindly tell me her flight isn't today; she is excited to see me in two days. I don't know that she will help protect me from myself, that she is stronger than anyone I will ever meet. I don't know that one day after she comes home from yoga, a day after I've spoken to her father over the phone, I'll ask her first to wait a second before she showers, and then if she will make me the luckiest man alive by marrying me. I don't know that somehow I will become a college professor, that we'll move together to southern California and Texas. That she is superhuman and that two times she will give birth to starlight—a son, Felix, and four years later a daughter, Alma.

The bus slowing as it nears Ariane's stop, I know nothing.

I stand and let her out of her seat. I say it was great talking. This is the truest thing I've spoken in years. She says maybe she'll see me tomorrow.

The bus door bursts open. The blizzard rushes in as Ariane crunches down the steps, but before she's gone, into the falling snow, I call out that I know a great breakfast place—would she ever want to go?

10. "Do the Trick" by Dr. Dog

After unpacking boxes, I ride my bike around to see what my new home is like. I learn that I live on the poor side of town, where all the small, ramshackle houses are. It's nearly impossible to ride a bike to the new subdivisions and fancy neighborhoods separated from us by highways.

But there is an old museum up the street from our house and it owns a size thirty-seven shoe that once belonged to Robert Wadlow—the tallest man ever—who was from Alton, half an hour away. With no friends, I go to see the shoe three times in our first week there. It's chained to a podium, but I can stretch the links out and hold it up to my torso. I wonder if I am flexible enough to fit into it. I'm shoulder-deep in the shoe when, behind me, the museum receptionist clears her throat. Each day I've walked into the museum she's turned red and shad-owed me as I rummaged through the museum's books and artifacts, and thumbed each picture of the dead dig-nitaries and industries of southern Illinois.

After I pull myself from the shoe, she says that if I've seen enough and don't have any questions it's probably time for me to go. I've seen everything there is to see. Surely someone wants me home.

The next week I start taking guitar lessons from my mumbly neighbor, a Slash look-alike whose band will fail years before Guns N' Roses falls apart. I crush on a girl who lives with a rotating cast of parent types, but no matter how many times I nonchalantly pedal past her house, Jeneeca wants nothing to do with me. She won't even say hi at school.

That spring I am in fifth grade and I am the only

white Beatle in the school musical. We sing "She Loves
You" poorly but passionately and loudly and the parents
love it. My classmate Larry can't remember the words
even though we've practiced for months. One kid doesn't
even show up. The third Beatle is my friend Jason, whose
cranky grandfather coaches our football team.

Jason also plays second base on our baseball team.
We kick ass, slaughtering every other team in the league.
D'juan dances at shortstop, his hat tipped back so far on
his head that some kind of magic must keep it from falling off. When he runs, legs lengthening like an Olympic
sprinter's, he smears the humid air. He is comic book
fast. Sometimes, instead of sprinting from third base
to score a run, I catch myself standing still, watching
D'juan blaze a curve around first and fly toward second.
Melvin bats third. He bulges with muscles and he's gone
from practice all the time because he has a job. But he
never misses a game. Melvin punishes baseballs, hits line
drives so hard that everyone on the team is afraid to get
in front of one. We practice on the old college field and
each ball Melvin smokes off his bat rattles the top of the
outfield fence. When I strap the catching gear on and
squat behind the plate, I am giddy to watch Gus. Gus hits
cleanup or fifth. We goad him into uppercutting at some
of the pitches, hammering them as high as he can. He is
taller than most of the fathers and built like a strongman.
He launches his whole body at each pitch, blasting moon
shots over the outfielders. Our best pitcher is the coach's
son, Matt, a short, pudgy white kid with huge glasses.
His curly mullet peeks from the back of his cap. Everyone
on the team can throw harder than he does—but Matt
has the slowest, most arcing pitch I've ever seen, almost

like an underhand softball pitch, and no one can hit it. Batters on the other team will swing and miss so violently they spin, sometimes falling to the ground. Coach has to tell us over and over not to laugh at them.

That summer—oblivious to how middle school will change everything and we'll hardly say hello to each other anymore; a year before I will move to Iowa; years before I will speak to Kelly, a friend from sixth grade, on the phone about a shooting at the roller-skating rink—we cannot be beaten, we will not lose. Matt is a hero and Melvin slaps everyone's back so hard our legs go numb and Jason smiles as he sprints down the baseline and for three months we love each other more than anything.

11. "That Dude" by Consequence

"Who's bringing treats today, Dada?" Felix asks from the backseat. We've just begun the drive to his soccer game. Before I can answer he tells me how much more he likes the car seat in the silver car. "This car is better because it's the lizard car, but I can't move in this seat."

"Nathan is," I say as I watch him squirm in the rearview mirror. He sucks applesauce from a packet. "I think, anyway."

This is the first thing he asks each Saturday after I buckle him in. Then, as we head west out of Fort Worth to the complex of soccer fields in Benbrook, he goes over who brought what treat every week of the season, stopping only to correct himself or point out a raptor circling above us.

"Tony brought Powerade and crackers and gummies,

right?" But Felix doesn't want to hear my answer. "That was last week," he goes on. "Before that Zach brought those peanut butter things and juice boxes. Right?"

Before the season, I promised myself I wouldn't coach, but this week I've volunteered again. It doesn't entail much, only organizing the chaos as one half of the team plays against one half of the other team. For Felix and his teammates I figure the best coach they can have is one who helps them have fun.

Last week, before we shouted, "One! Two! Three! Go Dragons!" and broke our huddle to play, I call-and-answered with the boys. "Which way we going?" I shouted. "That way!" they yelled, and pointed. "Which way you say?" I asked. "That way!" they laughed. Then I cheered each boy for every little thing, for each pass, each kick. I knelt in front of each one during time-outs to tell them how awesome they were doing.

After the game I was so exhausted I slept through dinner.

I know more about dark matter than about soccer, and though last week went fine, all morning I've been nervous. I woke with a floppy stomach and cottonmouth. A dozen times Ariane or Felix has asked me a question and caught me staring into space, thinking about the day's game.

"I brought Gatorade and fruit tape and fig bars the

second week," Felix says. "Right, Dada? After the game, I peed in the tall grass." He smiles to himself as our Subaru merges with the westbound traffic. "And then we got slushies!" The fields we whiz by are a grim brown, bone dry and ready for fire. The highway is packed with huge trucks and SUVs.

"Boring, boring, boring," Felix says as we pass a handful of blocks on which nearly identical homes have been built. The houses sit tightly beside each other. They look like Monopoly pieces. Only the paint color or trim or bush in front of the picture window differentiates them. "Boring, right, Dada?"

I smile severely, say, "Yup."

I'd pointed them out to him on one of our previous drives. I thought it was the perfect moment to teach him that he should never be afraid of being his own person. I said the homes looked boring even though *boring*, like *hate*, is a word we don't use in our house. How often must I break the rules I make for him? How confusing it must be to be my son.

Because it took forever to find a green shirt so I would look like one of the Dragons, we're running late. I push the pedal to the floor and zoom across three lanes of traffic. In the far-left lane I gun it and the old hatchback's engine hums.

"WHEEEEEE!" Felix yells. "GO GO GO!" I check the mirror again. His eyes are closed. His window is down and his hair waves around his head. "Zoom, Dada, zoom." He knows I dip the rearview when I check on him, and the next time I look back he's smiling right at me. "Go, go, go!"

In Texas the road construction never ends. I have to·

slow as 120 funnels to one lane. I hammer with my palm because I am sure we're going to be late. All my life I've felt that being late is one of the rudest things a person can do. It's disrespectful and unkind and flames an anger in me like nothing else can. So now I'm not only a bad dad, I'm a hypocrite. When the road widens, I speed up.

"Dada," Felix says. He's gazing intently out at the moonscape of brittle brush and occasional oil wells. There is no shade. I don't understand how the horses and cows out there can graze. Power lines droop and rise endlessly beside us. "Dada," he repeats. "The world is just a big cage."

I study him. Each day more of the kid in his face vanishes. He is smart enough to be as good or as bad as he will ever want to be at anything he might ever want to do. There are times, when Felix and I are alone, that I feel as if I am in the presence of something impossibly large and powerful. As if I am standing on a cliff at the edge of an ocean.

I put more weight on the pedal and drive silently for a few minutes.

"But it's good," Felix says. "It's OK."

We whiz by a Lexus and a Silverado and Felix says "Bye-bye" to each vehicle. The speedometer rises past eighty. The entire car shakes as if we are a spaceship hurtling back toward Earth. "Bye-bye," he says. I look and he's waving at each car when he shouts it. "Buuh-biiiiiiiii!"

"You can't wave at them, man," I say over my shoulder. "That's just mean." But I can't stop myself from laughing, and together, until we exit the highway, Felix and I shout "Bye-bye" to each car we speed by.

12. "Keep It between the Lines" by Sturgill Simpson

Yesterday Alma had her four-month checkup, and right now, at two in the afternoon, it's tummy time. Her cheeks are pink, her chubby legs churn. Band-Aids cover the places where she got vaccination shots. I hold my hands like paddles, flat against her sides but not too tight. I want to feel her every puff and heave. Feel every ounce of her fifteen pounds working so hard to keep her head up and looking around. She reaches for the squeaky moose dangling above her and shakes and quivers. She moans, a guttural monotone that sounds like *I like pieeeeee!*

I'm sweaty, just in from pruning the peach and plum and fig trees, but, for all the old reasons, I am sad and scared. It's a struggle to be around anyone today. It's a struggle to speak kindly, act from a place of love, be a good partner and father.

On days like this, I do not like the man I am.

I lie behind Alma on the carpet. I listen to Felix playing with Legos in the front room, loudly singing "Freaks Come Out at Night" over and over, and to the hot water heater whirring to life as Ariane turns on the shower. I hope Alma doesn't roll over and look up at me. I hope Felix doesn't come in and ask what's wrong. And then I am weeping.

"I love you so dearly," I sing into her hair.

Alma rolls onto her side, then gurgles at me. I wonder what she sees.

I imagine a better me nuzzling Alma's fat-rolled neck. That man would be filled with joy, dreaming of the full and beautiful life she will grow into. The amazing brother she has, already filled with more goodness than anyone I know. But there are too many days when I wallow in the grit and grime of the world.

I hold her tighter, listen to her breath and to Ariane's singing in the shower, try to fill myself with it. I holler for Felix. "Guess what?"

A second later he yells back. "I know, Dada. Same brain!"

Outside the living room window, spring has thickened the oak with deep-green leaves. The storm that is supposed to come this afternoon makes them spin deliriously.

"Well? What is it? What am I going to say?" Alma reaches for her toy squirrel, then stuffs half her hand in her mouth.

"Dada, I can read your brain," he replies. The focus in his voice tells me he's concentrating hard on whatever he's building.

"No way you got into this brain! Tell me."

"That you love me. I know it. Right? I know your brain."

Closing my eyes, I hear him climbing the pantry shelves, trying to find a snack that hasn't been approved for his consumption. Scramble, thud, thump, scamper, scamper. Then everything goes so quiet, all I can hear is Alma's heavy breathing.

When I open my eyes, Felix is right there, standing in front of us in just Batman underwear. His arms are flexed and his chest is scribbled with a tornado of blue marker. He takes a bite of a granola bar. "I was right, right?" He smiles, chocolate chinned.

I shake my head. I tell him that I was going to say that I *really, really* love him.

"Dada." He puts his hands on his hips the way Ariane sometimes does. "I was totally right. I can read your brain. Easy." He looks Alma and me over, then asks what we're doing. "Tummy time," I say. "You remember doing this?"

He frowns and says he never did that stuff. He looks at the window as rain starts streaking the glass, and stuffs the rest of the bar into his mouth before turning back to us.

"Is it almost time to start teaching her about monsters?" he asks.

I tell him it's going to be a few more months, maybe when she starts eating solid food. I explain how he'll have to grind up everything she eats into a soupy mush. Peas. Squash. Carrots.

"You gotta be strong to do it," I tell him. "But you're ready. Show me those muscles again."

He drops the empty wrapper to the floor, jumps up onto the couch, and flexes again. His face reddens until we are both roaring with laughter. He starts bouncing on the cushions. A bit higher each time, and then—hanging a few inches from the ceiling—he asks if, when we're done with tummy time, we want to practice doing some flips.

NOTES

I Was Already Ready When I Was Dead:
This title was taken verbatim from something my son, Felix, said over breakfast one morning.

Migrants in a Feverland:
This piece is for America. Burn to the ground. Live forever.

King of the Rats:

36   *In January 2005* See Andrei Miljutin, "Rat Kings in Estonia," *Proceedings of the Estonian Academy of Sciences, Biology and Ecology* 56, no. 1 (2007): 77–81, http://www.kirj.ee/public/Ecology/2007/issue_1/bio-2007-1-7.pdf.

36   *"the heavy-metal kings of the 1970s"* "Black Sabbath Bio," *Rolling Stone*, http://www.rollingstone.com/music/artists/black-sabbath/biography.

37   *while on the other side* See Nick Davies, Jonathan Steele, and David Leigh, "Iraq War Logs: Secret Files Show How US Ignored Torture," *Guardian*, October 22, 2010, https://www.theguardian.com/world/2010/oct/22/iraq-war-logs-military-leaks.

37   *advocate of torture* See *Meet the Press*, "Transcript," NBC News, December 14, 2014, http://www.nbc-news.com/meet-the-press/meet-press-transcript-december-14-2014-n268181.

37   *Dick Cheney was thirty-seven* See "Health & Medical History of Richard 'Dick' Cheney," Doctor Zebra, http://www.doctorzebra.com/prez/a_cheney.htm.

38   *In a study published* See Claudia Hopenhayn et al., "Arsenic Exposure from Drinking Water and Birth Weight," *Epidemiology* 14, no. 5 (September 2003): 593–602, doi: 10.1097/01.ede.0000072104.65240.69.

38   *"A dark, oily liquid"* *Oxford Essential Dictionary of the U.S. Military*, s.v. "lewisite," http://www.oxfordreference.com/view/10.1093/acref/9780199891580.001.0001/acref-9780199891580-e-4558.

38   *"the advantage in this mode"* Winford Lee Lewis, "Why Not Gas Warfare?" *The Science News-Letter* 36, no. 19 (November 4, 1939): 298–299, https://www.jstor.org/stable/25171441?seq=1#page_scan_tab_contents.

40   *"large, painful, fluid-filled blisters"* Joel A. Vilensky and Pandy R. Sinish, "Weaponry: Lewisite—America's World War I Chemical Weapon," *MHQ: The Quarterly Journal of Military History* 17, no. 3 (Spring 2005): http://www.historynet.com/weaponry-lewisite-americas-world-war-i-chemical-weapon.htm/2.

40   *"One of the 1948"* Ibid.

40   *On May 13, 2004* See Steve King, "Press Release," https://steveking.house.gov/media-center/press-releases/king-abu-gharaib-heidi-fleiss-and-political-cannibals-statement-by-iowa.

43   *"no one gets to heaven"* Yusef Komunyakaa, "Ode to Maggots," *Talking Dirty to the Gods: Poems* (New York: Farrar, Straus & Giroux, 2000).

My Misogyny:

60   *In 2006 almost seventy-eight thousand children* See US Department of Health and Human Services, Administration on Children, Youth and Families, *Child Maltreatment 2006* (Washington, DC: US Government Printing Office, 2008).

60   *"confronting child sexual abuse"* This mission statement, as well as the statistic that follows, are taken from Darkness to Light's old website: "Statistics Surrounding

Child Sexual Abuse," Darkness to Light, http://oldsite. d2l.org/KnowAbout/statistics_2.asp. Their new website, with the mission to "End Child Sexual Abuse," can be found here: http://www.d2l.org/.

Heartdusting:

65   *It is a felony* See Iowa Code §717D.2 (2016), https://www. legis.iowa.gov/docs/code/717D.pdf.

66   *"chicken chow Wayne"* Urban Dictionary, s.v. "chicken chow wayne," October 20, 2006, http://www.urban-dictionary.com/define.php?term=chicken%20chow%20 wayne.

67   *Promoting the film* See Chris Chase, "At the Movies; Maud Adams Finally Taken Seriously," *New York Times,* October 9, 1981, http://www.nytimes.com/1981/10/09/movies/ at-the-movies-maud-adams-finally-taken-seriously.html.

67   *Adams vehemently denied this* Ibid.

67   *In Britain, consumption of chicken* See Ray Moseley, "Spread of Mad Cow Disease Is Turning Britain's Beefeaters to Chicken," *Washington Post,* January 4, 1996, https://www.washingtonpost.com/archive/politics/ 1996/01/04/spread-of-mad-cow-disease-is-turning-brit-ains-beefeaters-to-chicken/b7531b60-1d1d-4bdc-a1ea-9069e7d530d1/?utm_term=.8e2de0b53ded.

68   *"The only Maybelline"* Michael Heatley, *The Book of Rock Quotes* (London: Omnibus Press, 2010).

69   *"plump, meaty bodies"* Food Safety and Inspection Service, "Chicken from Farm to Table," United States Department of Agriculture, July 2014, https://www. fsis.usda.gov/wps/wcm/connect/ad74bb8d-1dab-49c1-b05e-390a74ba7471/Chicken_from_Farm_to_Table. pdf?MOD=AJPERES.

69   *In a Northwestern University study* See X. Meng et al., "Detection of *Helicobacter pylori* from Food Sources by a Novel Multiplex PCR Assay," *Journal of Food Safety* 28, no. 4 (November 2008): 609–619, http://onlinelibrary.

wiley.com/doi/10.1111/j.1745-4565.2008.00135.x/ abstract.

70   *"The fact or state" Oxford English Dictionary*, 3rd ed., s.v. "ownership," http://www.oed.com/view/Entry/135518? redirectedFrom=ownership&.

72   *"A melody contains a thing"* Quoted in Kristen Hanssen, "Ingesting Menstrual Blood: Notions of Health and Bodily Fluids in Bengal," *Ethnology* 41, no. 4 (Fall 2002): 365–379, http://search.ebscohost.com/login. aspx?direct=true&AuthType=cookie,ip,url,cpid&cus-tid=s8427950&db=keh&AN=8896922&site=ehost-live.

74   *"blinded the animals"* W. N. P. Barbellion, *Enjoying Life and Other Literary Remains* (London: Chatto & Windus, 1919).

74   *"bone, cartilage, and tendon"* Ibid.

Things That Are: On Pleasure:

80   *"This movie is about the fact"* Gary Ross, quoted in Edward Johnson-Ott, review of *Pleasantville, NUVO Newsweekly*, 1998, http://www.imdb.com/reviews/149/14904.html.

80   "Pleasure—1: desire; inclination" *Merriam-Webster's Collegiate Dictionary*, 11th ed., s.v. "pleasure."

81   *"Pleasure is our first"* Epicurus, "Letters to Menoeceus," *Greek and Roman Philosophy after Aristotle*, trans. Jason L. Saunders (New York: Free Press, 1966).

84   *"Pleasure is never as pleasant"* Arthur Schopenhauer, translated and quoted in H. L. Mencken, *The Philosophy of Friedrich Nietzsche* (Boston: Luce and Company, 1908).

87   *One must pay dearly* Friedrich Nietzsche, *The Portable Nietzsche*, trans. Walter Kaufmann (New York: Penguin, 1976).

87   *To sue to live* William Shakespeare, *Measure for Measure*, ed. Edgar C. Morris (New York: The Macmillan Company, 1912).

87   *As long as you do not know* Adapted from Johann Wolfgang van Goethe, "The Holy Longing," in *News of the Universe:*

Poems of Twofold Consciousness, trans. and ed. Robert Bly (San Francisco: Sierra Club Books, 1995).

87   *We are in a world* William Blake, *The Portable Blake*, ed. Alfred Kazin (New York: Penguin, 1974).

Like So Many Nightmares:

95   *"And that brief madness"* Friedrich Nietzshe, *The Portable Nietzsche*, trans. Walter Kaufmann (New York: Penguin, 1976).

95   *"I live my life"* Rainer Maria Rilke, *Rilke's Book of Hours: Love Poems to God*, trans. Anita Barrows and Joanna Macy (New York: Riverhead, 2005).

98   *"Nothing but* being" Rainer Maria Rilke, "Dedications for Lulu Albert-Lazard," *Poems 1906 to 1925*, trans. J. B. Leishman (New York: New Directions, 1957).

99   *"It has been from the beginning"* Auguste Rodin, quoted in Albert E. Elsen and Rosalyn Frankel Jamison, *Rodin's Art: The Rodin Collection of the Iris & B. Gerald Cantor Center for Visual Arts at Stanford University*, ed. Bernard Barryte (New York: Oxford University Press, 2003).

105   *Over a million homes* See Mark Prigg, "The Astonishing Interactive Map That Shows Every German bomb Dropped on London during WW2 Blitz," *Daily Mail*, December 6, 2012, http://www.dailymail.co.uk/science-tech/article-2243951/The-astonishing-interactive-map-EVERY-bomb-dropped-London-Blitz.html.

105   *The bomb injured* See Mike Duval, "Meeting on LaGuardia Airport Explosion," December 30, 1975, Box 19, John Marsh Files, Gerald R. Ford Presidential Library, Ann Arbor, MI, https://www.fordlibrarymuseum.gov/library/document/0067/7829641.pdf.

105   *Khmer Rouge leaders apologized* See Keith B. Richburg, "A Small Apology to the Dead," *Washington Post*, December 30, 1998, https://www.washingtonpost.com/archive/politics/1998/12/30/a-small-apology-to-the-dead/f9cbfdad-48b9-483b-92b8-85d2b5b54d5d/?utm_term=.7bc7bb6601b3.

106   *a 1916 article on anal eroticism* Lou Andreas-Salomé, "'Anal' und 'Sexual'," *Imago* 4: 249–273.

106   *Locals started calling it* See Natasha Geiling, "This Hellish Desert Pit Has Been on Fire for More Than 40 Years," *Smithsonian*, May 20, 2014, http://www.smithsonianmag.com/travel/giant-hole-ground-has-been-fire-more-40-years-180951247/.

107   *"the patient sees"* Sigmund Freud, *An Outline of Psycho-Analysis*, trans. and ed. James Strachey (New York: W. W. Norton & Company, 1989).

107   *Freud called this* Ibid.

108   *"Men are not gentle creatures"* Sigmund Freud, *Civilization and Its Discontents*, trans. and ed. James Strachey (New York: W. W. Norton & Company, 1961).

109   *"None of us stands outside"* C. J. Jung, "The Undiscovered Self," *The Collected Works*, vol. X, trans. R. F. C. Hull (New York: Routledge, 2014).

Migrants in a Feverland:
This piece is for Nick. I'll never be able to repay you for your kindness and compassion and laughter and honesty—but know that I appreciate it, appreciate you, with all of my being. Anytime you need a handyman, I'm your man.

112   *the rich old men* See discussion of "shunamitism" in Steven Shapin, "Abishag's Revenge," review of *Mortal Coil: A Short History of Living Longer*, by David Boyd Haycock, *London Review of Books* 31, no. 6 (March 26, 2009): 29–31, https://www.lrb.co.uk/v31/n06/steven-shapin/abishags-revenge.

Rabbit Hole Music:
Jake Adam York comes to me each time I read this piece, whispering his beautiful poems. Miss you, Jake.

124   *Freudian psychoanalytical theory views* See Ariel Glucklich, *Sacred Pain: Hurting the Body for the Sake of the Soul* (New York: Oxford University Press, 2003).

126   *Often they bite* See "Congenital Insensitivity to Pain," Genetics Home Reference, US National Library of Medicine, https://ghr.nlm.nih.gov/condition/congenital-insensitivity-to-pain.

126   *the father of neurology* See David R. Kumar et al., "Jean-Martin Charcot: The Father of Neurology," *Clinical Medicine & Research* 9, no. 1 (March 2011): 46–49, doi: 10.3121/cmr.2009.883.

128   *In the British girl group* See "Sugababes—Hole in the Head [OFFICIAL VIDEO]," YouTube video, music video 2003, posted by "Emil D," December 8, 2012, https://www.youtube.com/watch?v=rn1qHqCQUJk.

128   *the movie trailer for the documentary* See "A Hole in the Head—Trailer from the Documentary," YouTube video, movie trailer, posted by "trepanned," October 4, 2007, https://www.youtube.com/watch?v=YoU_-ru8yEc.

140   *"favorably alters movement"* "ITAG: International Trepanation Advocacy Group," last modified March 19, 2016, http://www.trepan.com.

140   *Its website documents* See ibid.

140   *After monitoring the brain's blood flow* In ITAG's own words: "The study shows that the blood flow enhancement attained by skull trepanation resembles the blood flow characteristics of youth and on this basis the reduced flood flow through the brain characteristic of middle age can be restored to a youthful level."

Way Up High Way Down Low:

144   *But the posttraumatic stress* See Hope R. Ferdowsian et al., "Signs of Mood and Anxiety Disorders in Chimpanzees," *PLoS ONE*, June 16, 2011, doi:10.1371/journal.pone.0019855.

144   *"To suffer is to find oneself"* Alphonso Lingis, *Phenomenological Explanations* (Dordrecht, Netherlands: Martinus Nijhoff Publishers, 1986).

147   *Almost half of all teenagers do it* See "Nail-Biting—Topic Overview," WebMD, last updated February 20, 2015,

http://www.webmd.com/anxiety-panic/tc/nail-biting-topic-overview.

147 *but some studies report* L. A. Pennington, "The Incidence of Nail-Biting among Adults," *American Journal of Psychiatry* 102, no. 2 (September 1945): 241–244, http://ajp.psychiatryonline.org/doi/abs/10.1176/ajp.102.2.241.

148 *Freud argued that parental conflict* See Sigmund Freud, *Three Essays on the Theory of Sexuality*, trans. James Strachey (New York: Basic Books, 2000).

148 *we know Freud was a coke fiend* See Howard Markel, *An Anatomy of Addiction: Sigmund Freud, William Halsted, and the Miracle Drug Cocaine* (New York: Vintage, 2012).

148 *In folktales from around the world* Examples throughout this paragraph are taken from A. H. Godbey, "Ceremonial Spitting," *The Monist* 24 (1914): https://archive.org/details/monistquart24hegeuoft.

151 *Some theorize two types* See Chris G. Sibley and James H. Liu, "Differentiating Active and Passive Littering: A Two-Stage Process Model of Littering Behavior in Public Spaces," *Environment and Behavior* 35, no. 3 (May 2003): 415–433, doi: 10.1177/0013916503035003006.

153 *Swayambhunath means* Keith Dowman, "A Buddhist Guide to the Power Places of the Kathmandu Valley," *Kailash* 8, no. 3–4 (1981): 183–291.

156 *"I have never seen"* Michel de Montaigne, "Of Cripples," *Essays of Michel de Montaigne*, vol. 3, ed. William Carew Hazlitt, trans. Charles Cotton (London: George Bell and Sons, 1908).

157 *that killed 230,000 people* See Alan Taylor, "Ten Years since the 2004 Indian Ocean Tsunami," *Atlantic*, December 26, 2014, https://www.theatlantic.com/photo/2014/12/ten-years-since-the-2004-indian-ocean-tsunami/100878/.

158 *"The Romans exempted"* Michel de Montaigne, "Of Thumbs," *Essays of Michel de Montaigne*, vol. 2, ed. William Carew Hazlitt, trans. Charles Cotton (London: George Bell and Sons, 1908).

158 *"I found ancestors"* Eugène Ionesco, interviewed by Shusha

Guppy, "Eugène Ionesco, The Art of Theater No. 6," *Paris Review* 93 (Fall 1984): http://www.theparisreview.org/interviews/2956/the-art-of-theater-no-6-eugene-ionesco.

Migrants in a Feverland:
This piece is dedicated to the Balizet family.

Becoming Animal: A History:

176 *Of the parts of animals* Excerpts throughout the essay are taken from Aristotle, "History of Animals," trans. D'Arcy Wentworth Thompson, Internet Classics Archive, http://classics.mit.edu/Aristotle/history_anim.html.

188 *Bird-watchers in Brazil* See Bryan Bernard Lenz and Alaercio Marajó dos Reis, "Harpy Eagle-Primate Interactions in the Central Amazon," *Wilson Journal of Ornithology* 123, no. 2 (June 2011): 404–408, http://wjoonline.org/doi/abs/10.1676/10-171.1?journalCode=wils.

193 *an apocryphal story* See A. C. Greene, *Sketches from the Five States of Texas* (College Station: Texas A&M University Press, 1998).

How Long Before You Go Dry:

201 *"The past is not closed"* Czesław Miłosz, "What Did I Learn from Jeanne Hersch," trans. Adam Zagajewski, quoted in Rob Riemen, *Nobility of Spirit: A Forgotten Ideal* (New Haven: Yale University Press, 2008).

202 *Montaigne argued* See Michel de Montaigne, "Apology for Raimond de Sebonde," *Essays of Michel de Montaigne*, vol. 2, ed. William Carew Hazlitt, trans. Charles Cotton (London: George Bell and Sons, 1908).

202 *Freud believed* See Sigmund Freud, *On Dreams*, trans. M. D. Eder (Mineola, NY: Dover Thrift Editions, 2001).

204 *For thousands of years* See M. A. Screech, "Good Madness in Christendom," *The Anatomy of Madness: Essays in the History of Psychiatry*, ed. W. F. Bynum et al. (New York: Routledge, 2004).

206   *studied him constantly* See Larry R. Squire, "The Legacy of Patient H.M. for Neuroscience," *Neuron* 61, no. 1 (January 2009): 6–9, doi:10.1016/j.neuron.2008.12.023.

210   *But medical professionals* See "Symptom Checker: Excessive Crying," WebMD, http://symptomchecker.webmd.com/single-symptom?symptom=excessive-crying&symid=400.

210   *My words are my tears* Samuel Beckett, *Stories and Texts for Nothing* (New York: Grove Press, 1994).

210   *Tears are the silent language* Voltaire, "A Philosophical Dictionary," *The Complete Works of Voltaire*, vol. 14, trans. William F. Fleming (Akron, OH: Werner Company, 1905).

210   *I didn't want my picture* Sylvia Plath, *The Bell Jar* (New York: Harper Perennial, 2005).

210   *It is such a secret place* Antoine de Saint-Exupéry, *The Little Prince* (New York: Mariner Books, 2000).

210   *You left and I cried* Rumi, "Rubaiyat," *The Pocket Rumi*, ed. Kabir Helminski (Boston: Shambhala Publications, 2008).

210   *Keep me away from the wisdom* Kahlil Gibran, *Mirrors of the Soul* (New York: Philosophical Library, 1965).

210   *The fine line between* "Interview with Roald Dahl," by Scholastic Kids Book Clubs, https://clubs-kids.scholastic.co.uk/clubs_content/1491.

210   *Cry me a river* Justin Timberlake, "Cry Me A River," *Justified*, Jive Records, 2002.

210   *A number of studies* See Lorna Collier, "Why We Cry: New Research Is Opening Eyes to the Psychology of Tears," *Monitor on Psychology* 45, no. 2 (February 2014): 47, http://www.apa.org/monitor/2014/02/cry.aspx.

211   *In a 2002 experiment* See Suzanne Corkin, "What's New with the Amnesic Patient H.M.?" *Nature Reviews Neuroscience* 3 (February 2002): 153–160, doi:10.1038/nrn726.

213   *Neuroscientists have learned* See Danielle Venton, "Big

Question: Can My Brain Get Too Full?" *Wired,* June 16, 2015, https://www.wired.com/2015/06/can-my-brain-get-too-full/.

215 *Between 1966 and 2000* See Steven Shapin, "The Man Who ForgotEverything,"*NewYorker,*October14,2013,http://www. newyorker.com/books/page-turner/the-man-who-forgot-everything.

All Night the Cockroaches:

233 *Researchers at North Carolina State University* See Matt Shipman, "Researchers Use Video Game Tech to Steer RoachesonAutopilot,"*NCStateNews,*June25,2013,https:// news.ncsu.edu/2013/06/wms-bozkurt-roach-autopilot/.

Migrants in a Feverland:

This piece is for Dr. J.

ACKNOWLEDGMENTS

I give all of my love, all of myself to the people who made this book, this life possible. Ariane, Felix, Alma—you are my everything. I'm grateful to the amazing people at Milkweed Editions—you are family, friends, and I so appreciate everything you do. Joey, this book owes an incredible amount to your crazy-good editing. The completion of this book was made possible by the generous support of TCU, which helped during the years it took to write this collection by awarding me a TCU-IS grant, a JFSRP grant, a Mid-Career Summer Fellowship, and a semester-long research leave. Thank you to my colleagues in the Department of English, especially our chair, Dr. Karen Steele, Dean of AddRan Andrew Schoolmaster, Dean Bonnie Melhart, Provost Nowell Donovan, Chancellor Victor Boschini (who always asks about the welfare of my family, and amazingly knows each of our names), and everyone associated with Ashland University's MFA program.

Big love to the editors of the following publications for editorial suggestions and for publishing these pieces, sometimes in different iterations:

AGNI: "My Misogyny"
Copper Nickel: "Rabbit Hole Music"

Gulf Coast: "Becoming Animal: A History"

Literary Review: "EKG"

River Teeth: "How Long Before You Go Dry"

Rumpus: "King of the Rats"

Southern Review: "Heartdusting"

Sycamore Review: "Like So Many Nightmares"

Ariane Balizet

ALEX LEMON is the author of *Happy: A Memoir*, and the poetry collections *Mosquito, Hallelujah Blackout, Fancy Beasts,* and *The Wish Book*. His writing has appeared in *Esquire, The Best American Poetry 2008, AGNI, Gulf Coast,* the *Kenyon Review,* and *Tin House,* among others. He was awarded a 2005 Literature Fellowship in poetry from the National Endowment for the Arts, and he contributes and reviews frequently for a wide range of media outlets. He lives with his wife and two children in Fort Worth, and teaches at Texas Christian University and in Ashland University's low-residency MFA program in creative writing.

The Editor's Circle of Milkweed Editions

We gratefully acknowledge the following individuals for their
annual leadership support of the literary arts.

milkweed
editions

Founded as a nonprofit organization in 1980, Milkweed Editions is an independent publisher. Our mission is to identify, nurture and publish transformative literature, and build an engaged community around it.

milkweed.org

Interior design by Mary Austin Speaker
Typeset in Wilke

Wilke was designed by Martin Wilke in 1988 for the Linotype
foundry. His design was inspired by classical
inscriptions, the Caslon typeface and the Book of Kells.
Its high x-height and round, broad letterforms make it
extremely legible for setting book text.